Analysis and Valuation of Golf Courses and Country Clubs

by Arthur E. Gimmy, MAI, and Buddie A. Johnson

Readers of this text may also be interested in the following publications from the Appraisal Institute:

- *The Appraisal of Real Estate*, 12th edition
- *Appraising Residential Properties*, 3d edition
- *The Dictionary of Real Estate Appraisal*, 4th edition
- *Land Valuation: Adjustment Procedures and Assignments*

Appraisal
Institute®

Professionals Providing
Real Estate Solutions

Analysis and Valuation of Golf Courses and Country Clubs

by Arthur E. Gimmy, MAI, and Buddie A. Johnson

Reviewers: Frank E. Harrison, MAI, SRA
Stephen A. Manning, MAI, SRA
Michael S. MaRous, MAI, SRA
John A. Schwartz, MAI

*Vice President, Educational
Programs and Publications:* Larisa Phillips
Director, Publications: Stephanie Shea-Joyce
Manager, Book Design/Production: Michael Landis
Production Specialist: Lynne Payne
Senior Coordinator, Publications: Colette Nicolay

FOR EDUCATIONAL PURPOSES ONLY

NONDISCRIMINATION POLICY

Printed in the United States of America

LIBRARY OF CONGRESS CATALOGING-IN-PUBLICATION DATA

Gimmy, Arthur E
    Analysis and valuation of golf courses and country clubs / by Arthur E. Gimmy and Buddie Johnson.
        p. cm.
    ISBN 0-922154-78-3
        1. Golf courses–Valuation–United States. 2. Country clubs–Valuation–United States. 3. Golf courses–United States–Finance. 4. Country clubs–United States–Finance. I. Johnson, Buddie. II. Title.

    GV975.G55 2003
    796.352'06'873–dc22

2003063703

CONTENTS

FOREWORD

Golf is big business in communities across the United States
and around the world. Golf courses are recreational enterprises
that represent an investment in real estate, personal property,
inventory, personnel, and intangibles. To manage these complicated investments, golf course owners and managers need
help from real estate appraisers and analysts who can provide
sound feasibility studies and accurate value estimates.

Analysis and Valuation of Golf Courses and Country Clubs is
an entirely new valuation manual that replaces the classic appraisal text on the subject, *Golf Courses and Country Clubs: A
Guide to Appraisal, Market Analysis, Development, and Financing.* The popularity of golf, the supply of facilities, and the profitability of courses have all changed dramatically since that book
was published in 1992. This new text reflects these changes and
will help appraisers and other analysts describe and classify
golf courses, understand current industry trends, identify and
analyze golf markets, and estimate property value.

Investigating the feasibility and value of a golf course is a
challenge for even the most experienced appraiser because valuing a course requires analysis of the total business enterprise,
not just the facility's physical assets. Most appraisal assignments
involve analysis of the sales revenues and operating expenses
of various departments of the business, which vary widely at
different facilities in different geographic markets. The unique
aspects of municipal facilities, daily fee courses, private golf

clubs, and residential golf communities are all covered in this text as are all of the necessary steps in the valuation process.

Alan E. Hummel, SRA
2003 President
Appraisal institute

ABOUT THE AUTHORS

Arthur E. Gimmy, MAI, is president of Arthur Gimmy International, a nationwide real estate appraisal and consulting firm whose California offices are in Corte Madera and Newport Beach. Mr. Gimmy received the MAI designation in 1965 and is a prolific author, having published nearly 50 articles on a wide variety of appraisal topics and written various books in use by appraisal professionals. Books previously published by the Appraisal Institute include *Fitness, Racquet Sports, and Spa Projects; The Analysis and Valuation of Health Care Enterprises; Senior Housing: Looking Toward the Third Millennium;* and *The Business of Show Business: The Valuation of Movie Theaters.* He has taught many appraisal courses during his career, including ones at San Jose State, UCLA, SMU, the University of Tampa, and the University of Connecticut. He has also served on numerous local and national committees of the Appraisal Institute, including 10 years as a member of the Appraisal Journal Editorial Board. A pioneer in the analysis of difficult, unique, or specialized properties, Mr. Gimmy is frequently an expert witness in litigation matters involving complex appraisal issues. He recently received the George L. Schmutz Memorial Award from the Appraisal Institute for his special contribution to the advancement of appraisal knowledge.

Buddie A. Johnson was associated with Arthur Gimmy International in the 1970s and 1980s and rejoined the firm in 2001. From 1969 to 1975, Johnson was Western Region Facility Development Consultant for the National Golf Foundation. In

1975 he formed his own consulting company, providing feasibility, golf course financial planning, appraisal, and operational consultation to clients and other consulting firms.

From 1984 to 2000, Johnson was president of a development company in Arizona. He oversaw the development of a 2,100-acre, mixed-use real estate project, including planning, financing, construction, and operation of an 18-hole championship golf course that has been ranked among the finest in the state.

As Director of the Division of Golf at AGI, Johnson's work centers on the appraisal and analysis of golf course projects. Much of this work includes real estate development land associated with golf course projects. These assignments are typically performed for financing, estate valuation, condemnation, sales and purchases of golf courses, and feasibility analysis. Golf course assignments may include stand-alone golf courses, resort golf facilities (including hotel and development real estate), private country clubs, and golf courses associated with large residential real estate projects.

PREFACE

The golf industry is not immune to the economic woes of the new millennium. Golf was born in 15th century Scotland, raised to renown at St. Andrews, and developed a huge following in the United States. The sport yields a gross economic product of more than $23 billion and is considered a lifestyle choice by 10 million avid players.

Golf courses require vast economic and ecological resources that are in limited supply. Only a finite number of acres are suitable for productive golf course development and much of the remaining supply of land for this purpose is marginal at best, which will discourage new development until the economy reaches a new growth cycle.

Analysts and appraisers, especially those involved in assessing the potential of proposed projects, have a responsibility to their clients and the market to provide accurate recommendations and feasibility analyses. Their reports must be based on realistic estimates of future revenues and income and a logical assessment of the ability of the facility to support the costs of development.

The success of a project is the responsibility of management and other professionals. Appraisers should be able to recognize the difference between good and bad practices and communicate the levels of performance attained at a project to clients. This text focuses on analysis and valuation techniques that will allow appraisers to give clients, whether they are financial institutions, developers, operators, investors, or newcomers to the business, the best possible evaluations or appraisals of their existing or proposed projects.

INTRODUCTION

This new valuation manual, which replaces a text previously published by the Appraisal Institute,[1] will help appraisers and other analysts describe and classify golf courses, understand industry trends, measure and analyze golf course markets and competition, and estimate property value, considering all appropriate techniques and the contribution of non-realty assets.

Golf courses are part of the leisure and entertainment industry; they are recreational enterprises that represent an investment in real estate, personal property, inventory, personnel and intangibles. Golf courses fall into three primary categories: private country clubs, daily fee courses that are privately owned and open to the public, and municipal or publicly owned courses. Many golf courses are called *clubs*, even those that lack a membership structure.

For valuation purposes, a golf course or country club must be considered a business enterprise, not just an assemblage of physical assets. In most assignments value is based on an analysis of the sales revenues and operating expenses of various departments of the business, rather than capitalization of net rental income, which is typical in the appraisal of an investment property.

The data and techniques described in this text will assist the appraiser or analyst in conducting all of the necessary steps in the valuation process.[2]

Chapter One examines the process of describing and classifying a golf course. To describe a property for analytical purposes, factors such as size, type, par, ownership, layout, topography, location, difficulty, and physical components must be considered.

1. *Golf Courses and Country Clubs: A Guide to Appraisal, Market Analysis, Development, and Financing* (Chicago: Appraisal Institute, 1992).

2. *The Appraisal of Real Estate*, 12th ed. (Chicago: Appraisal Institute, 2001).

Chapter Two focuses on the golf course industry and observed trends. It includes numerous statistics regarding the number of players and courses, the distribution of facilities, playing characteristics, participation rates, and rounds played and sets the stage for market analysis, the next step in any valuation assignment.

Chapter Three explores market analysis, probably the most important step in the valuation process. In today's competitive market, where many segments are oversupplied, proposed projects must meet the test of feasibility and the income capitalization approach is of vital importance. Current trends in the market are emphasized.

Chapter Four presents information and a series of questions which the analyst must answer to measure the management and performance of the enterprise (both statistically and financially) in relation to its competitors. The key to such a determination is analysis of the intangible factors that define the success or failure of a golf course or country club.

Chapter Five provides statistics on municipal courses (financial and performance data) from the National Golf Foundation (NGF) and a discussion of the special considerations involved when a property is owned by an agency.

Chapter Six examines the daily fee course, the type of golf course that is most commonly appraised and analyzed. This most popular type of course is typically appraised as an investment using the income capitalization and sales comparison approaches. Financial data is provided for climate regions.

Chapter Seven deals with performance data for private golf courses and country clubs. This subject is controversial because some of these projects are nonprofit and are rarely sold in the open market. Statistics indicate that some of these clubs can be profitable, but questions can arise regarding the classification and ownership of assets.

In Chapters Eight through Ten, the traditional valuation approaches are applied to profit-oriented golf courses and country clubs. Chapter Eight explores the cost approach and provides the methodology for preparing a separate estimate of the business component of the enterprise. Typical and unusual land valuation practices are explained. Chapter Nine covers the income capitalization approach and examines all of the components of a golf course investment that should be reflected in the net income projection. The discounting and capitalization of income to derive the overall value of the assets are described, applying direct capitalization and discounted cash flow analysis techniques. The allocation of value to each component of the investment is also explained. The sales comparison approach is the subject of Chapter Ten. In this chapter, units of comparison are identified and the use of adjustment factors and grids is demonstrated. More than 80 recent sales of golf courses and country clubs are analyzed.

Chapter Eleven provides an overview of golf courses in residential communities and presents data on development issues, planning and design, marketing, and financial performance. The transfer of value to the residences within a golf course community project is explained.

The findings of the authors' research and recommendations are summarized in Chapter Twelve. Conclusions concerning the future of golfing and the analysis of a golf course business are presented. Unique valuation problems that will continue to challenge analysts are explored, and predictions for the future of the industry are presented as they relate to development, feasibility, and valuation.

Analysts and other professionals who conduct comparative analyses of competing clubs, prepare feasibility studies, and undertake appraisals of golf courses should be familiar with all the material in this book. Helpful ideas and ways of analyzing data can be found in several chapters. Much of the statistical data presented applies to the performance of a typical golf course enterprise. By consulting the references indicated, readers can access percentile data for the nine U.S. climate regions classified and surveyed by the National Golf Foundation.

The National Golf Foundation (NGF) is the recognized source of research and studies on the golf industry. A full list of publications that will be of assistance to appraisers, analysts, and others is included in the appendix to this text.

The authors are indebted to NGF for many of the statistics presented herein, especially those in Chapters Two, Three, Five, Six, and Seven, which were derived from the following NGF publications:

- Operating and Financial Performance Profiles
  Daily Fee Facilities (2001 Edition)
  Municipal Facilities (2001 Edition)
  Private Facilities (2001 Edition)
- *Golf Participation in the U.S./2002*
- *Golf Facilities in the U.S./2002*

The statistics published by NGF are derived by sampling participants who are willing to provide confidential or proprietary data to NGF. Data are reported for nine climate regions, which are grouped by similarities in climate, turfgrass, facility density, and cultural factors (see the map on page xvii). This regional organization facilitates meaningful data analyses and comparisons among facilities. There is no guarantee that the data presented is applicable to a particular golf facility or project. Rather, it represents information that is significant to the industry and a starting point for individualized, in-depth analysis of actual or proposed facilities.

NGF may be contacted at:

National Golf Foundation
1150 South U.S. Highway One, Suite 401
Jupiter, FL 33477
http://www.ngf.org.

U.S. Climate Regions*

Region 1
New England

Region 2
Middle Atlantic

Region 3
East North Central

Region 4
West North Central

Region 5
South Atlantic

Region 6
East South Central

Region 7
West South Central

Region 8
Mountain

Region 9
Pacific

* Hawaii is included in Region 8; Alaska is included in Region 9.

Source: National Golf Foundation

CHAPTER ONE

DESCRIBING AND ANALYZING COURSE FACILITIES

The characteristics of the golf course site ultimately determine the type of golf course built and its routing and design. The five basic design options are: core, single-fairway continuous, single-fairway with returning nines, double-fairway continuous, and double-fairway with returning nines. Variations of these basic designs or combinations may be considered distinct types by some golf course architects.

Course design is greatly influenced by the amount of land available, the investment objectives of the project sponsor, the type and density of adjacent land uses, and other factors such as the perception of quality, supportable operating costs, and the need to differentiate between competitive courses.

Recognized qualitative differences between golf courses relate to playability, aesthetics, condition, reputation, and location. There are no set criteria for classifying courses qualitatively, but certain facilities are described as "trophy" or "signature" courses. A signature course is one that has been designed by a well-known golf course architect. A trophy course is a signature course with a world-class reputation, an expensive clubhouse, a unique location, exceptional design and layout, and other amenities. Qualitative considerations influence value, but they are subjective in nature. To assess qualitative factors appraisers must examine a variety of courses or facilities and develop the ability to evaluate critical differences.

The construction of a golf facility cannot be covered in detail in this chapter, but the reader will become acquainted with various improvements and equipment, the importance of careful design, and the functional relationships reflected in the overall operation and use of various parts of the property. For additional information, the reader is referred to the specialized texts listed in the appendix.

In most appraisals, the process of describing a golf course begins with the raw land before any improvements have been made.

SITE FEATURES

A golf course site description includes consideration of site size (in acres), shape, topography, utilities (especially water), accessibility, soils, vegetation (especially trees), and other factors.

Golf course sites vary greatly in size. A regulation 18-hole course generally covers 120 to 180 acres; a site of 160 to 180 acres is typical for a 6,500-yard course on gently rolling land. Core courses require the least amount of land, double fairways require more, and single fairways require the most land and are the least efficient. A developer who wants to include a golf course as a project amenity, but has a limited amount of land, might consider a short course such as a 9-hole, par-3 course built on 35 acres or an 18-hole executive course built on less than 100 acres.

A regulation-sized course may be designed in one of five basic configurations:

1. Core course
2. Single-fairway, continuous 18-hole course
3. Single-fairway, 18-hole course with returning nines
4. Double-fairway, continuous 18-hole course
5. Double-fairway, 18-hole course with returning nines

These five layouts are shown in Figure 1.1

Various design options or combinations are available, so the shape of sites can be highly variable. When a golf course is part of a real estate development, the design of the course must be integrated with surrounding land uses. There are no set rules for determining the ratio of golf course frontage to residential or resort parcels. Developers will attempt to maximize the highest and best use of the land, as measured by the internal rate of return (*IRR*). They want to achieve the highest price or profitability for the entire mixed-use project in a balanced manner that does not penalize any one land use. A successful golf course design will win the acceptance of the target market and maximize and enhance the price and marketability of the entire project. Topography becomes a critical factor in the siting process.

FIGURE 1.1

Golf Course Layouts

Core golf course

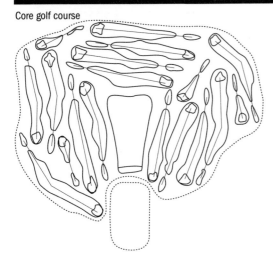

Single-fairway, continuous, 18-hole course

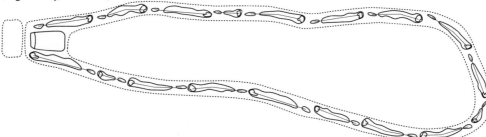

Single-fairway, 18-hole course with returning nines

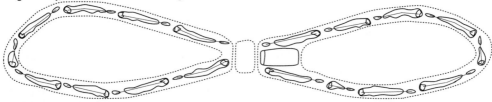

Double fairway, continuous, 18-hole course

Double-fairway, 18-hole course with returning nines

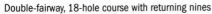

Source: Urban Land Institute

The slope and contours of the terrain determine the course layout and routing plan, especially when the course is associated with adjacent building sites. Fairways should be at the same or lower elevations than housing sites to promote visibility. On undulating terrain, the course designer must locate tees on flat or cut-and-fill areas and greens in landing areas that are visible, not too hilly, and framed by natural or landscaped site features. A good golf course architect also considers safety elements and the location of trees, hills, water, sand, and other features (see Figure 1.2). The optimal design will provide a variety of hole lengths, difficulty, and style. A combination of two, par-3 holes, five, par-4 holes, and two, par-5 holes will yield a total par of 36 over nine holes. If the holes can be designed in a sequence of 4-5-4-3-4-5-4-3-4 or 4-3-4-5-4-3-4-5-4, no two consecutive holes will have the same par. This combination may be ideal, but it is atypical. The only firm criteria are that par-3 holes should not be at the beginning or end of the course (although there are exceptions) and that the holes should be spaced to avoid backups.

The basic utilities required for a golf course project or country club include electricity, domestic and irrigation water, and a sanitary sewer or septic system. Because water to irrigate the course is essential, the adequacy and quality of the water supply must be thoroughly investigated and verified. Typical sources of water include local water companies; on-site wells, canals, or aqueducts; lakes or streams; and effluent from waste water treatment plants. Except for the latter source, which has become generally acceptable, public water sources tend to be too expensive.

The securing of sufficient water over a long period of time may be a critical problem for proposed courses and some existing courses in areas subject to water shortages or fluctuations in water supplies. Actual water requirements and pumping costs can vary greatly. An 18-hole, regulation-sized course may use between 250,000 and 500,000 gallons of water per day, depending on the amount and type of ground cover, climatic conditions, and the means of irrigation. Desert-type courses often require 1,000,000 gallons per day during the summer.

The appraiser should consider the status of current and future water supplies, potential alternative sources, and factors that could result in future restrictions or supply interruptions. Competition for water will increase in the future, resulting in higher water costs for most projects that depend on an outside source.

One important positive trend is the use of treated effluent for golf course irrigation. In many areas the disposal of waste water is a problem for local sanitation districts. It can be quite cost-

FIGURE 1.2

Design Safety Elements

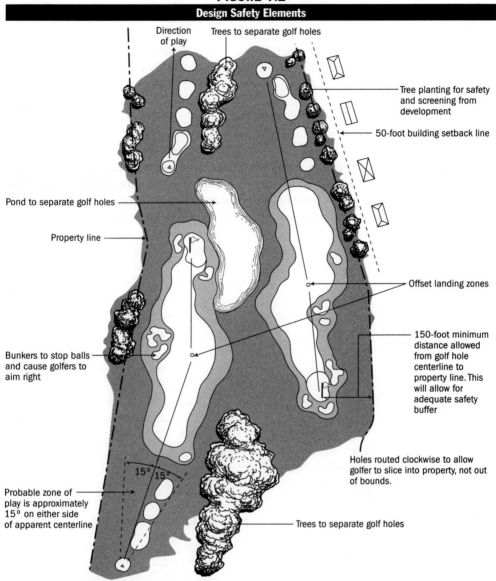

Direction of play

Trees to separate golf holes

Tree planting for safety and screening from development

50-foot building setback line

Pond to separate golf holes

Property line

Offset landing zones

Bunkers to stop balls and cause golfers to aim right

150-foot minimum distance allowed from golf hole centerline to property line. This will allow for adequate safety buffer

15° 15°

Holes routed clockwise to allow golfer to slice into property, not out of bounds.

Probable zone of play is approximately 15° on either side of apparent centerline

Trees to separate golf holes

Hurdzan design guidelines can be used as a starting point and adjusted to suit the topography, vegetation, altitude, prevailing winds, adjacent land uses, and anticipated play level of the specific site or project.

Source: *Golf Course Architecture*, Dr. Michael J. Hurdzan

effective for a golf course developer or operator to make use of this water. In some cases the ability to develop a course has hinged on the availability of treated effluent.

Soils of all types can support golf course construction, but differences in soil quality can greatly affect development costs and operating expenses. The best soils are alluvial, sandy loam soils which have good drainage characteristics and support healthy turf and ground cover. Soils that are rocky, clayish, mucky, or gravelly are undesirable because they can result in drainage problems, higher construction costs, and/or excessive maintenance expenses. In recent years some golf courses have even been built on lava fields such as those in Hawaii, but these courses were built at great expense.

Courses are sometimes developed on floodplains and seasonal wetlands when more desirable sites are not available. However, the advantage of lower land costs may be offset if the course is unplayable during wet periods and maintenance costs are high. Design features such as crowned fairways and drainage systems can overcome many of the problems of low-lying land and improve the appearance of a property.

Geographic conditions in the United States divide golf course locations into two general categories: Frostbelt and Sunbelt. The length of the playing season in Frostbelt and Sunbelt locations can vary by several months, which affects the number of rounds played and the project's operating income and expense.

This general discussion of site characteristics is only a starting point for the serious analyst. Many factors must be considered in selecting and describing a golf course site. Site factors can play an important role in estimating land value and in comparing golf course sales with a subject property.

COURSE CHARACTERISTICS

Golf courses are designed to meet the requirements of a specific market or markets. Typical or desirable features for regulation courses designed for specific markets are described below.

MUNICIPAL COURSES

The simplest of courses, municipal golf courses are designed to accommodate heavy daily play throughout the year or season and to appeal to a wide variety of players. Typically a core design is used to create a course with playability and enough complexity to challenge a wide range of players. Municipal courses tend to be flat and have few rough areas where balls can be lost. Development and operating costs are typically low due to a concentrated irrigation system, easily mowed grounds, reduced landscape maintenance costs, and few course obstacles. Municipal courses are shorter than most (approximately 6,000 to 6,500 yards) and fairways tend to be wide.

COUNTRY CLUBS

Country club or private courses must appeal to a wide range of golfers, but they are typically more difficult than municipal courses. The level of play is less intensive and social interaction is emphasized at country clubs so playing time is a less important consideration. A great many of these courses have a core design and most exhibit more intensive maintenance practices. New country clubs are typically associated with a golf course community. These projects emphasize residential development and use a combination of single and double fairways so that many of the lots have golf course frontage or views.

RESORT COURSES

Resort courses are the most complicated type of courses. They are designed to appeal to serious golfers and to serve as a marketing tool to attract convention business to the course or residents to a related housing development. Resort courses have memorable holes, scenic beauty, a feeling of privacy or spaciousness, "signature" designers, lakes, and a variety of hazards. They usually feature a core or double-fairway layout and have high construction and maintenance costs.

RETIREMENT COMMUNITY COURSES

The typical player at a retirement community course is older, but plays often, so the course should not be situated in difficult terrain. These courses are shorter, have wide fairways for faster play, and are challenging in terms of visibility and the placement of hazards. Retirement community courses range from 5,500 to 6,500 yards in length. They may have a single- or double-fairway layout to maximize the frontage of surrounding lots and simplify maintenance.

In addition to the three basic course types described here, desirable design characteristics may be combined to produce hybrids and variations. For example, a semi-private course in a residential setting might include features to attract a wide market without compromising playability and the need for challenging holes. If land is available and market dynamics warrant it, a 27-hole course can be built to provide three distinct, 18-hole combinations designed to appeal to players of varying expertise. Generally, 27-hole facilities increase golf course capacity by two-thirds, but such courses are only 50% more expensive to develop. Of course, the objective in golf course development is to realize the highest return from a particular piece of land.

Describing the Course

To describe and analyze a golf course for valuation purposes, the appraiser must understand its functional parts. A typical hole includes two tees, a fairway, greens, roughs, and hazards (see Figure 1.3). These elements are combined in different ways to form unique golf courses. Starting with a basic understanding of golf courses, the appraiser can develop the ability to describe, critique, compare, and rate them through practice and exposure to a variety of facilities.

Tees

As the starting point for each hole, the tee must be carefully placed and sized. Because tee shots generally range from 150 to 250 yards, it is desirable to have three or four sets of tees at varying locations to meet the needs of a wide range of golfers. The tees are often spaced over a distance of 25 to 75 yards and identified as gold (for a drive of 250 yards), blue (for a drive of 225 yards), white (for a drive of 175 yards), and red (for a drive of 150 yards). A good course design relates the overall size of tees to the number of annual rounds played; there is a direct relationship between the amount of play and tee damage or wear. A general rule of thumb is 100 to 200 square feet of tee surface is required for each 1,000 rounds played per year. Tees should be level and planted with sturdy turf.

Designing a tee requires careful consideration of a number of factors: proper soil and drainage, adequate exposure to sunshine and air movement, a moderate slope for mowing purposes, and appropriate fairway orientation to minimize damage to adjacent property from errant drives. Tees are subject to a great deal of hard use and need constant attention. When they are sized properly, the tee markers can be frequently changed to allow for an even distribution of wear. Tees on par-3 holes should be twice the size of others since iron shots cause divots and destruction of the turf at a far greater rate than is experienced at par-4 or par-5 holes.

Fairways

The fairway is the playing area between the tee and the hole. It is generally 40 to 65 yards wide and surrounded by rough consisting of longer turf grass, tall natural grasses and weeds, or unplanted natural terrain. The combination of the fairway and rough can reach 100 yards in side dimensions. The playing area of each hole is designed in accordance with critical principles that are not apparent to most players. Fairway length determines par: up to 250 yards is needed for a par-3 hole, up to 470 yards

FIGURE 1.3
A Typical Hole

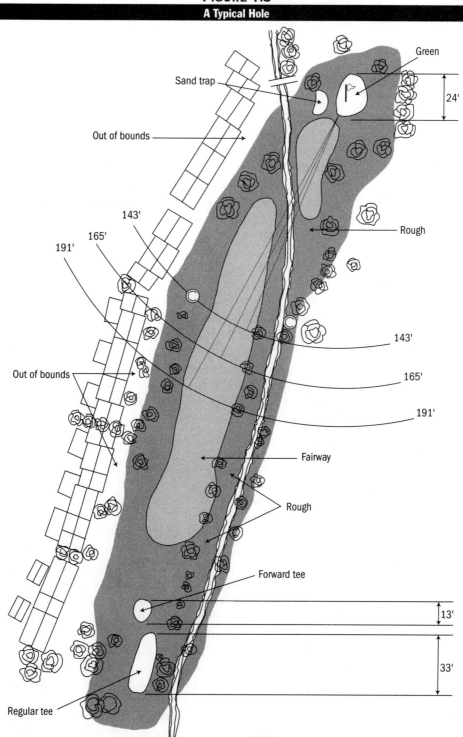

Green

Sand trap

24'

Out of bounds

Rough

143'

165'

191'

143'

165'

191'

Out of bounds

Fairway

Rough

Forward tee

13'

33'

Regular tee

for a par-4 hole, and more than 470 yards from golf tees for a par-5 hole. Fairway width can vary greatly.

Narrow fairways require greater expertise; wider fairways favor less talented golfers. Landing areas, where most golf shots should fall, are planned at predetermined distances from the tee. If the surrounding area is wooded, the fairway should be wider. Rough areas need to be carefully planned because they increase playing time. They can, however, materially reduce the costs of course construction if they are interspersed and extended between planned landing areas that are planted with turf, as in a traditional links design. The placing of hazards materially affects the difficulty or rating of the hole and the speed of play.

A path for golf cars may be an integral part of the fairway design. Such a path usually runs parallel to the length of the fairway, except where there are obstacles, and should be designed to follow the contours of the land. Paved paths are necessary for courses that receive a great deal of play and in areas that receive a lot of rain. The surface of the path may consist of gravel and rock, asphalt, or concrete over a base or over dirt. Using low-cost surface material may produce initial savings, but the path could require excessive maintenance due to wear and tear, drainage problems, and exposure to the elements. Golf car paths are typically five to eight feet wide and approximately 20% to 40% longer than the course when they run throughout the course. However, many courses only have golf car paths over portions of the course, usually near the tees and greens.

GREENS

The putting area of a hole, or the green, is carefully manicured to provide an even surface. Golfers need to study the terrain when putting because greens usually have a slight slope (for visibility and drainage) and grass has surface irregularities. Typical greens range in size from 3,000 to 5,000 square feet, but some are larger. Smaller greens are suitable for short approach shots; larger greens, which may be up to 1/3 acre in total area, are needed if the shape of the course is highly variable and gets heavy play or the typical approach is long or difficult. The green should be large enough to allow for frequent changes in the location of the cup so that wear and tear on the surface is evenly distributed.

Greens vary not only in size and shape, but also in the variety of hazards that surround them. Most golfers, as well as course designers and architects, believe that the green should be contoured and visible from the location of the typical approach shot.

The construction of greens requires careful subsoil preparation and drainage. The site is prepared to a depth of eight to 24 inches with layers of gravel, sand, and soil mix over drainage tiles. The Greens Section of the U.S. Golf Association establishes specifications for site preparation. Other specifications include the so-called "California Greens Construction." Both are illustrated in Figure 1.4. In preparing a golf course appraisal, the quality and condition of the greens should be observed because this is where the typical golfer spends a large percentage of his or her playing time. Greens are a key item in the rating of a golf facility.

FIGURE 1.4

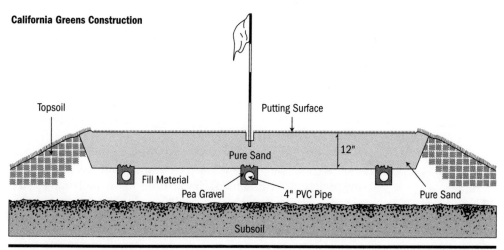

USGA Greens Construction

Topsoil
Putting Surface
12"
Amended Soil
2" Sand Layer
Fill Material
4" PVC Pipe
4" Pea Gravel
Subsoil

California Greens Construction

Topsoil
Putting Surface
12"
Pure Sand
Fill Material
Pea Gravel
4" PVC Pipe
Pure Sand
Subsoil

Source: *Golf Course Architecture*, Dr. Michael J. Hurdzan

PRACTICE RANGE

Two-thirds of the golf facilities in the United States have a golf practice range. The features of these practice ranges are shown in Table 1.1.

Modern driving ranges have evolved into practice facilities that include the traditional driving range, sometimes on two levels, plus putting greens and practice bunkers. Such facilities encourage more extensive use of all golf properties. By providing teaching programs as well as practice opportunities, these ranges help develop new golfers and retain old ones.

Nationwide data shows that 78% of private facilities have practice ranges as do 61% of daily fee facilities and 58% of municipal courses. The average on-course practice range has 24 tee stations.

HAZARDS

Sand bunkers, lakes, rough areas, and trees are typical golf course hazards. Hazards can be natural or man-made features designed for a particular purpose. They make a course more challenging and some provide other functions such as water storage, drainage, boundaries, and visual beauty. Their placement is important to the game and can greatly influence the speed at which the typical golfer plays. Hazards add to the development and maintenance costs of a course.

TYPE OF HOLES

Individual hole styles fall into three broad categories: strategic, penal, and heroic (see Figures 1.5, 1.6, and 1.7).

Most golf course holes have a strategic style, which means that golfers can select various ways to reach the hole depending on their skill and the location of hazards. Strategic holes have wider fairways, but they offer alternative routes to the green such as a shot over a hazard that can reward the golfer with a lower score.

To play penal holes, all shots must go directly over hazards such as lakes, sand bunkers, or rough areas. Errant shots result in penalties, lost balls, and increased playing time. Courses with penal holes tend to be designed for expert golfers and professional tournaments.

Heroic golf holes represent a combination of strategic and penal styles. They are included in a regulation course to provide variety and challenges. Heroic holes are usually long holes over a water hazard that reward the successful golfer with the opportunity for a subpar score. Alternative routes (e.g., around the lake) are available for less skillful players and usually result in over-par scores.

Well-designed golf courses provide a blend of styles with many strategic holes and a few heroic holes.

TABLE 1.1

Practice Ranges		
Feature	All Ranges	Built in Last Three Years
Night lights	51%	62%
Putting green	58%	51%
Short game area	43%	51%
Teaching pros on staff	38%	43%

Source: National Golf Foundation

FIGURE 1.5
Strategic Golf Hole

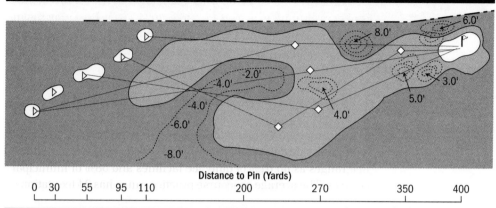

Distance to Pin (Yards)

0   30   55   95   110   200   270   350   400

FIGURE 1.6
Penal Golf Hole

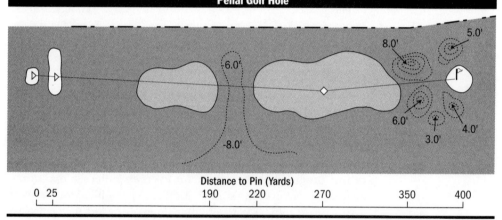

Distance to Pin (Yards)

0   25   190   220   270   350   400

FIGURE 1.7
Heroic Golf Hole

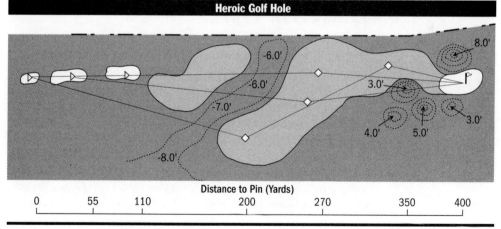

Distance to Pin (Yards)

0   55   110   200   270   350   400

Source: *Golf Course Architecture*, Dr. Michael J. Hurdzan

COURSE RATINGS

According to the U.S. Golf Association, par is "the score a scratch golfer would be expected to make for a given hole. Par means errorless play without flukes and under ordinary weather conditions, allowing two strokes on the putting green." Par is also a range of horizontal distances for men and women that should not be applied arbitrarily, but should allow for the configuration of the ground, difficult or unusual conditions, and the severity of hazards. A par-3 hole allows for one shot off the tee to reach the putting green plus two strokes on the putting green; a par-4 hole allows for two shots to reach the putting green plus two strokes on the putting green; and a par-5 hole allows for three shots to reach the putting green plus two strokes on the putting green.

The U.S. Golf Association suggests the following yardages for computing par:

Par	Men	Women
3	Up to 250 yards	Up to 210 yards
4	251-470 yards	211-400 yards
5	471 yards or more	401-575 yards

Slope is a measure of the difficulty of obstacles and hazards encountered on a golf course. This measure, developed by the U.S. Golf Association, takes into account the placement of hazards and the degree of difficulty of a hole within 150 yards of the green. Distance is only part of the formula. The higher the slope rating, the tougher the course for average golfers. Slope rating also makes an average golfer's handicap portable. More strokes are given on courses with a higher slope rating and fewer strokes are given on those with a lower rating.

IRRIGATION SYSTEM

Climatic conditions dictate the size and complexity of golf course irrigation systems. Almost all modern systems are computer-controlled for great efficiency. Double-row systems with lines on each side of a fairway are popular, but in a wet climate a less costly, single-row layout down the center of the fairway may be adequate. Irrigation lines should be strategically placed considering the terrain and design of the course. Sprinkler heads should be spaced so that the water coverage of the heads overlap and all watering needs are met. Automatic systems are used to save labor costs and courses without them suffer a significant deficiency. A storage system designed as a staged series of interconnected lakes can provide a continuous flow of water to the sprinkler system, which might not be possible with the typical combination of wells, pumps, and tanks.

Carefully controlled, cost-effective irrigation systems are a necessity in today's market. Water will be an increasingly important economic issue in the future. Aside from the availability and cost of land, water for golf course irrigation will be the most decisive factor in the development of future golf courses. Opposition to golf courses is common in areas where water quality and quantity are critical community issues. One possible solution is more extensive use of treated effluent, a trend which is expected to increase in the near future.

An appraiser valuing a golf course should obtain information about the irrigation system– i.e., the linear feet of lines, number of sprinkler heads, number of valves, size and number of pumps and wells, and type and capacity of the storage system. The appraiser should also examine the system to understand the amount of accrued depreciation and to estimate annual reserves for replacement.

THE CLUBHOUSE

The type of golf course and the objectives of the owners will dictate the size of the clubhouse and its facilities. A brief checklist is provided in Table 1.2. Functional considerations must be carefully analyzed before a clubhouse is designed and built. Inappropriate clubhouses exist wherever there are golf courses, and many of these structures have incurable problems.

Because of high construction and operating costs, clubhouse architects must maximize the utility of each square foot of building area. Efficient management can then direct and control the workforce to minimize operating expenses.

Table 1.2 also lists the rooms or functional areas that may be included in a clubhouse. Within each area a number of specialized activities may be conducted. A kitchen, for example, could conceivably include a chef's office, receiving area, dry storage area, meat and vegetable coolers, freezers, hot food preparation area, salad and dessert area, raw food preparation area, bakery, ice machines, dishwashing area, pot and pan washing area, serving stations, and garbage room.

More mistakes are probably made in designing and sizing clubhouses than in any other aspect of golf course development. In the recent past developers of some upscale clubs with no insight into the negative economic impact of excessive size built clubhouses of up to 70,000 square feet which cost $200 to $300 per square foot. Such extravagant investments of capital can lead to excessive obsolescence.

On a practical level, clubhouse architects should be able to analyze the specialized needs of the users of a facility through systematized research. Once the functions of the clubhouse are

TABLE 1.2

Functional Components of a Clubhouse and Other Structures (in Square Feet)			
Clubhouse Component	**Municipal Course**	**Daily Fee Course**	**Country Club Course**
Pro shop	500	1,000-1,500	1,500
Office/administration	100	250-400	1,000-1,500
Storage	250	450	500-1,000
Snack shop*	450	-	-
Bar and grill	-	750	750-1,000
Dining room	-	-	4,000
Banquet room	-	-	0-6,000
Kitchen	-	400-1,500	2,500
Card/meeting room	-	-	2,000
Locker rooms	-	1,500-5,500	5,500-9,500
Fitness area	-	-	2,500-4,000
Car and bag storage	3,000	5,500	7,500
Subtotals	4,300	9,850-15,600	27,750-40,500
Maintenance building	2,500	6,000	6,000
Shop/garage	-	2,500	3,500
Miscellaneous	200	650-900	750-1,000
Total	**7,000**	**19,000-25,000**	**38,000-51,000**

* Includes restrooms

Additional areas that could be part of a clubhouse include:

- Control fee collection
- Changing room for pro shop
- Steam rooms
- Saunas
- Whirlpools
- Attendants' storage space
- Lounge
- Ancillary kitchen facilities
- Service pantry
- Library
- Nursery/children's room
- Boiler room

- Patios/terraces
- Car maintenance
- Mechanical rooms
- Employee lounge
- Maintenance offices
- Linen/janitorial
- Cold storage
- Dry storage
- Service corridor/transport
- Wine storage
- Loading dock
- Service pantry

Source: Arthur Gimmy International

identified, the analyst can consult architects and other specialists and determine the percentage of club members or the playing public that will be engaged in each function and the frequency of use over a specified time period. This information will help developers optimize the use of available funds.

There are no hard-and-fast rules for determining clubhouse functions, but some general concepts and expectations can be cited. Obviously, all golf courses need a sheltered area for the collection of fees and the start of play. The size of the pro shop or restaurant at a golf course is determined by studying competitive properties, the size and affluence of the membership, and the overall objectives of the management or owners. Overdevelopment of food and beverage facilities is a common problem in country clubs. In a resort complex, facilities such as restaurants, lounges, lockers and showers, kitchens, and offices can be provided by a hotel that is part of the project.

The appraisal analysis typically involves three clubhouse-related, revenue-producing departments: pro shop sales, food and beverage sales, and golf car rentals. With few exceptions, the performance of the clubhouse as a functional part of the golf course or country club is reflected in the income and expenses generated by these three departments. The financial viability of a clubhouse can be evaluated with careful cost accounting and analysis of the net gains or losses of individual departments.

In the application of the cost approach to value, economic data on clubhouse operations is needed to identify appropriate categories and amounts of depreciation and external obsolescence. This data is also needed in the sales comparison approach to adjust for differences between the clubhouses of sale properties and the subject property. Such comparisons depend on relative measures of productivity, which may be based on pro shop sales per member or per round, food and beverage sales per square foot or per round, and car rentals per member or per round.

It is prudent to make the clubhouse smaller if there is any question about its ultimate service requirements. Designing a clubhouse for expansion over its projected life cycle is difficult, but it is preferable to building a facility that is too large or elaborate.

OTHER IMPROVEMENTS AND FACILITIES

A golf course and clubhouse cannot exist without a substantial number of ancillary land improvements and buildings. At a bare minimum, a course must have golf car storage space, which is frequently found on the lower or basement level of the clubhouse, and a maintenance building for the storage of equipment and supplies such as fertilizer. Additional structures may include a starter's station, repair shop, guard shack, rest stations, and pump houses. Regulation courses typically have up to 8,000 square feet of enclosed storage area, usually in a prefabricated metal structure that is out of view but efficiently sited.

Other recreational facilities associated with country clubs, exclusive real estate subdivisions, and resorts include tennis courts and swimming pools. These amenities may be housed in separate clubhouse facilities with dressing rooms, a snack bar, offices, restrooms, and a lounge. Fitness facilities should be sized and equipped to maximize their use by members and spouses who do not golf. Site improvements on a golf course include golf car paths, parking lots, a driving range, a practice area, service and entry drives, landscaping, and outdoor lighting.

FURNITURE, FIXTURES, AND EQUIPMENT

In any analysis or valuation of a golf course, real property aspects of the project are emphasized. However, every golf facility includes a significant investment in furniture, fixtures, and equipment (FF&E), especially course maintenance equipment. It is common for a facility to have a variety of furniture in the lobby, office, and dining areas; office and kitchen equipment; pro shop furnishings; and maintenance tools and equipment.

Golf cars are among the personal property included in the FF&E category. They may or may not represent a large capital investment. Many clubs lease golf cars and other major equipment to reduce the amount of equity needed to develop and operate the course. The leased items are an expense rather than a depreciable asset.

The total cost of FF&E can range from 3% to 9% of total assets. The market tends to dictate that the return on FF&E will be higher than the return required for real property. Moreover, furniture, fixtures, and equipment have a much shorter average life expectancy, typically ranging from five to ten years for individual items.

An appraisal should include an itemized inventory and estimate of the depreciated value of FF&E. The treatment of FF&E is covered in the discussion of the valuation approaches in Chapters Seven through Ten. A sample equipment inventory for a new course is shown in the appendix.

USE OF A GOLF FACILITY RATING FORM

To facilitate a golf course appraisal, a consistent format should be applied to the comparison of rental and sales data, greens fees, and other golf course characteristics. Golf course analysts can use golf course rating data to study the competition and identify the special benefits and unique aspects of a particular golf course facility. Rating data can assist in the preparation of a capital improvement program, help to identify deficiencies, and provide a reference for future market research.

The golf course rating form shown in Figure 1.8 illustrates the minimum information that would be gathered in analyzing competitive golf courses.

SPECIAL ENVIRONMENTAL CONSIDERATIONS

Proposed golf courses must satisfy planning and zoning requirements and address environmental concerns. Environmental impact studies are required in many jurisdictions. Organized opposition to golf courses usually relates to the use of pesticides and fertilizers; the loss of open space, farmland, or wildlife habitat; and the inappropriate use of water.

Some of these problems can be alleviated with good management. For example, the seepage of pesticides and fertilizers can be reduced through controlled application. Water use can be managed effectively with computer-controlled irrigation systems and the substitution of drought-tolerant plantings. Objections relating to the loss of agricultural land and employment are difficult to contest, but may be countered by promoting the beneficial aspects of a golf course, such as employment opportunities, increased revenue from property and sales taxes, higher real estate values, and open space. In drought-prone areas of the country, the water issue can be most important. A golf course cannot exist without proper irrigation. As mentioned earlier, the increased use of treated effluent from waste water facilities is a contemporary solution to this problem. Future golf course locations will be influenced by their proximity to waste water plants. For golf courses in residential communities, onsite package plants can be used to reclaim domestic waste water for use on the golf course.

No investment in a prospective golf development should be made without first obtaining the services of professional consultants who can provide advice on environmental problems as well as planning and financial considerations.

FIGURE 1.8

Golf Course Rating Data

Name: _____

Address: _____

Metropolitan area: _____

No. of holes: _____   Acres: _____   Length: _____

Par/course rating: _____   Slope: _____   Age: _____

Annual rounds played: This year (est.)_____   Last year: _____

Description of buildings:

Type	Area in sq. feet	Condition/Design
_____	_____	_____
_____	_____	_____
_____	_____	_____

Type of irrigation:

List of amenities: (please check)

Practice greens _____   Driving range _____

Chipping green _____   Practice sand trap(s)_____

Lockers_____   Bag storage _____

Restaurant _____   Snack bar_____

Bar/lounge_____   Golf cars_____

Rain shelters _____   Restrooms (on course) _____

Drinking water (on course)_____   Snack bar (on course)_____

Tennis courts_____

Swimming pool _____

Other (list items) _____

Course rating: Use 1 to 5 points for each:

Excellent = 5; good = 4; average = 3; fair = 2; poor = 1

Greens/fairways_____   Clubhouse/pro shop _____

Tees/range/hazards _____   Trees/scenic beauty_____

Layout/design _____   Practice facilities _____

Food/beverage facilities   Other amenities _____

                                                                                Social atmosphere_____

                                                                                Total points_____

Note: A score over 45 is excellent; 35–44 points is good; 25–34 points is average; 15–24 points is fair; and less than 14 points is poor.

Course prices:

9-hole weekday $_____   9-hole weekend $_____   18-hole weekday $_____

18-hole weekend $_____   Golf car 9-hole $ _____   Golf car 18-hole $_____

Special rates-senior $_____   Junior $_____   Twilight $_____

Financial:

Gross revenue $_____   Net income $_____   Sale price $_____

Date_____   OAR _____   TRM_____

PPR _____   GFM _____   Other_____

Date of rating: _____   Name of analyst: _____

Person contacted: _____   Telephone: _____

Source: Arthur Gimmy International

CHAPTER TWO

GOLF INDUSTRY DATA AND TRENDS

There is much research data on golf courses available to the appraiser. Most of the data is developed by golf industry groups and other professionals, including the Professional Golfers Association of America, Golf Course Superintendents Association of America, Golf Course Builders Association of America, American Society of Golf Course Architects, and the National Golf Course Owners Association. State and local chapters of these groups can provide data as can other groups.

The major source of golf industry data and research, however, is the National Golf Foundation (NGF), headquartered in Jupiter, Florida. Since 1936 NGF has gathered and published industry data on golf course development, golfer characteristics and profiles, costs for the development and operation of facilities, player spending habits, and other factors that impact the game. Most of this data is updated annually and some is updated quarterly. Appraisers would be wise to become familiar with NGF and its research data, which can be viewed on its website.

This chapter examines issues related to supply and demand, player characteristics, participation rates, and trends in the industry and discusses how available data may be best used in the appraisal of a particular golf course. It is important to remember that the supply of golf courses and the degree of participation in the game varies by geographic region; national statistics do not adequately describe local conditions. Most of the statistics provided in this chapter have been compiled by NGF. Much of this data is derived from a national population sample and is subject to error and interpretation. While NGF is constantly improving its research efforts, the appraiser is cautioned to use these statistics in combination with actual field research and other primary data.

To use the data presented in this chapter effectively, an understanding of the basic terminology used by researchers is needed.

- *Golf capacity utilization* is the number of rounds played on a course divided by the desired number of rounds at a facility. A private course may prefer to express capacity utilization as the actual number of club members divided by the maximum number of members desired.
- *Golf participation rate* is the percentage of the total population in a defined area, age five and older, who have played golf at least once within a calendar year.
- *Golf frequency rate* is the average number of rounds played per year by a defined segment of the golfing population.
- *Golf accessibility rate* is the total population of a defined area compared to the number of golf holes available; the rate is expressed in terms of the number of persons per 18 holes.

GOLF COURSE SUPPLY

Golf has not always been the public game it is today in the United States. Groups of wealthy persons living near major metropolitan areas developed the vast majority of the nation's original golf courses. This predominance of private courses continued well into the twentieth century. There were approximately 5,000 golf courses in the United States in 1950, and more than 60% of them were private clubs. The ratio of golfers to golf courses was 400 to one. In 2000 NGF reported a total of 17,108 golf courses of all types in the United States (see Table 2.1), including 4,773 private courses (28%) and 12,335 public courses (72%). Public courses are divided into two major categories: municipal and daily fee. Municipal courses are owned by public entities, while daily fee courses are privately owned and operated for profit.

One important figure the appraiser will want to establish is the number of golf rounds that are available in a given market. To accomplish this, a survey is made of courses within the defined market to ascertain the number of *desired* rounds. This will vary from course to course based on a number of variables, including management policy, course conditions, location in the market, budget requirements and operating history. For example, a daily fee operator who wants to maximize income while minimizing "wear and tear," may desire to achieve 60,000 rounds per year. A municipal golf course, which operates to provide the

TABLE 2.1

Course Types	Daily Fee	Municipal	Private	Total
U.S. Golf Course Totals				
Regulation				
9-hole	2,671	674	950	4,295
18-hole	5,651	1,664	3,570	10,885
Total regulation courses	8,322	2,338	4,520	15,180
Executive				
9-hole	452	134	75	662
18-hole	260	45	62	367
Total executive courses	712	179	137	1,029
Par-3				
9-hole	482	143	98	723
18-hole	121	38	17	176
Total par-3 courses	603	181	115	899
Total courses	9,637	2,698	4,772	17,108
Total holes	141,021	40,005	75,798	256,824

Source: National Golf Foundation

most availability to the largest number of citizens, may desire to host 80,000 rounds. The numbers will differ in each market, and the goals of each course operator must be considered. The appraiser will want to analyze each course in the market area to develop an accurate assessment of the supply of golf rounds.

The number of *desired* rounds will almost always be greater than the number of actual rounds played, even in an undersupplied market, due to weather, cost and time restrictions, and course difficulty. In many markets, the number of rounds played is close to the desired number of rounds. This is demonstrated by national statistics, which showed an average of 36,333 rounds played per 18 holes in 2000, down from 45,265 rounds per 18 holes in 1990. This decline is a result of the dynamic growth in the number of golf courses in the 1990s.

The appraiser will also want to know the capacity utilization (or occupancy factor) in the subject's market area. To ascertain capacity utilization for a public course, the number of actual rounds played is divided by the number of desired rounds. For instance, if a course desires to host 60,000 rounds but only receives 52,000 rounds, the capacity utilization is 87%. For a private course, with 460 members and a capacity for 500, the utilization factor would be 92%. Some courses, usually municipal facilities, achieve a capacity utilization of more than 100% by accepting more players than would normally be recommended to ensure good course conditions and acceptable playing times.

The supply of golf courses and the capacity utilization of courses vary greatly by region and by state.

GOLF COURSE DISTRIBUTION

There are various types of golf course operations (e.g., private club, daily fee, resort, municipal, military) and various types of courses which are generally categorized by their lengths (e.g., regulation, executive, par-3). The reader is encouraged to refer to the glossary in the addenda for definitions of these and other golf terms. Each year the National Golf Foundation publishes a tabulation of golf course facilities titled *Golf Facilities in the United States*, which sets forth the particulars of golf course development and total golf facility supply. This publication also presents statistics on accessibility by state, region, and metropolitan statistical area (MSA). The most meaningful statistic to be gleaned from this data is the golf accessibility rate, which expresses supply in terms of the total area population.

The 2001 edition of *Golf Facilities in the United States* provides a breakdown of population per 18 holes at the national, state, and regional levels and population per hole at the MSA and national levels. Table 2.2 that sets forth this information for 2000. Careful analysis of this data by the appraiser is important. According to NGF, golf accessibility is defined as the relationship of golf supply and potential demand in a given area and is measured by dividing the area population by the number of holes to determine the number of persons per hole for that area. When combined with other information on golf participation rates, demographic trends, and socioeconomic considerations, the golf needs of a particular area may be assessed. A full analysis of all competing courses in a particular market area is required to complete this assessment.

Table 2.3 ranks each state by the number of public and private courses. A high ranking generally indicates an underserved market, while a low ranking may suggest that a state has an adequate supply or an oversupply of golf courses. It is not uncommon for golf courses to be unevenly distributed. For instance, a major metropolitan area may be underserved even though the state shows an adequate supply for its population. Another significant variable in certain areas is the number of resort courses that cater to large numbers of vacationing golfers.

Returning to Table 2.2, which shows overall golf accessibility by state (excluding Alaska), the lowest ranking state is California, which has 38,749 persons per 18 holes, while the highest ranking state is North Dakota, with 10,038 persons per 18 holes. For public courses, these states retain the same ranking. Private course figures show Florida is the highest ranked with 32,979 persons per 18 holes, while Utah is the lowest with 161,210. The overall number of golf courses per population is important, but

TABLE 2.2

State and Regional Golf Accessibility—2000

State and Region	2000 Population	Total Holes	Total Pop. Per 18 holes	Total Rank	Public Holes	Public Pop. Per 18 holes	Public Rank	Private Holes	Private Pop. Per 18 holes	Private Rank
Connecticut	3,286,710	2,790	21,205	37	1,530	38,667	42	1,260	46,953	9
Maine	1,259,783	1,746	12,987	12	1,512	14,997	11	234	96,906	45
Massachusetts	6,192,844	5,274	21,136	36	3,537	31,516	34	1,737	64,175	23
New Hampshire	1,211,496	1,539	14,170	15	1,305	16,710	13	234	93,192	40
Rhode Island	992,905	765	23,362	40	432	41,371	44	333	53,671	14
Vermont	597,455	999	10,765	4	864	12,447	2	135	79,661	32
New England	**13,541,193**	**13,113**	**18,588**		**9,180**	**26,551**		**3,933**	**434,558**	
New Jersey	8,180,016	4,878	30,185	47	2,601	56,609	48	2,277	64,664	24
New York	18,218,649	13,185	24,872	44	9,135	35,899	40	4,050	80,972	36
Pennsylvania	12,021,139	11,610	18,637	26	7,803	27,730	28	3,807	56,838	16
Middle Atlantic	**38,419,804**	**29,673**	**23,306**		**19,539**	**35,394**		**10,134**	**68,241**	
Illinois	12,180,495	10,746	20,403	34	7,776	28,196	30	2,970	73,821	28
Indiana	5,982,403	7,425	14,503	16	5,877	18,323	15	1,548	69,563	26
Michigan	9,912,884	15,021	11,879	7	12,483	14,294	6	2,538	70,304	27
Ohio	11,299,135	12,717	15,993	20	9,513	21,380	18	3,204	63,478	21
Wisconsin	5,289,691	7,506	12,685	11	6,516	14,612	9	990	96,176	42
East North Central	**44,664,608**	**53,415**	**15,051**		**42,165**	**19,067**		**11,250**	**71,463**	
Iowa	2,880,573	4,626	11,208	5	3,627	14,296	7	999	51,902	13
Kansas	2,672,533	3,240	14,847	18	1,971	24,407	22	1,269	37,908	4
Minnesota	4,822,750	6,912	12,559	9	6,012	14,439	8	900	96,455	44
Missouri	5,508,242	5,103	19,429	30	3,510	28,247	31	1,593	62,240	19
Nebraska	1,678,625	2,691	11,228	6	2,016	14,988	10	675	44,763	6
North Dakota	637,393	1,143	10,038	1	1,017	11,281	1	126	91,056	39
South Dakota	739,478	1,323	10,061	2	1,026	12,973	3	297	44,817	7
West North Central	**18,939,594**	**25,038**	**13,616**		**19,179**	**17,775**		**5,859**	**58,186**	
Delaware	760,314	729	18,773	27	342	40,017	43	387	35,363	3
District of Columbia	517,659	90	103,532	51	90	103,532	51	0	0	0
Florida	15,351,873	20,907	13,217	13	12,528	22,057	19	8,379	32,979	1
Georgia	7,887,700	7,227	19,646	31	4,905	28,946	33	2,322	61,145	18
Maryland	5,217,014	3,312	28,353	46	1,917	48,986	47	1,395	67,316	25
North Carolina	7,747,726	10,017	13,922	14	7,038	19,815	17	2,979	46,814	8
South Carolina	3,930,581	6,822	10,371	3	4,968	14,241	5	1,854	38,161	5
Virginia	6,940,092	5,499	22,717	39	3,339	37,413	41	2,160	57,834	17
West Virginia	1,810,928	1,755	18,574	25	1,350	24,146	21	405	80,486	35
South Atlantic	**50,163,887**	**56,358**	**16,022**		**36,477**	**24,754**		**19,881**	**45,418**	
Alabama	4,405,925	4,419	17,947	24	2,817	28,153	29	1,602	49,505	11
Kentucky	3,991,110	4,212	17,056	23	2,826	25,421	24	1,386	51,833	12
Mississippi	2,789,503	2,601	19,305	29	1,539	32,626	37	1,062	47,280	10
Tennessee	5,541,822	4,599	21,690	38	3,006	33,185	38	1,593	62,619	20
East South Central	**16,728,360**	**15,831**	**19,020**		**10,188**	**29,555**		**5,643**	**53,360**	
Arkansas	2,575,028	2,826	16,401	22	1,440	32,188	36	1,386	33,442	2
Louisiana	4,401,013	2,394	33,090	48	1,368	57,908	49	1,026	77,211	30
Oklahoma	3,380,866	3,177	19,155	28	2,376	25,613	25	801	75,975	29
Texas	20,342,007	13,383	27,360	45	8,667	42,247	45	4,716	77,641	31
West South Central	**30,698,914**	**21,780**	**25,371**		**13,851**	**39,895**		**7,929**	**69,691**	
Arizona	4,889,201	5,481	16,056	21	3,906	22,531	20	1,575	55,877	15
Colorado	4,121,552	3,663	20,253	33	2,736	27,115	27	927	80,030	34
Idaho	1,272,513	1,449	15,808	19	1,197	19,136	16	252	90,894	38
Montana	892,844	1,278	12,575	10	1,026	15,664	12	252	63,775	22
Nevada	1,862,453	1,683	19,919	32	1,350	24,833	23	333	100,673	46
New Mexico	1,766,409	1,287	24,705	42	954	33,328	39	333	95,482	41
Utah	2,176,333	1,629	24,048	41	1,386	28,264	32	243	161,210	49
Wyoming	482,929	711	12,226	8	612	14,204	4	99	87,805	37
Mountain	**17,464,234**	**17,781**	**18,297**		**13,167**	**23,875**		**4,014**	**78,315**	
Alaska	626,788	243	46,429	50	243	46,429	46	0	0	0
California	33,498,246	15,561	38,749	49	10,269	58,717	50	5,292	113,940	48
Hawaii	1,195,682	1,467	14,671	17	1,197	17,980	14	270	79,712	33
Oregon	3,366,679	2,925	20,718	35	2,295	26,405	26	630	96,191	43
Washington	5,840,330	4,239	24,800	43	3,276	32,090	35	963	109,165	47
Pacific	**44,527,725**	**24,435**	**32,801**		**17,280**	**46,383**		**7,155**	**112,019**	
U.S. Totals	**275,148,319**	**256,824**	**19,284**		**181,026**	**27,359**		**75,798**	**65,340**	

Source: National Golf Foundation, *Golf Facilities in the United States*, 2001 edition.

GOLF INDUSTRY DATA AND TRENDS

TABLE 2.3

State Total Course Supply Ranked by Type—2000

State	Daily Fee Courses	2000 Rank	1999 Rank	Municipal Courses	2000 Rank	1999 Rank	Private Courses	2000 Rank	1999 Rank	Total Courses	2000 Rank	1999 Rank
Alabama	146	21	24	36	31	31	105	16	16	287	23	24
Alaska	16	50	T49	3	T48	T48	0	T50	T50	19	50	50
Arizona	202	16	T16	43	26	26	92	20	22	337	19	19
Arkansas	95	T30	32	16	42	T38	91	T21	T20	202	T30	T29
California	477	5	6	207	1	1	323	2	2	1007	2	2
Colorado	95	T30	28	93	9	9	55	30	31	243	26	26
Connecticut	67	T36	37	37	30	29	81	T24	T24	185	32	32
Delaware	19	49	T49	2	T50	T50	22	38	38	43	49	49
District of Columbia	3	51	51	4	47	47	0	T50	T50	7	51	51
Florida	654	2	2	112	5	5	495	1	1	1261	1	1
Georgia	260	15	15	53	20	19	146	10	10	459	13	13
Hawaii	64	38	38	8	45	45	17	41	T39	89	45	44
Idaho	57	42	43	31	33	T33	15	T45	T43	103	T41	41
Illinois	341	11	10	191	T2	2	193	T6	7	725	8	8
Indiana	313	12	12	73	T10	12	96	18	19	482	12	12
Iowa	266	14	14	59	T14	15	81	T24	T24	406	15	15
Kansas	103	28	29	61	13	14	95	19	T17	259	25	25
Kentucky	143	23	T21	52	T21	22	91	T21	T20	286	24	23
Louisiana	67	T36	36	28	35	35	72	27	27	167	34	34
Maine	110	26	26	9	44	44	16	T42	42	135	35	35
Maryland	79	34	35	40	28	27	83	23	23	202	T30	31
Massachusetts	196	17	T16	52	T21	21	115	13	14	363	16	17
Michigan	721	1	1	96	8	8	154	9	9	971	3	3
Minnesota	343	10	11	104	7	7	54	31	30	501	11	11
Mississippi	82	33	33	18	41	T38	79	26	T24	179	33	33
Missouri	194	18	T16	56	T17	16	109	15	15	359	17	16
Montana	62	39	39	23	T36	T36	16	T42	T43	101	43	42
Nebraska	123	25	25	49	23	23	47	33	33	219	27	27
Nevada	60	T40	41	23	T36	T36	20	T39	41	103	T41	43
New Hampshire	92	32	T30	3	T48	T48	16	T42	T43	111	38	T38
New Jersey	108	27	27	55	19	20	142	11	11	305	20	20
New Mexico	38	T45	46	30	34	T33	23	37	37	91	44	45
New York	504	4	4	134	4	4	248	4	4	886	5	5
North Carolina	389	9	9	38	29	30	176	8	8	603	9	9
North Dakota	50	44	44	47	24	24	10	47	47	107	40	40
Ohio	514	3	3	108	6	6	193	T6	6	815	6	6
Oklahoma	97	29	T30	70	12	11	50	32	32	217	28	28
Oregon	145	22	T21	19	T39	41	39	34	34	203	29	T29
Pennsylvania	471	6	5	46	25	25	234	5	5	751	7	7
Rhode Island	27	T47	48	5	46	46	20	T39	T39	52	48	48
South Carolina	295	13	13	11	43	43	114	14	13	420	14	14
South Dakota	60	T40	40	34	32	32	24	36	36	118	37	37
Tennessee	142	24	23	56	T17	T17	101	17	T17	299	21	21
Texas	411	7	7	191	T2	3	304	3	3	906	4	4
Utah	38	T45	45	57	16	T17	15	T45	T43	110	39	T38
Vermont	56	43	42	2	T50	T50	8	48	48	66	46	46
Virginia	174	T19	19	41	27	28	138	12	12	353	18	18
Washington	174	T19	20	59	T14	13	61	28	28	294	22	22
West Virginia	77	35	34	19	T39	42	28	35	35	124	36	36
Wisconsin	390	8	8	73	T10	10	59	29	29	522	10	10
Wyoming	27	T47	47	21	38	T38	7	49	49	55	47	47

Note: T before number indicates tie in ranking.
Source: National Golf Foundation, *Golf Facilities in the United States*, 2001 edition.

ANALYSIS AND VALUATION OF GOLF COURSES AND COUNTRY CLUBS

the analyst should give more weight to the population/course ratios relative to the particular type of course under consideration.

At first glance, golf course accessibility statistics indicate a wide variance in course supply so it is difficult to establish a national norm for measuring accessibility. Many states are underserved although capacity utilization rates as low as 85% can be found in some Sunbelt states. Weather can make a huge difference in the number of playing days available in a Frostbelt state as compared to a Sunbelt location. Consequently, 10,038 persons per 18 holes in North Dakota can indicate nearly the same accessibility as 19,646 persons per 18 holes in Georgia.

A more refined analysis is facilitated by referring to NGF statistics for the 314 MSAs where supply is ranked according to population per hole (PPH). The national average in 2000 was 1,071 persons per hole, compared to 1,452 in 1990. Public courses averaged 1,520 PPH in 2000, compared to 2,503 in 1990, while private courses at about 3,635 remained unchanged during that decade. These figures indicate increases in the supply of golf courses. NGF has figures on population and the total number of golf courses for each MSA. Using these figures the analyst can refine the research further by determining the ratio of public and private courses in the MSA from current data.

When using the PPH as an analytical tool, care must be taken to consider the results within context. For example, Florida and Arizona attract a large number of tourists and seasonal residents, so population data for permanent residents will not reflect the true demand for golf in those areas. A careful analysis of demographic characteristics such as age and income can often bring the dynamics of supply and demand into focus because people who are over 50 or retired tend to play more frequently than persons who are younger.

NEW AND PLANNED GOLF COURSES

In analyzing a particular golf market, new and planned golf course facilities are important. Since 1994 the number of new courses built has continued at a record pace. This trend is primarily due to the maturing of the U.S. population, its affluence, and the appeal for new resort-style upscale golf courses. Table 2.4 shows new course openings from 1994 through 2000. Note that the number of courses opened in 2000 was 20% higher than the number opened in 1995.

In 2000 the leading state for new golf courses (as opposed to 18-hole equivalents) was Florida, with 41 of the nation's 524 new courses. The top ten states in new course openings are shown in Table 2.5.

TABLE 2.4

Golf Course Openings in 18-Hole Equivalents (1994–2000)							
	1994	**1995**	**1996**	**1997**	**1998**	**1999**	**2000**
Daily Fee	190.5	242.0	238.5	245.0	239.5	272.5	318.5
Municipal	38.5	45.0	41.5	35.0	40.0	40.0	21.0
Private	33.5	49.0	39.5	36.0	48.0	63.0	59.0
Total	**262.5**	**336.0**	**319.5**	**316.0**	**327.5**	**375.5**	**398.5**

Source: National Golf Foundation, *Golf Facilities in the United States*, 2001 edition.

TABLE 2.5

Top Ten States in Golf Course Openings—2000	
Florida	41
Texas	38
California	31
Michigan	28
Pennsylvania	25
Minnesota	24
New York	20
North Carolina	19
Indiana	19
Wisconsin	18
Total	**263**
U.S. Total	**524**

At the end of 2001, a total of 377 new golf courses were opened and 629 new courses were under construction. At the same time, NGF reported that another 905 were in the planning stage. History shows that about 60% of these new courses will open on schedule. In 2001, 82% of the new courses completed were public facilities. This trend is expected to continue as 86.3% of the planned courses and 84.3% of those under construction are public courses. These figures include expansion of existing facilities. Figures on new courses are reported quarterly in the NGF publication, U.S. Golf Course Construction–Activity Report, which includes the names and addresses of the courses by city and state.

GOLF PARTICIPATION

Participation rates for golfers in the United States vary widely and NGF has developed categories of golfers to reflect their playing patterns and frequency of play. These categories are broad, but provide the analyst with a quick snapshot of who plays the game.

- *Golfers*–Adults age 18 or above who played at least one regulation round in 2001
- *Juniors*–Juniors between ages 5-17 who played golf or visited a golf practice facility
- *Alternative participants*–Adults age 18 or above who participate in golf only by utilizing an alternative course (executive short course, par-3 course, pitch and putt course) or driving range.
- *Golf participants*–The combination of golfers, juniors and alternative participants
- *Best customers*–Golfers age 18+ with household golf spending of $1,000 or more, and/or personally played 25+ rounds of golf in 2001[1]

In the past, NGF has reported on the playing frequency of golfers, placing them in categories such as core golfers (age 18

1. National Golf Foundation.

and above who played eight or more rounds in 2000), occasional golfers (age 18 and above who played one to seven rounds), and Junior Golfers (age 12 to 17 who played at least one round). The research shown in Table 2.6 indicates that the average core golfer was 46 years old, had a household income of $75,200, and played 44 rounds per year. This compares with the occasional golfer with an average age of 39, who had a household income of $72,100 and played three rounds per year. Junior golfers averaged 14 years of age, played 11 rounds, and had a household income of $76,700, reflecting the relative affluence of families that produce young golfers. A powerful group among golf participants are senior golfers (age 50+) who typically have more leisure time and above-average incomes, two important attributes of active golfers. The typical senior golfer played an average of 39 rounds per year and had a household income of $67,619.

Table 2.6 indicates that one of the golf industry's biggest opportunities lies in the ability to increase the rate of participation for occasional golfers. It also shows that most junior golfers are from wealthier families who can provide access to golf facilities for their children.

TABLE 2.6

Average Participation of Golfer Types				
	Core Golfers	Occasional Golfers	Junior Golfers	Senior Golfers
Age	46	39	14	62.2
Household income	$75,200	$72,100	$76,700	$67,619
Annual rounds	44	3	11	39

Source: National Golf Foundation

NUMBER OF GOLFERS

At the end of 2001, there were 37,100,000 golf participants in the United States, an increase of 1.1 million, or 3 %, over 2000. These figures include golfers of all ages and also 4,900,000 exclusive driving range users. Table 2.7 shows a breakdown of golf participants.

One major goal of the industry is to increase continually the number of participants in the golfer (18+) category. The number of golfers can best be increased by retaining the interest of junior golfers into adulthood and by encouraging the skill development of those who play short courses and visit golf practice ranges.

TABLE 2.7

U.S. Golf Participants			
	2001	**2000**	**% Change**
Golfers (18+)	25,800,000	25,400,000	1.6%
Juniors (5-17)	4,400,000	4,000,000	10.0%
Alt. participants	6,900,000	6,600,000	4.5%
Alt. course types	2,000,000	1,700,000	18.0%
Exc. range users	4,900,000	4,900,000	0.0%
Total participants	37,100,000	36,000,000	3.0%

Source: National Golf Foundation

DISTRIBUTION OF GOLFERS

The nation's 25,800,000 golfers are spread throughout the United States. The percentages of U.S. golfers within nine separate regions are set forth in Table 2.8.

The distribution and participation rates of golfers are closely associated with the accessibility of golf facilities. The number of golf courses per population in the East North Central Region (Illinois, Indiana, Ohio, Michigan, and Wisconsin) far exceeds the number in the East South Central Region (Kentucky, Tennessee, Mississippi and Alabama). Other key factors include general affluence, weather, and age groupings. The South Atlantic Region, which ranges from Virginia to Florida, has good weather year round for golfing, is economically vibrant, and has a large number of retired persons. Regions with the lowest participation rates tend to be the least affluent.

A word of caution to the appraiser: it is misleading to use national averages when analyzing a specific golf market. For example, the percentage of golfers in the national population has grown dramatically since the 1960s when 3.5% of the U.S. population played golf. In the 1990s, 11.7% of the population played golf and the participation rate was about 11%. This growth trend may not be reflected in all markets. The analyst must consider other factors such as gender, age, household income, education, occupation, number of retirees, and climate.

TABLE 2.8

Regional Distribution of Golfers		
Region	2001	2000
East North Central	21.3%	21.1%
West North Central	9.5%	8.5%
New England	5.1%	5.2%
Mountain	6.8%	6.6%
Pacific	15.5%	14.5%
Mid Atlantic	12.5%	13.2%
South Atlantic	16.1%	16.6%
West South Central	8.8%	9.5%
East South Central	4.3%	4.9%

Source: National Golf Foundation

GOLFER DEMOGRAPHICS

An abundance of demographic data is available for all markets. It is recommended that the appraiser analyze the data carefully to ascertain the characteristics of the market being studied. NGF annually compiles and publishes demographic profiles of golfers which provide national averages for participation rates according to gender, age, income, education, and occupation. This data, which is shown in Table 2.9, indicates these golfer characteristics:

TABLE 2.9

Demographic Profile of Golfers in the U.S.

	2001	2000
Total Golfers	25,800,000	25,400,000
Gender		
Male	76.2%	80.7%
Female	23.8%	19.3%
Age		
Under 18	3.3%	1.3%
18–29	22.1%	18.7%
30–39	25.6%	28.3%
40–49	21.5%	22.7%
50–59	13.1%	13.3%
60–64	4.6%	4.7%
65+	9.8%	11.0%
Income		
Under $20,000	6.9%	6.6%
$20,000–$29,999	8.0%	7.9%
$30,000–$39,999	10.1%	10.3%
$40,000–$49,999	10.8%	11.3%
$50,000–$74,999	17.2%	24.6%
$75,000–$99,999	21.3%	22.8%
$100,000+	25.7%	16.5%
Education		
Non-HS graduate	2.6%	2.9%
HS graduate	16.9%	15.1%
Some college	32.5%	36.3%
College graduate	48.0%	45.8%
Occupation		
Professional/mgt./adm.	38.6%	43.6%
Clerical/sales	16.5%	14.8%
Blue collar	23.8%	21.6%
Other	6.8%	7.4%
Retired	14.3%	12.7%

Source: National Golf Foundation, *Golf Participation in the United States*, 2002 edition.

- Golf is predominantly played by males (76.2% men vs. 23.8% women)
- Almost 70% of all golfers are between the ages of 18 and 50, with about 47% between the ages of 30 and 50.
- Golf is still more available to the affluent: 47% of all golfers have annual incomes of more than $75,000 and nearly 26% have incomes of more than $100,000.
- Golfers are educated. Only 2.6% of golfers are not high school graduates. Nearly half of all golfers have a college degree.
- More than half (53%) of all golfers are white-collar professionals, work in management, or are retired. An encouraging sign of the ever-increasing popularity of golf, especially in the Tiger Woods era, is that 23.5% of golfers work in blue-collar jobs.

GOLF'S BEST CUSTOMERS

The driving force in the golf industry is a group newly defined by NGF as "golf's best customers." This group accounts for the vast majority of rounds played and they spend the most money on golf. These golfers either play more than 25 rounds each year or play fewer than 25 rounds but have household golf spending that exceeds $1,000.

There were 9.8 million best customers in the United States in 2001, representing 38% of total golfers. Amazingly, this group was responsible for more than 80% of all golf spending and rounds played. NGF has a distinct demographic profile for best customers.

- 61% are between the ages of 35 and 64
- Their average household income is $84,300.
- More than half (55%) hold bachelor or graduate degrees.
- 46% live in two-person households, usually with no children in the home.

POTENTIAL FOR GROWTH

The national participation rate for golfers has remained somewhat static since 1995 and the golf industry is struggling to find the key to future growth. In 1999 the National Golf Foundation Board of Directors decided to prepare a study on the future of golf in the next ten years. The study was accomplished with the participation of key players in the industry and was published as *A Strategic Perspective on the Future of Golf.* Highlights of this report provide an honest overview of golf's future and suggestions to address some its major challenges.

The supply of golf courses has increased dramatically since 1990, but participation rates have generally remained flat. Many golf course owners and operators have experienced a shrinking bottom line because of an imbalance between supply and demand–i.e., new courses are being built and the number of golfers has not kept pace. It is estimated that golf loses about the same number of players as it gains each year (more than three million). This trend is creating a "demand gap" of approximately 100 million annual rounds, indicating that the industry must find a way to increase the number of rounds played. Currently, the number of rounds played increases by only 1.5% per year.

Golf is now a mature industry and is beginning to experience cyclical characteristics, particularly in relation to supply and demand issues. Most insiders agree that the game can and will continue to sustain its historical growth rate of 1.5% to 2%. The main concern is how golf can grow at a greater rate to meet the needs of owners and serve the available pool of potential golfers on an ongoing basis.

One major finding of the NGF study was that approximately 40 million people would either like to participate in the game or are already playing and would like to play more frequently. This group was designated as "highly interested players." It was immediately recognized that the industry would not have to "sell" the game to these persons, but find ways to accommodate their desire to play golf. If only a small proportion of these highly interested players can be stimulated, an annual participation rate increase of 3% to 4% for rounds played could be achieved over the current rate of 1.5%. Few industries have this kind of latent market waiting to be tapped.

In 1998 NGF conducted a series of surveys of current and former golfers, non-golfers, and junior players. Major findings of the surveys follow:

- Of the 24 million golfers 18 or older, 14 million are highly interested in the game and desire to play more.
- Of the 42 million former golfers, 12 million are highly interested in the game and desire to take up golf again.
- Of the 130 million adult non-golfers, seven million are interested in golf and are open to trying the game.
- Of the 51 million who are between the ages of 5 and 17, eight million either currently plan or desire to play or are very open to trying the game.

Among the millions of potential players who want to become active participants, the best opportunity lies with current players who want to play more and former golfers who want to come back to the game. The industry's main focus, then, will be to stimulate less active golfers to become more committed players.

With golf awareness at an all-time high around the world, what prevents these potentially committed players from moving to the next level? Although golf courses offer lessons, most operations are not geared to assist new or returning golfers to overcome their lack of skill or fear of failure. They provide few opportunities for golfers to learn or improve at a comfortable pace with others who are at a similar stage. Overall, the NGF study identified these critical reasons why golfers play: enjoyment of early experiences with the game; encouragement from family, friends, and golf course personnel; becoming more connected to the game; understanding the game; affordability; and accessibility.

The key to a successful golf industry is the committed golfer, defined as playing at least eight rounds per year. Committed golfers make up about 50% of total players, but contribute 87% of total spending and 95% of all rounds played. The creation of new committed golfers will determine the success of golf in the future, both locally and nationally. Growth opportunities have not been tapped for a number of reasons.

- Historically, the industry has experienced success.
- The industry is somewhat fragmented with little communication or agreement on strategies for improvement.
- Relatively few customers account for the vast majority of spending.
- The game has unique barriers to participation by juniors, women, seniors, and minorities.
- Course owners resist changes that may alienate current avid golfers.

The future economic health of golf will be determined by how well these problems are addressed by the industry. Appraisers and analysts must be familiar with these issues and understand how they will be addressed by particular golf course facilities and markets.

TRENDS

Certain trends have developed within the golf industry since 1998. Some of these trends should be of short duration, while others may be more lasting. Today, more than any time in history, practically all segments of the golf industry are acting cooperatively to meet and solve its problems and take advantage of its opportunities. Some of the emerging trends are discussed below.

- *Increased participation.* The supply of new golf courses is outpacing the development of new golfers and increases in participation. Golf courses are increasing at an annual rate of more than 2.5%, while the number of rounds played is relatively flat, increasing at 1.5% per year since 1995. The industry has identified a ready market of about 40 million new, former, and existing golfers who would like to play more. Industry experts want to develop programs that will increase participation.
- *Consolidation.* Since the early 1990s, consolidation of golf course ownership and operations has steadily increased. Local, regional, and national companies now own multiple courses. Real estate developers have had difficulty operating golf facilities and municipalities have grown weary of high operating costs and residents' opposition to increasing fees. Many golf course operation companies have experienced financial problems in recent years and some have gone out of business. Others have sold golf courses from their inventory or consolidated with other companies. The trend toward consolidation is expected to continue.

- *Upscale facilities.* Another trend in the golf business is development of the upscale golf facility. These courses have been built to attract an increasing number of affluent golfers who travel frequently and are willing to pay significantly higher-than-normal fees to play. Most of these facilities have been developed at traditional resort/golf destinations and around major metropolitan areas; others are located in remote areas that offer privacy and total exclusivity. The projects are almost always accompanied by expensive second-home communities and luxury hotel accommodations.

- *Aging population.* As the baby boom generation passes 50 years of age, they reach the most productive years of their lives and have more time and money to spend on the game. In 1998 there were 74 million persons in the United States who were 50 or older. That number will increase to 95 million by 2010. This group will account for a 12% increase in rounds played between 1998 and 2010.

- *Internet usage.* The majority of golfers are on-line and the Internet has become a major factor in the lives of golfers. More than one in three golfers book over the Internet when they travel to play golf and the trend is increasing. As more golf courses develop their own Web sites, golfers can obtain information about the locations, conditions, fees, and amenities at these courses and confirm tee times from their own desks. The trend to book online has affected airlines and hotels in recent years and astute golf course operators will exploit this resource to their benefit in the future.

CHAPTER THREE

MARKET ANALYSIS

A critical component of any golf course appraisal assignment is an analysis of the subject market, with the major emphasis on supply and demand. Based on this analysis, the analyst can make projections regarding the feasibility of a new golf course or expansion of an existing facility. To the appraiser with little or no experience with such assignments, market analysis may appear to be a daunting task, but considerable data on golf courses is available. This chapter will identify some key resources and methods of compiling, organizing, and interpreting golf course information, focusing on analyses of golf course supply in the subject market and golfer demand characteristics.

As previously mentioned, golf course supply and the degree of participation by golfers varies widely by geographic region. Factors that impact both supply and participation include weather, economics, land availability, population density, and age characteristics. Consequently, national statistics and averages have only limited usefulness in analyzing a specific market. Most data provided by the National Golf Foundation, for example, relates to major regions identified as groups of states that share similar geographic and climatic characteristics. The data for a given region may help the appraiser analyze a specific local market, but great care must be taken to recognize and interpret local demographic and market characteristics.

To supplement the statistics and data provided by the National Golf Foundation, the appraiser can gather meaningful information from local and area golf associations, golf course owners, municipal planning departments, and institutional research departments. Some private companies can also provide fairly accurate demographic information for a given market area based on official data from the U.S. Department of the Census. For example, data might be provided for an area within a 20-mile radius of the subject property, which is the typical size of a golf market in an urban area.

The appraiser's analysis will include both primary and secondary data. Primary data relates to characteristics found within the subject's specific market area and requires careful investigation by the appraiser. Secondary data refers to information that relates to state, regional, or national trends. NGF and other organizations provide an abundance of secondary data, but this information is generic and cannot usually be accurately applied to a specific market.

An article by Stephen F. Fanning, MAI, published in *The Appraisal Journal* alerts appraisers to the submarket segmentation that should be considered in the market analysis of a golf course.[1] To define the various segments of a golf course market, Fanning first identifies the "demanders" for a specific course and the competing facilities in the same market.

There are many golf course submarkets within a given geographical area that do not correspond with the three traditional types of golf courses—i.e., municipal, daily fee, and private. Today analysts find resort courses, upscale daily fee courses, regional ultra-private residential golf clubs, corporate clubs, senior retirement developments, and other facilities. Moreover, each type of course is further stratified by the income, age, social status, and other characteristics of the golfers who use it.

In other words, the traditional approach, in which the analyst considers only local population, age, income, type of course, and driving time to the facility, is usually inadequate. A true picture of a golf course's feasibility and value can only be obtained by analyzing the market factors that are most significant to a particular course. The journal article includes an outline that sets forth one approach to the segmentation process. This outline is shown in Figure 3.1.

ANALYZING LOCAL GOLF COURSE SUPPLY

The purpose of a golf course market study is to determine the number of rounds that may be supported by a specific market area. The first step in making this determination is to survey all the golf courses in the competitive market. The appraiser will want to prepare a chart showing the following information for each course: course name, location, distance from subject, number of holes, yardage, range of fees (or membership costs), golf car fees, basic facilities (e.g., clubhouse, restaurant, health club),

1. Stephen F. Fanning, MAI, "Segmentation of Golf Course Markets" *The Appraisal Journal* (January 2003).

FIGURE 3.1

Golf Course Market/Marketability Study Process*

1. What golf market segment(s) does the subject golf course have the ability to serve? (property productivity analysis)
   Factors that determine market segment:
   - Course design and quality
   - Facilities design and quality
   - Legal requirements (deed restrictions, club bylaws, etc.)
   - Social and economic characteristics of the club and community
   - Location, including how the golf course fits with the community growth structure and with competitive courses
2. What are the characteristics of the consumers for this golf market segment?
   - Market area delineation
   - Consumer profile of most likely users
     - Type
       - Tourist
       - Second home residents
       - White collar executives
       - Corporate outing groups
       - Local residents
     - Characteristics
       - Income
       - Age
       - Social and family structure
       - Employment categories (e.g., high tech, service)
3. What is the competition for this market segment?
   - Current competitive courses
   - Planned competitive courses
4. What is the future golf course demand for this market segment?
   - Inferred methods
     - Current market conditions
     - General growth trends of city and subject submarket
   - Fundamental methods
     - Actual current demand forecast methods
     - Potential new demand forecast methods
5. What is the market condition for this market segment? (comparing supply with current and future demand)
6. How much of this market segment can the subject golf property capture?
   - Current capture analysis methods
   - Competitive course rating methods
7. What are the financial implications of the property?
   - Is it a good investment? (investment value to an individual or specific groups)
   - Is the property's value more than its cost? (feasibility)
   - Does this market segment produce a higher net income than another segment? (highest and best use)
   - What is the golf course's market value? (appraisal)
   - Can redirected management or marketing increase income? (management practices)

---

* The outline is based on Fanning & Associates' study process. Others may have different styles and content, but segmentation should be required near the start of the study process.

Source: Stephen F. Fanning, "Segmentation of Golf Course Markets," *The Appraisal Journal* (January 2003): 63.

---

condition, and estimated number of rounds played. The chart may also show information or comments that complete the golf course profile. A sample of such a chart is provided in Table 3.1.

TABLE 3.1

Public Golf Courses in Same Competitive Market as Friendly Hills Golf Course

Golf Course	Location	Holes	Yardage	Par	Weekday 18-Holes	Weekend 18-Holes	Golf Car	Estimated Rounds	Year Opened	Miles From Subject
Oak Tree	Springfield	18	6,725	72	$30*	$38	$13†	85,000‡	1967	12
Hidden Valley	Springfield	9	2,769	35	$22	$25	$11	50,000	1963	9
Hilltop	Springfield	27	7,000	72	$55	$70	$12	75,000	1996	11
Green Hills	Springfield	18	6,949	72	$73	$108	$12	45,000	1998	14
Mt Vista	Upton	18	6,466	72	$31	$41	$13	65,000	1963	21
Canyon Lakes	Lakeside	18	6,373	71	$55	$70	$12	62,000	1987	24
Locust Hills	Lakeside	18	7,220	72	$63	$83	$12	55,000	1999	21
St Andrews	Littlefield	36	6,200/6,900	72/72	$28	$42	$12	90,000	1967	28
River Bend	Littlefield	9	3,104	36	$15	$20	$10	50,000	1999	10
Indian Valley	Littlefield	18	6,478	72	$18	$24	$13	72,000	1966	15
The Ridge	Littlefield	18	6,400	70	$18	$20	$10	40,000	2001	15
Ocean View	Auburn	18	6,928	72	$18	$23	$10	60,000	1967	16
Cottonwood	Auburn	18	6,407	72	$18	$23	$10	70,000	1952	20
The Farm	Auburn	18	7,000	72	$38	$53	$12	55,000	1999	18
Blue Sky	Rock Hills	18	6,608	73	$38	$53	$12	60,000	1994	15
Sunnyside	Rock Hills	18	6,701	71	$58	$78	$12	35,000	2002	16
Deer Valley	Oakton	18	7,000	72	$43	$68	$12	50,000	2000	20
Canyon Ranch	Oakton	18	6,481	72	$22	$32	$12	82,000	1957	22
Average—18-holes			6,696	71.82	$35.72	$48.38	$11.66	61,058		

* Fees for 9-hole courses shown for 18 holes of play.

† At some courses, golf cars are mandatory. Figures split greens fee and golf car fees as separate fees.

‡ Rounds estimated where not provided by operator.

Note. Executive (short) and par-3 courses not included in above schedule.

Source: Arthur Gimmy International

SUPPLY AND ACCESSIBILITY

The analyst must first identify the type of golf facility under consideration to define the market's comparable supply. For instance, if the subject property is a daily fee facility, the private courses in the market area do not directly compete with the subject.

Each competitive golf course must be inspected and evaluated by the analyst. One of the major purposes of this part of the appraisal is to determine the extent to which the existing supply is meeting market demand. Interviewing the operator or a key staff person will often help determine the number of desired rounds for each course. The term *desired rounds* means the number of rounds that will optimize income without creating golfer resistance due to longer playing times, unacceptable course conditions, and general overcrowding. The desired number of rounds will vary by course because each facility will have its own goals. For example, a daily fee course operated for profit will normally have fewer desired rounds than a municipal course, which is operated to serve the greatest number of golfers at the lowest possible fee.

UTILIZATION AND CAPACITY

The utilization rate for a golf course is similar to the occupancy rate for a hotel, office building, or apartment building. It is calculated by dividing the number of actual rounds played by the number of desired rounds. For example, a public golf course that desires 75,000 rounds but actually hosts only 68,000 has a *capacity utilization rate* of 91%. By analyzing each course in the market area, the appraiser can develop an accurate picture of the capacity for additional play at existing competitive facilities. A private course with 440 members and a capacity of 500 will have a capacity utilization rate of 88%. By analyzing each golf course in the subject market area, the appraiser can determine how many additional rounds of golf may be accommodated in the local market.

Other comparison methods are also available to the analyst. As noted in Chapter Two, NGF publishes data on the number of 18-hole golf courses in each state and MSA in the United States (see Table 2.2). It is important to note that NGF data may refer to "golf courses" or "golf facilities." Golf facilities often will have more than one course but are reported as a single facility. The total population for the subject market area can be divided by the number of 18-hole golf courses present to arrive at the number of persons per course. For instance, if a local market area in Oregon has a population of 363,000 and there are seven existing 18-hole public courses, the average population per course is 51,857. The population per 18 holes for the state is 26,405, indicating that the subject market may be underserved when compared to the state as a whole. The national average in 2000 was 27,359 persons for each 18-hole public golf course.

It is important to carefully evaluate and consider the types of courses in the market area. If the subject is a regulation-length public facility, greater consideration should be given to daily fee and municipal regulation courses. Resort courses should also be studied along with public facilities. Executive and par-3 courses should be reported, but only regulation courses will typically be included in the primary analysis of market supply.

The appraiser will also want to include a narrative description of each competitive course. This description should include information on design, ownership, operating philosophy and history, facility condition, the size of the clubhouse, fees and services, operating budgets (if available), location and access, and any other factors that may impact the operation and inform those who read the report.

In summary, the analyst's goal is to make an accurate estimate of utilization rates for existing golf courses in the subject market area. By comparing this estimate to the estimated demand, the analyst can determine if the subject market is being adequately served or requires additional facilities to meet demand.

If additions to the area's golf course supply are planned, information on these additions may be obtained by interviewing current golf course owners and operators and local municipal officials, particularly planning departments. The analyst should try to identify and interview key persons associated with planned projects and include data on potential new supply in the market analysis.

ANALYZING GOLFER DEMAND
ROUNDS PLAYED

The National Golf Foundation reports that there were approximately 25,800,000 golfers in the United States in 2001, compared with 25,400,000 in 2000. To learn how many rounds these golfers played annually, NGF partnered with the National Golf Course Owners Association (NGCOA) to survey all 15,720 facilities in the country. Replies were received from 2,426 facilities, a response rate of just over 15%. Previous surveys had targeted golfers aged 12 and older and asked them to estimate the number of rounds played. However, golfers tend to think they play more golf than they actually do, so this survey targeted facilities in hopes of producing more accurate results.

The NGCOA/NGF study (which divided the country into 11 regions rather than nine) showed that in 2001 about 518,100,000 rounds were played at regulation facilities, compared to 518,400,000 in 2000. The reasons cited for this small decline included weather, renovations, the economy, and the terrorist events of September 11, 2001. A breakdown of survey results is provided in Table 3.2.

TABLE 3.2

Rounds Played in the United States		
Region	Total Rounds in 2001 (in Millions)	Total Rounds in 2000 (in Millions)	% Change
	518.1	518.4	−0.1%
1. Northeast	71.1	69.4	2.4%
2. Mid Atlantic	31.7	30.6	3.7%
3. Southeast	65.8	64.8	1.5%
4. Central/S. Florida	36.5	35.4	2.9%
5. Gulf Coast	28.8	29.2	−1.4%
6. S. Central	32.5	32.3	0.9%
7. Lower Midwest	90.5	92.3	−1.9%
8. Upper Midwest	55.0	58.3	−5.7%
9. Mountain	19.7	18.4	7.2%
10. Southwest	64.5	65.0	−0.8%
11. Northwest	22.0	22.7	−3.0%

Source: 2002 survey by National Golf Association and National Golf Course Owners Association.

NGCOA and NGF plan to continue tracking the volume of rounds played and will report their findings to the industry on a quarterly basis beginning in 2003. Such data can help appraisers measure the overall playing activity of golfers and may help them analyze participation rates and rounds played in specific market areas.

While the analyst must be aware of both national and regional demand levels, this data alone is not sufficient to make a decision concerning a golf course project. To create a meaningful market analysis of demand in a specific market, survey data on competitive golf courses in the market area must be combined with demographic data. The primary indicators of golf participation are age and income.

MARKET DEMOGRAPHICS

Once the primary market area is determined for a golf facility, the appraiser can study its demographic structure and apply national and regional research data. Golfer demand in a given market area can be estimated by analyzing the population of the primary market and the relationship that exists between age and income. In this way the number of potential golfers and rounds played can be projected.

The sample golf market demand analysis that follows is based on data developed by NGF and Claritas, a private research firm. In this analysis, market size estimates are derived independently from two separate models—one based on age characteristics and the other on household income characteristics. Such data can be confirmed and supported by studying the actual performance of golf facilities in the subject market. The following demand analysis is based on a county-wide market in Florida, where 2000 participation rates were approximately 10.1%, but the methodology employed is also applicable to smaller and larger market areas.

Using statistics compiled in NGF's golf participation surveys, estimates of the market size for this county may be developed from the figures in Table 3.3. These estimates are shown in Tables 3.4 and 3.5.

OTHER VARIABLES TO BE CONSIDERED

Sometimes other variables affect the demand for golf in a given market area. For example, if the subject property is located in a resort area, the impact of visitors must be considered in estimating both supply and demand. Most resort areas have a large number of motels and hotels to accommodate tourists. The appraiser will want to estimate the number of potential rounds generated by these tourists, usually by studying the total room nights (i.e., number of occupied rooms per night) at area hotels.

TABLE 3.3

Demographic Summary		
2000 Population	249,436	
2005 Population projection	282,295	
2000 Households	101,829	
2005 Household projection	116,584	
2000 Median household income	$31,822	
2005 Median household income projection	$35,015	
2000 Median age	42.5	
2005 Median age projection	41.2	
2000 Households by income		
Total number of households	**101,829**	**% of Total**
Less than $15,000	20,225	19.86%
$15,000 to $25,000	19,945	19.59%
$25,000 to $35,000	18,227	17.90%
$35,000 to $50,000	18,491	18.16%
$50,000 to $75,000	15,556	15.28%
$75,000 to $100,000	5,081	4.99%
$100,000+	4,304	4.23%
2005 Households by income		
Total number of households	**116,584**	**% of Total**
Less than $15,000	19,951	17.11%
$15,000 to $25,000	21,236	18.22%
$25,000 to $35,000	19,823	17.00%
$35,000 to $50,000	22,321	19.15%
$50,000 to $75,000	19,109	16.39%
$75,000 to $100,000	7,353	6.31%
$100,000+	6,791	5.82%
2000 Population by age		
Population	**249,438**	**% of Total**
Under 5 years	15,640	6.27%
5 to 14 years	30,917	12.39%
15 to 19 years	16,432	6.59%
20 to 24 years	10,164	4.07%
25 to 34 years	30,866	12.37%
35 to 44 years	32,068	12.86%
45 to 64 years	58,149	23.31%
65+	55,202	22.13%
2005 Population by age		
Population projection	**282,295**	**% of Total**
Under 5 years	17,304	6.13%
5 to 14 years	34,335	12.16%
15 to 19 years	18,789	6.66%
20 to 24 years	12,254	4.34%
25 to 34 years	33,549	11.88%
35 to 44 years	34,062	12.07%
45 to 64 years	69,974	24.79%
65+	62,028	21.97%

Source: National Golf Foundation and Claritas, Inc.

TABLE 3.4

Household Income	Estimated Population	Potential Golfers	Potential Number of Rounds		
			Public	Private	Total
Estimated Market Size By Income—2000					
Less than $15,000	46,432	1,718	33,157	18,726	51,883
$15,000 to $24,000	45,801	3,105	87,570	39,127	126,697
$25,000 to $34,999	41,850	4,348	94,356	47,830	142,186
$35,000 to $49,999	42,458	5,800	128,174	109,615	237,789
$50,000 to $74,999	35,724	5,076	84,269	41,119	125,388
$75,000 to $99,999	11,667	1,884	17,711	16,392	34,103
$100,000+	9,890	1,801	32,236	34,577	66,814
Total	233,822	23,732	477,473	307,386	784,860

Source: National Golf Foundation

TABLE 3.5

Household Income	Estimated Population	Potential Golfers	Potential Number of Rounds		
			Public	Private	Total
Projected Market Size By Income—2005					
Less than $15,000	45,340	1,678	32,377	18,266	60,663
$15,000 to $24,999	48,281	3,273	32,377	41,246	133,558
$25,000 to $34,999	45,048	4,681	101,568	51,486	153,054
$35,000 to $49,999	50,746	6,932	153,194	131,012	284,207
$50,000 to $74,999	43,432	6,172	102,450	49,991	152,441
$75,000 to $99,999	16,721	2,700	25,384	23,494	48,878
$100,000+	15,422	2,808	50,271	53,922	104,193
Total	264,990	28,244	497,621	369,417	936,994

Source: National Golf Foundation

In a typical recreational area with destination-type hotels, the analyst may estimate 0.03 to 0.04 golf rounds per room night. In areas like Phoenix, Myrtle Beach, and Palm Springs where golf is a top attraction, a higher ratio may be applied.

Many golf courses associated with real estate development projects become part of the local public golf market, particularly in their initial years of operation. Often these facilities are converted to private membership clubs when a certain number of housing units are sold. If such facilities are present in the local market, the analyst should interview their managers to determine if any change of status is planned for the golf course in the future.

Demand may also be influenced by the presence of certain population segments that alter the results of the analytical methods typically applied. For example, some golf markets have a large retirement population or a population that varies at particular times of the year. Such variances are common in warm southern states, but they also affect demand in northern states such as Michigan, Colorado, Oregon, and Montana, which tend to have moderate summers.

CONCLUSION

By combining data on rounds played with NGF guidelines for golfer participation and the specific demographics of the subject area, the analyst can estimate general demand in the subject golf market. This information is compared to the appraiser's estimate of the current supply of golf courses to gauge the facilities' ability to meet present and projected demand. The analysis of local supply and demand is refined using other data and information gathered in the research process to arrive at a complete picture of the market in which the subject golf course competes.

Additional data on local supply and demand may be developed by personally interviewing managers of golf courses in the market area. Such interviews usually lead to other sources that will provide further data and add refinement to this crucial segment of the appraiser's analysis.

CHAPTER FOUR

VALUATION PROCESS AND SPECIAL CONSIDERATIONS

The valuation process is a methodology used to answer a client's specific questions about property value. This process begins with identification of the valuation problem to be solved and ends when a solution is reported to the client. This valuation process is described in detail in the Appraisal Institute's textbook *The Appraisal of Real Estate.* Figure 4.1 is based on the valuation process chart in that book, but here the process has been revised to apply specifically to the valuation of golf courses and country clubs. The revised chart addresses the unique characteristics of golf facilities and the valuation problems they create.

All three of the traditional approaches to value (cost, income capitalization, and sales comparison) may be appropriate in the appraisal of golf courses and country clubs. If properly applied, these approaches will indicate the value of the physical assets (real property and personal property or FF&E) as well as the value of the entire facility as a going concern or business enterprise. The valuation of a golf enterprise as an operating business will include a component of value attributed to the intangible assets of the business, if the facility is profitable.

To meet the requirements of accepted appraisal standards, the value of the real property assets must often be segregated from the values of personal property and the intangible aspects of the ongoing business. The need to segregate value in this way is determined by the requirements of the assignment. Segregation of the various components of value is typically required for mortgage financing and property tax purposes, but is often not necessary for feasibility analyses, investment decision making,

FIGURE 4.1

The Valuation Process

Definition of the Problem

Identification of client/ intended users	Intended use of appraisal	Purpose of appraisal (including definition of value)	Date(s) of opinion of value	Identification of characteristics of golf course (including location and property rights to be valued)

Scope of Work

Data Collection and Property Description

Market Area Data	Subject Course Data	Comparable Property Data
General characteristics of region, city, and neighborhood	Specific characteristics of land, rounds played, etc.	Sales and trend analysis

Market (Feasibility) Analysis

Trends, Competitive Courses, Golf Course Usage

Highest and Best Use

Site as though vacant

Golf course improvements

Financial Performance Analysis

Statistical Analysis of Revenue and Expenses by Percentages and Rounds

Application of Approaches to Value

Cost (Less depreciation)	Sales comparison techniques	Income capitalization (direct or DCF)

Reconciliation of Value Indications and Final Opinion of Value

Allocation of Appraised Value

Real Property

Personal Property

Intangible Assets

Source: Based on *The Appraisal of Real Estate*, 12th ed. (Chicago: Appraisal Institute, 2001). Figure revised by author.

or determining a sale price. It may also be appropriate to allocate a sale price to reflect various property components and their associated income tax implications. It is the responsibility of the analyst to determine when separate values are required and to provide information on these separate values to the client.

Chapter Eight (Cost Approach), Chapter Nine (Income Capitalization Approach), and Chapter Ten (Sales Comparison Approach) include detailed information on valuation processes, applications, and sources of supporting data. The information presented in this chapter relates to the overall scope of an appraisal and the analyst's role in analyzing the components, operations, and management of a complex enterprise. For many real estate appraisers, valuing a golf course is a new and challenging experience and requires special training and experience.

The analyst is not a golf course management consultant, but he or she should be able to recognize the difference between good and bad policies and comment on management activities that have a detrimental effect on value. To analyze a golf course facility as a business enterprise, the analyst must recognize that the net operating income from a successful golf course includes income produced by one or more intangible assets. Valuing intangible assets is difficult. In today's market most golf courses show variable results in each department due to changing economic conditions. With continued increases in competition, the overall results of many facilities may be stagnant or declining. The appraiser can deal with this problem by first analyzing the components of each revenue-producing department (e.g., greens fees and rounds, number of restaurant patrons and average cover, number of merchandise sales and average price per sale). Then, through market analysis, he or she can determine the facility's fair share of future patronage within the competitive trade area and create a discounted cash flow projection of annual departmental revenues and expenses.

HIGHEST AND BEST USE AND THE APPROACHES TO VALUE

A golf facility must be valued at the most profitable competitive use to which it can be put. Virtually all golf courses have greater value than the land value alone. Sometimes, however, a greater value could be realized by changing the tangible or intangible characteristics of the enterprise such as course size, condition, improvements, fee structure, or services. The appraiser should advise the owner if this is the case.

In the cost approach, value is estimated by determining the cost to develop an equivalent facility, including land, and deducting an appropriate amount for the depreciation evident in the subject property. Because the cost approach is founded on the principle of substitution and replacement sites are usually impossible to procure, this approach is generally inapplicable to golf courses. It is especially difficult to estimate external obsolescence in the current market where many prices have fallen 50% or more from the transactional levels achieved in the late 1990s.

The income capitalization approach assumes that value is based on the price market participants would pay to receive the future income that the subject property will produce. This financial consideration is driving current price trends. Buyers have realized that golf market revenues are not going to increase forever and that markets can be overbuilt. They may not recognize how good management can change the future performance of a property, however, because the impact of poor management is difficult to quantify.

To estimate future revenues and expenses properly, the analyst needs to gather data on the performance of efficiently run golf courses and country clubs and to understand the estimated expenditures required to bring the subject's performance up to an equivalent level. To address this concern, Chapters Five, Six, and Seven include a variety of operating and financial statistics for municipal courses, daily fee courses, and private courses and country clubs.

To apply the sales comparison approach the appraiser studies the prices currently being paid for golf courses and country clubs throughout the nation. However, this data may not be indicative of the value of the subject golf course if the transactions only involve problem properties. The analyst needs to be able to discern the performance differences between the subject property and sale properties and determine whether indicators of value developed from the transactions will be applicable to the subject. The discussion of the sales comparison approach includes information on five units of comparison or multipliers that are applicable in the appraisal of an existing or proposed golf course.

OPERATIONAL CONSIDERATIONS

In addition to good management policies and practices, many other factors must be considered in developing and operating a golf course. One of the most important requirements is a data collection and compilation system that allows the operator to understand and analyze revenues and expenses by department and subcategories of departments. The informational software used should provide statistics on units as well as dollar amounts. Data overload should be avoided, but a management company that oversees portfolio properties and funds will need extensive data (on a weekly basis) for detailed statistical analysis of properties scattered across the country. Figure 4.2 shows the type of extensive information that can be provided through an integrated accounting system.

FIGURE 4.2

Sample Chart of Accounts

Golf Operations

Revenue

Greens fees_____

Golf car fees_____

Rentals_____

Other_____

Expenses

Officer salaries_____	Over & short _____
Employee salaries_____	Professional fees_____
Bonus_____	Rental of equipment_____
Employee benefits_____	Printing_____
Accounting_____	Promotion _____
Advertising_____	Replacement_____
Amortization_____	Repairs & maintenance—general _____
Bad debt _____	Repairs & maintenance—vehicles_____
Bank services_____	Repairs & maintenance—golf cars_____
Chemicals_____	Repairs & maintenance—course_____
Computer support_____	Repairs & maintenance—equipment_____
Consulting fees_____	Repairs & maintenance—irrigation _____
Contributions_____	Repairs & maintenance—greens_____
Dues & subscriptions_____	Sand, seed & gravel _____
Fertilizer_____	Shop supplies_____
Fungicides_____	Taxes—income_____
Freight _____	Taxes—payroll _____
Gas, oil & equipment_____	Taxes—properties_____
Insurance—vehicles_____	Taxes—other_____
Insurance—general_____	Taxes—fuel_____
Insurance—health _____	Travel_____
Insurance—workers comp_____	Training _____
Interest_____	Utilities & telephone_____
Landscaping_____	
Laundry & uniforms_____	
Legal _____	
Licenses & permits_____	
Meeting & seminars_____	
Miscellaneous_____	
Office expense_____	
Outside labor_____	

Practice Range

Revenue

Range fees_____

Sales_____

Sales returns & allowances_____

Expenses

Employee salaries _____

Bonus _____

Employee benefits _____

Insurance—general _____

Insurance—health _____

Insurance—workers comp_____

Interest _____

Miscellaneous expense_____

Office expense _____

Outside labor_____

Range balls_____

Repairs & maintenance _____

Shop supplies_____

Taxes—income _____

Taxes—payroll _____

Taxes—property _____

Taxes—other_____

Taxes—fuel_____

Utilities & telephone_____

51

FIGURE 4.2

Sample Chart of Accounts *(continued)*

Food Services

Income	**Expenses**
Restaurant food ____	Employee salaries ____
Banquet food ____	Bonus ____
Banquet room rental ____	Employee benefits ____
Sale returns & allowances ____	Accounting ____
Cost of sales ____	Advertising ____
	Bad debt expense ____
	Bank service charge ____
	Computer support ____
	Contributions ____
	Dues & subscriptions ____
	Employee meals ____
	Gas, oil, auto and equipment ____
	Insurance–auto/truck ____
	Insurance–general ____
	Insurance–health ____
	Insurance–workers comp ____
	Interest ____
	Janitorial supplies ____
	Laundry & uniforms ____
	Legal ____
	Licenses & permits ____
	Meetings & seminars ____
	Miscellaneous expense ____
	Office expense ____
	Outside labor ____
	Over & short ____
	Professional fees ____
	Rental of equipment ____
	Penalties & fines ____
	Printing ____
	Promotion ____
	Repairs & maintenance ____
	Kitchen supplies ____
	Supplies ____
	Taxes–income ____
	Taxes–payroll ____
	Taxes–property ____
	Taxes–other ____
	Taxes–fuel ____
	Travel ____
	Utilities & telephone ____

FIGURE 4.2

Sample Chart of Accounts *(continued)*

Beverage Services

Income

Income	Expenses
Liquor	Employee salaries
Wine	Bonus
Beer	Employee benefits
Banquet liquor	Accounting
Banquet wine	Advertising
Banquet beer	Bad debts
Bar snacks	Bank services
Merchandise	Computer support
Soda	Insurance—general
Coin machine	Insurance—health
Tobacco	Insurance—workers comp
Sales return & allowances	Interest

Cost of sales

Liquor	Laundry
Wine	Licenses & permits
Beer	Miscellaneous
Mixes	Office expense
Tobacco	Outside labor
Others (snacks)	Over & short
Soda	Equipment rental
Inventory adjustment	Printing
	Promotion
	Repair & maintenance
	Bar supplies
	General supplies
	Taxes—income
	Taxes—property
	Taxes—other
	Taxes—fuel
	Travel
	Utilities & telephone

Golf Shop

Income

Income	Expenses
Clothing	Employee salaries
Gloves	Bonus
Club repair (labor)	Employee benefits
Clubs	Accounting
Bags	Advertising
Shoes	Bad debt expense
Balls	Computer support
Other merchandise	Dues & subscriptions
Sales returns & allowances	Freight
Discounts	Insurance—general

Cost of sales

Clothing	Insurance—health
Gloves	Insurance—workers comp
Club repair	Interest
Clubs	Miscellaneous
Bags	Outside labor
Shoes	Over & short
Balls	Promotion
Other merchandise	Repairs & maintenance
Inventory adjustment	Supplies
	Taxes—income
	Taxes—payroll
	Taxes—property
	Taxes—other
	Travel
	Utilities & telephone

FIGURE 4.2

Sample Chart of Accounts *(continued)*

General & Administrative

Expenses

Salaries—management _____

Salaries—administrative _____

Taxes—property _____

Taxes—payroll _____

Taxes—other _____

Insurance—general _____

Insurance—health _____

Insurance—other _____

Maintenance _____

Travel _____

Dues & subscriptions _____

Utilities & telephone _____

Promotion _____

Supplies _____

Computer support _____

Other _____

Source: Mark Gurnow, Integrity Golf Company

The golf course analyst must address these questions: What is good management? Is it measured by the size of the bottom line? Are there larger philosophical considerations involved? To understand management the analyst should first look to the mission statement of the facility. A typical mission statement might read as follows:

> It is our goal to provide a great golf experience with high quality facilities and services that maximize profitability and maintain loyal customers, operating with integrity and professionalism using sound and cost effective business tactics, astute marketing strategies with promotional and community outreach programs, while protecting natural resources and habitats.

One way to measure the quality and success of management is by reviewing the management's system of checks and balances relating to accounting, purchasing, hiring, training, and supervising personnel. A well-managed facility has club policies and procedures and an employee relations program. In judging the quality of management, it is difficult to say which of these three factors is most important:

- Maintenance and payroll, which are the largest expenses
- The marketing program, which brings in new player/customers
- The revenue management systems, which maximize profits

The analyst may wish to use a checklist like the one shown in Figure 4.3 to keep track of the items that contribute to good management.

54

FIGURE 4.3

Sample Management Checklist

Marketing

1. Is there a marketing plan?
2. How is it being implemented?
3. Who is responsible for marketing and monitoring the results?
4. Is there a program for hiring, training, and supervising marketing and/or membership sales personnel?
5. Are printed materials available?
6. Is there a branding program?
7. What is the fee structure?
8. Who is responsible for feasibility or market studies, media relations, advertising, special events, etc.?

Maintenance

1. Is there a systematic plan for the periodic review and assessment of the condition of the golf course and irrigation system, building and site improvements, FF&E, and argonomic operations?
2. How is maintenance being implemented and reported?
3. Is there a detailed budget?
4. Are there detailed employee job descriptions and sufficient full- and part-time personnel?
5. What are the qualifications of the facility superintendent?

Administrative

1. Is there a human resources program covering hiring, training, and review; health insurance plans; 401k plan administration; staff motivation and development; and union relationships?
2. Is there accountability for financial services such as accounts payable, accounts receivable, sales and other taxes, management forecasts, payroll processing, monthly revenue and expense statements and balance sheets, annual budgeting, daily cash reconciliation, and insurance coverage?

Source: Arthur Gimmy International

FUNCTION OF MANAGEMENT COMPANIES

Facility owners who are not qualified to manage or wish to have a passive role in operations can turn to golf management companies, which provide turnkey management services for private, semi-private, daily fee, resort, and municipal operations. Some golf management companies are listed below.

- American Golf Corporation, Santa Monica, California
- Arnold Palmer Golf Management, Orlando, Florida
- Billy Casper Golf, Vienna, Virginia
- ClubCorp., Dallas, Texas
- CourseCo, Corte Madera, California
- Crown Golf, Glenview, Illinois
- Freedom Golf Services, Hershey, Pennsylvania
- I.R.I. Golf Management, Rancho Santa Fe, California
- Kemper Sports Management, Northbrook, Illinois
- Meadowbrook Golf Group, Champions Gate, Florida
- Medallion Golf Management, San Diego, California
- OB Sports, Scottsdale, Arizona

- Troon Golf Management, Scottsdale, Arizona
- Western Golf Properties, Santa Ana, California

These management companies will work on a fee, lease, or ownership basis. Fees are typically set at a percentage of gross revenue plus a percentage based on bottom-line performance. Depending on the degree of services provided, the cost of management can range from 3% to 10% of total revenue.

CHAPTER FIVE

THE MUNICIPAL COURSE

Municipal courses are owned by government entities such as cities, counties, states, and the armed forces. They are the fewest in number and are operated on a daily fee basis. Government agencies may manage and operate their courses on a nonprofit basis or lease courses to private corporations, individuals, or concessionaires, who run them on a profit-oriented basis.

The statistical data presented in this chapter relates to a golf course operated by employees of a government agency. However, if proper allowances are made for rental expense and possessory taxes for real and personal property, it can be used for leasehold and leased fee valuations.

SUPPLY

There are approximately 2,700 municipal courses in the United States, accounting for about one in six golf courses in the nine climate regions. Most of these courses (87%) are regulation size, with the balance divided evenly between executive and par-3 layouts. A listing of the municipal courses and hole supply for 2000 is included in the appendix.

CHARACTERISTICS

Most, but not all, municipal golf courses are simple courses designed to accommodate heavy daily play throughout the year or season and to appeal to a variety of players. Typically a core design is used with emphasis on playability and enough flexibility to challenge a wide range of players. Municipal courses tend to be flat and have few rough areas where balls can be lost, thereby encouraging faster play. Development and operating costs are typically low because the courses have concentrated irrigation systems, reduced landscape maintenance, and fewer obstacles for easy mowing.

The average course acreage varies by climate region, with a low of 140 acres in Region 2 and a high of 218 acres in Region 5 (see Table 5.1). Course sizes range from 108 acres to 460 acres. The total course acreage maintained as turf also varies significantly with climate, from a low of about 68% turf in Region 6, which is one of the driest areas of the country, to a high of about 76% turf in Region 4. The irrigated portion of a course is generally expressed as a percentage of the total amount maintained as turf, generally in the range of 80% to 90%.

TABLE 5.1

Size, Operating, and Financial Data for Municipal Courses										
	Region 1	Region 2	Region 3	Region 4	Region 5	Region 6	Region 7	Region 8	Region 9	U.S.
Facility Characteristics										
Total median acreage	170	140	150	150	218	150	160	150	150	150
Acres maintained as turf	117	110	110	120	105	110	120	120	110	114
Acres maintained as irrigated	100	85	90	70	87	90	110	120	80	90

Source: National Golf Foundation, Operating and Financial Performance Profiles, 2001.

Municipal courses tend to be older than other types of golf courses because many were developed as community amenities before the explosive popularity of golf began in the 1960s. The median age for municipal courses is more than 30 years and 40% of these courses are more than 40 years old.

Few municipal facilities are associated with real estate developments (10% ±) and even fewer are associated with resorts (5% ±).

AMENITIES

Most municipal golf courses (83%) have a restaurant/lounge. These restaurant/lounges are generally modest in size with a limited menu, a full liquor license, and less than 100 seats (see Table 5.2). Many are run by concessionaires who specialize in operating restaurants and lounges in public facilities such as airports, hospitals, and government buildings. As will be discussed later, food and beverage sales are the third most important revenue department in a municipal course. Exceptional care must be employed in their design because the profit margin on food sales is low.

The second most important amenity in a municipal golf course is the driving range. Nationwide, approximately 76% of

TABLE 5.2

	Region 1	Region 2	Region 3	Region 4	Region 5	Region 6	Region 7	Region 8	Region 9	U.S.
Size, Operating, and Financial Data for Municipal Courses										
Facility Amenities										
Restaurant/lounge	86%	72%	92%	88%	90%	75%	87%	91%	89%	83%
Driving range	86%	70%	75%	67%	60%	88%	96%	100%	83%	76%
Golf school	67%	24%	35%	28%	30%	25%	17%	9%	12%	25%
Tennis court(s)	0%	9%	13%	11%	10%	13%	9%	0%	12%	10%
Swimming pool	0%	8%	4%	8%	10%	13%	4%	9%	0%	7%
Fitness facility	0%	0%	0%	2%	0%	4%	0%	0%	0%	1%

Source: National Golf Foundation, Operating and Financial Performance Profiles, 2001.

courses have ranges. The average number of tee stations is about 24. Other golf course amenities may include a golf school (present at 25% of courses) and tennis courts (10% nationwide). Very few have a swimming pool or fitness facility.

CAPITAL INVESTMENT

Due to the age of many municipal courses and the intense play they receive, constant capital investments are needed to maintain the integrity and market share of the facility. The average annual capital investment for U.S. courses in 1999 totaled about $590,000: $189,338 for golf course renovation, $136,724 for clubhouse renovation, $111,807 for irrigation upgrades, $57,152 for the maintenance of equipment and golf cars, $55,741 for maintenance building renovation, and $39,222 for infrastructure improvements.

Sixty percent of all U.S. facilities incurred a golf course renovation/reconstruction/expansion expense in 1999. Of those courses, 36% underwent clubhouse renovation/reconstruction, 18% had maintenance building(s) renovation/reconstruction, 65% had equipment maintenance or golf car purchases, 37% had an irrigation system installation or upgrade, and 30% had infrastructure improvements.

TOTAL ROUNDS PLAYED

The number of rounds played varies substantially from one climate region to another. The median for the United States was 45,000, but ranged from 27,000 in Region 6 to 110,000 in Region 8 (see Table 5.3).

Municipal courses generally have far more rounds than any other type of golf course because of their fee structure, which emphasizes affordability, and efficient design, which facilitates speedy play. In climates where golf can be played year round (Regions 1 and 8), the median number of rounds was 79,000, or 75% more than the national average. A significant number of

TABLE 5.3

	Region 1	Region 2	Region 3	Region 4	Region 5	Region 6	Region 7	Region 8	Region 9	U.S.
Size, Operating, and Financial Data for Municipal Courses										
Total Rounds Played										
Bottom 25%	60,000	30,000	44,000	33,000	32,000	27,000	30,000	81,932	52,712	34,000
Median	72,000	42,000	49,500	39,571	35,000	35,000	45,000	86,000	62,000	45,000
Top 25%	85,200	53,000	55,000	46,000	48,000	53,500	60,000	95,000	77,300	56,967
Top 5%	101,425	72,000	65,000	58,500	63,000	70,000	67,000	110,000	98,000	84,000

Source: National Golf Foundation, Operating and Financial Performance Profiles, 2001.

golf courses in these regions had more than 100,000 rounds played annually.

Nationwide, 24% of the rounds played in 1999 were in 9-hole rounds. Sixteen percent of rounds were played by visitors, 65% were during the peak season, and 36% were played on the weekend. Typically, actual rounds represent about 90% of the rounds desired by the owner/operator.

STAFFING

Statistics are available on the type and distribution of staffing for each department by region. Table 5.4 shows the staff breakdown for an average facility in each region.

TABLE 5.4

	Region 1	Region 2	Region 3	Region 4	Region 5	Region 6	Region 7	Region 8	Region 9	U.S.
Size, Operating, and Financial Data for Municipal Courses										
Staffing (Median Facility—All)										
Course maintenance	13	10	11	13	12	9	12	16	13	11
Golf shop	16	10	19	17	13	9	14	14	17	14
Food & beverage	5	4	0	7	7	3	6	6	10	5
Administrative	2	0	1	1	1	1	2	2	2	1
Other	3	3	3	2	3	0	3	6	2	1
Total staff	39	27	34	40	36	22	37	44	44	32
Employed year round	39	12	8	5	3	16	4	37	19	10

Source: National Golf Foundation, Operating and Financial Performance Profiles, 2001.

The nationwide average for full- and part-time staff is 32–11 for course maintenance, 14 for golf shop and player services, five for food and beverage, one for administration, and one for other work.

There are substantial differences in the number of course maintenance personnel by region, ranging from a low of nine staff members in Region 6 to 16 in Region 8. (The difference is primarily a function of seasonality and the number of rounds.) Similarly, the staff needed to operate the golf shop and food and beverage service vary by region, as does the number of administrative personnel needed. Total staff range from 27 in Region 2 to 44 in Region 8. These figures are difficult to understand without considering the breakdown of part-time and full-time staff, since part-time workers represent about two-thirds of total staff nationwide. Total staff also vary by the number of rounds and the fee structure, both of which are key factors in the budget determination.

Most of the staffing budget goes to golf course maintenance. Nationwide, maintenance costs represent 44% to 70% of the budget for a golf course, with busier courses spending more. Again, there is a strong relationship between revenue and staff size. The number of staff employed year round depends on the climate. In Region 5, 8.3% of the total staff works year round but in Region 1, 100% of the staff does. The nationwide median is 31%.

GREENS FEES

Greens fees, guest fees, and annual fees for regular players together represent total revenue from golf only. Dividing this figure by the total rounds played provides the golf revenue per total rounds played. The 1999 data in Table 5.5 indicates that the average price per round ranges from approximately $10 in Regions 5, 6, and 7 to a high of $18 in Region 3, with a nationwide average of $13.

In light of the recent increase in upscale golf clubs, these figures seem unrealistically low. However, government agencies that support public golf generally dictate that greens fees be kept at affordable levels. They seek to produce only enough revenue to operate and maintain the course and provide a reasonable reserve for periodic capital improvements. The highest greens fees are found in regions near the Atlantic and Pacific coastlines; the lowest rates are found in the "heartland" states.

The posted weekend rates shown in Table 5.5 indicate that these rates are 50% to 100% higher than the average greens fees. However, converting these fees into average revenue per round is prob-

TABLE 5.5

	Region 1	Region 2	Region 3	Region 4	Region 5	Region 6	Region 7	Region 8	Region 9	U.S.
Size, Operating, and Financial Data for Municipal Courses										
Greens Fees (Median Club)										
Average actual	$14	$11	$18	$15	$10	$10	$10	$16	$15	$13
Weekend rate	$34	$20	$30	$23	$26	$15	$20	$32	$25	$24
Golf Car Fees										
Average, all rounds	$8	$6	$5	$4	$4	$6	$3	$5	$3	$5
Weekend rate	$15	$10	$12	$12	$12	$10	$10	$12	$11	$12

Source: National Golf Foundation, Operating and Financial Performance Profiles, 2001.

lematic. If the actual weekend revenue from golf were converted to an average rate for all rounds played, it would have to be adjusted to reflect the percentage difference between the total rounds played and the number of rounds in which golf cars were used.

GOLF CAR FEES

Golf car fees represent a major source of revenue for all golf courses. Many resort and upscale daily fee operations require the use of golf cars by patrons and such fees are usually included in the greens fees. Municipal golf courses normally do not require the use of golf cars but rent them by the number of persons riding. Across the United States, golf car fees range from $10 to $14 per rider. Revenue projections may be made for this income category by multiplying the approximate number of riders by the appropriate rate.

REVENUE

Revenue sources by category include greens, guest, and annual fees; golf car rental; golf range; pro shop sales; food and beverage sales; and other revenue. NGF provides this data by region for the bottom 25%, median, top 25%, and top 5% of golf courses. The data in Table 5.6 relates to a median municipal course only and is presented as an example. The analyst can review information for the region in which the subject property is located and compare reported data for the property being appraised to the performance of other courses of similar financial status.

Municipal courses have modest revenues by choice. The total revenue per course varies greatly due to vast differences in the number of rounds played and the level of greens fees. For example, comparing the median club in Region 5, with a total revenue of $727,000, to the median club in Region 8, with $2,397,000 in total revenue, indicates a difference of 230%.

The data can best be understood by converting the revenue by category data into revenue per round. Here the differences between the lowest and the highest revenue producers are narrowed. Revenues per round range from $18 in Region 7 to $29.41 in Region 3, a difference of 63%. Revenue per round figures differ from one course to another and from one climate region to another due to a variety of factors, including management ability, course condition and quality, and competition. Every course is unique in terms of its financial performance on a per-round basis. The appraiser must not only analyze the subject property, but also compare it to other properties of a similar nature to understand and explain the estimates derived for the facility being appraised. The analyst can also research and analyze data

TABLE 5.6

Financial Performance of Municipal Courses (Median Data)

	Region 1	Region 2	Region 3	Region 4	Region 5	Region 6	Region 7	Region 8	Region 9	U.S.
Revenue by Category (in thousands)										
Greens & guest fees; annual dues	$1,032	$451	$894	$607	$365	$361	$429	$1,336	$1,027	$590
Golf car rentals	580	237	250	152	125	193	129	400	183	203
Golf range	74	34	49	28	22	24	36	99	81	38
Pro shop sales	150	87	68	66	62	108	123	212	163	91
Food & beverage sales	125	122	168	118	149	93	74	325	262	122
Other revenue	5	9	27	10	4	5	19	25	26	12
Total	$1,966	$940	$1,456	$981	$727	$784	$810	$2,397	$1,742	$1,056
Revenue per Round										
Greens & guest fees; annual dues	$14.33	$10.74	$18.06	$15.34	$10.43	$10.31	$9.53	$15.53	$16.56	$13.11
Golf car rentals	8.06	5.64	5.05	3.84	3.57	5.51	2.87	4.65	2.95	4.51
Golf range	1.03	0.81	0.99	0.71	0.63	0.69	0.80	1.15	1.31	0.84
Pro shop sales	2.08	2.07	1.37	1.67	1.77	3.09	2.73	2.47	2.63	2.02
Food & beverage sales	1.74	2.90	3.39	2.98	4.20	2.66	1.64	3.78	4.23	2.71
Other revenue	0.07	0.21	0.55	0.25	0.11	0.14	0.42	0.29	0.42	0.27
Total	$27.31	$22.38	$29.41	$24.79	$20.77	$22.40	$18.00	$27.87	$28.10	$23.47
Expenses per Round										
Payroll	$9.59	$7.82	$10.19	$9.24	$8.57	$8.47	$6.51	$9.63	$9.61	$8.29
General & administrative	1.38	0.60	0.71	0.81	0.43	0.43	0.58	1.30	0.69	0.53
Irrigation water	0.07	0.02	0.16	0.03	0.11	0.23	0.09	0.51	0.31	0.09
Fertilizers/chemicals	1.38	0.81	0.93	0.83	0.51	0.54	0.40	0.36	0.47	0.69
Lease expense/golf cars	1.04	1.33	1.33	1.09	1.06	1.14	0.69	0.81	0.74	1.09
Lease expense/equipment	0.18	0.52	0.99	0.61	0.69	0.83	0.76	0.94	0.90	0.64
Cost of merchandise sold	1.56	1.52	0.95	1.11	1.06	1.60	2.27	1.15	1.94	1.38
Cost of food & beverage	0.68	1.26	0.99	1.42	1.31	1.31	1.02	1.30	1.71	1.27
Advertising/marketing/promotion	0.14	0.21	0.16	0.23	0.29	0.23	0.18	0.36	0.19	0.20
Facility insurance	0.68	0.26	0.30	0.23	0.31	0.20	0.18	0.28	0.21	0.24
Utilities	0.47	0.52	0.65	0.48	0.51	0.71	0.24	0.40	0.52	0.49
Other expense	0.51	0.50	1.25	0.73	0.60	0.43	0.38	0.65	0.89	0.58
Subtotal	$17.68	$15.37	$18.61	$16.81	$15.45	$16.12	$13.30	$17.69	$18.18	$15.49
Other (see text)	3.63	1.64	4.03	3.27	2.41	2.70	0.56	2.38	3.18	2.93
Total expense	$21.31	$17.01	$22.64	$20.08	$17.86	$18.82	$13.86	$20.07	$21.36	$18.42

Source: National Golf Foundation, Operating and Financial Performance Profiles, 2001.

for clubs in a higher revenue category (e.g., the top 25%) or within a range (e.g., the 50th and 75th percentiles) to assist in the analysis and help determine if a property is underperforming based on its potential.

Looking at the total revenue derived from municipal courses shown in Table 5.6, it is obvious that a course with total revenue of $727,000, as reported for Region 5, has very little margin for error and may have insufficient funds to maintain the course and set aside reserves for future capital improvements. This uncertainty will affect the valuation.

Individual analyses can be performed within each category. For example, one can determine the level of golf car usage in a given region. In Region 7, for example, golf car rentals amount to only $2.87 per round and the rental rate is $10, so only 29% of the golfers are using cars. This means that most golfers are walking, which may result in longer playing times and reduce the number of rounds that can potentially be played. In hot regions such as Region 1, golf car usage is 54%. Obviously, it is important for management to maximize golf car rentals because the operating margin for this activity is high.

The appraiser can also analyze the subject property's other revenue departments to see how they compare with comparable courses and reported averages. For example, there may be a difference of $2.40 in food and beverage sales per round for a median performer in Region 9 compared to another course in that region that is in the top 25% revenue category. Differences such as this can assist the appraiser in the highest and best use study and in preparing a pro forma income statement that reflects market performance rather than individual performance. A facility's low food and beverage sales may reflect a management problem or, depending on the quality and condition of the clubhouse, a defect in design or maintenance.

When one considers the varied characteristics of a golf course, which combines a retail business, a restaurant and bar business, and various golf activities, it is apparent that one individual cannot be a specialist or expert in all of these areas. If the performance of one category is good, another may suffer, due to limited resources and the modest scale of individual departments. Disappointing revenues could lead to a recommendation that the food and beverage operation be leased to an outside operating company that specializes in this activity. The same considerations apply to pro shop sales and usage of the golf range, two potentially high-margin departments that underperform at many properties.

The appraiser should analyze the various categories of revenues produced by the facility to the greatest extent possible. Statistical units of comparison beyond revenue per round can be employed. For example, restaurant revenue can be analyzed on a sale-per-seat basis and compared with data provided by NGF. If an average facility with 107 seats produces sales of $125,000, a modest $1,168 in sales per seat is indicated. Another club in the same climate region may perform in the top 5% of food and beverage sales, with $2,682 in sales per seat, a difference of 130%. Part of the difference can be attributed to more customers and a greater number of rounds being played, but other factors are obviously involved including the quality of the facility, a desirable menu of food items, special events, on-course sales, and the quality of staffing and management.

EXPENSES

Golf course expenses are reported by NGF under the categories of payroll, general and administrative, irrigation water, fertilizer/chemicals, lease expense/golf cars, lease expense/equipment, cost of merchandise sold, cost of food and beverage, advertising/marketing/promotion, facility insurance, utilities, other expense, and total. All of this data for the nine climate regions and for the United States as a whole is converted into the expense-per-round statistics shown in Table 5.6. To derive the total expense, the analyst should not add up the expenses per round in each column, which would result in a total expense per round factor that is not representative of the total expense actually achieved. Instead, the analyst should use the NGF-reported statistics on average operating margins (subtracted from 100%). The operating margin, which is defined as net operating income before taxes, debt service, and depreciation, is most representative of median golf course performance.

A review of municipal golf course expenses will reveal that there are no deductions for real estate or personal property taxes because these courses are tax-exempt. Maintenance and other supplies, non-payroll office expenses, and certain replacement items not covered in another expense category could fall into a gray area between operating expenses and capital improvements to be depreciated. Expenses for salaries and benefits may differ greatly for private courses and municipal courses because government employees often have more expensive benefits and greater job protection. This can create a problem in some cases where management has no entrepreneurial motive to excel or upgrade.

Although a municipal facility is not subject to real and personal property taxes, it is taxed on a possessory or leasehold basis when it is operated by a lessee who pays rent to the government agency, but has not provided the entire capital investment to develop and operate the property.

In addition to analyzing expenses on a per-round basis, the analyst may also consider expenses as a percentage of total revenue or on a department basis. For example, comparing food and beverage sales in Region 1 ($1.74) with the cost of food and beverage ($0.68) indicates a 61% departmental profit, without consideration of other applicable undistributed expenses. As departmental revenue increases, departmental profit should also increase on an aggregate and percentage basis due to the fact that some departmental expenses are fixed in nature. For example, in Region 8 food and beverage sales are $3.78 and the cost of food and beverages is $1.30, indicating departmental profit of approximately 66%. For the entire nation, the average departmental profit for the food and beverage category is 53%. Comparisons such as these can help appraisers conduct more detailed studies of the business of a golf course.

A similar analysis can be made of the departmental profit of the pro shop. A typical pro shop is only modestly profitable because the management team often lacks retail business experience. The average pro shop in Region 1 makes a 25% profit, while the national average is 32%. It should be noted that the equipment and golf cars of a municipal course are leased and, for the appraiser, this lease expense represents an allocation out of the average operating margin. No other allowance need be made for the contributory value of these personal property items.

The units of revenue and expense shown in Table 5.6 can be considered along with the data in Tables 5.1 through 5.5 to compare one climate region to another. There are major differences between a seasonal golf operation in a cold climate (Region 5) and a year-round operation in a mild climate (Region 8). Fewer potential rounds can be played in the Frostbelt and there is no need for a full, year-round staff. For example, the typical course in Region 5 has a total staff of 36 but only three people are employed year-round; in Region 8 the typical staff is 44 workers with 37 employed year round. On an overall basis, therefore, a seasonal golf operation will be much less profitable than a year-round operation. This is indicated by the difference in the average operating margin, which is 14% in Region 5 and 28% in Region 8.

Very detailed analyses could be made of all of this statistical information, but it may be difficult to compare actual line items in the financial statement of an individual club with the NGF data due to the lack of uniform accounting in the golf industry. Business appraisers continually face this problem. Analysts must be creative in using statistical information and understand relationships between revenue and expenses, rounds, staffing, and other factors. Line items can vary significantly from standardized survey data and financial information from competing properties should be studied carefully, usually in consultation with the manager of the facility or its accountant.

OPERATING MARGINS

NGF only presents average or mean operating margins for all facilities in the nine regions and the United States as a whole (see Table 5.7). Obviously, individual operating margins or profit ratios can be substantially greater or less than the 14% to 28% range shown below. For example, Risk Management Association (*RMA 2002*) reports that 301 public courses had an average loss of 0.4% to 3.3% of net revenues in 2001. The only category of municipal courses that was profitable, with revenues between $5 and $10 million, achieved a net income before taxes of 1.5% of revenue.

One would expect courses that operate on a year-round basis to be more profitable and the NGF data supports that assumption. It is also reasonable to expect that those golf courses with the most rounds played, the top 25% and top 5%, should also be substantially more profitable. This can be determined from the NGF data by comparing the average total expense, say for the top 25% (or 75th percentile) performers, to the total revenues reported within the same category. This assumption is proven by the reported information. For example, in Region 8 the top 25% of performers had average expenses of $2,028,000 and revenues of $3,037,000, indicating an operating margin of 33%. The reader is again cautioned that the expense items discussed here are not necessarily representative of all the expenses a golf course can incur.

UNIQUE ASPECTS OF HIGHEST AND BEST USE

The concept of highest and best use, which considers whether a property should continue in its present use or be redeveloped to a higher use, is irrelevant when an assignment involves a municipal golf course. Such a facility was created for the good of the general public. (Of course, some may question whether a golf course really represents an amenity to the general public when it calls for extensive use of land resources and only 13% of the population are golfers.) Nevertheless, an appraiser may be asked to determine the highest and best use of the land used as a golf course because of the need to replace a facility or provide superior alternative facilities.

In any event, when the assignment involves an existing course, the highest and best use analysis should focus on the management and performance of the club compared to other competently managed courses.

TABLE 5.7
Operating Margins

Climate Region	Percent
1	22
2	24
3	23
4	19
5	14
6	16
7	23
8	28
9	24
U.S.	22

The appraiser may also be called on to appraise an existing course in response to a proposal for expansion or redevelopment. In a political sense, the internal rate of return *(IRR)* as a measure of the relationship between investment and income is irrelevant when the benefit to the general public is the reputed objective. These comments should not be taken out of context. In appraising a municipal course, the analyst must understand the environment in which this type of assignment is undertaken and the potential scrutiny that the appraisal report might receive from the public.

In the true sense of highest and best use, outside the political context, a municipal course will generally underperform an equivalent daily fee course in the same market, primarily because prices are kept low to provide the greatest public benefit.

The benefit to the public may be estimated by comparing how a municipal course would be operated by the private sector with its actual results as a governmental operation. The monetary difference between its value in use as a municipal course and its value at its highest and best use reflects the public benefit value. Once this calculation is made, a political decision can be made to determine whether the benefits produced by the course justify the dollars invested. This concept is demonstrated in the following example, in which the sales comparison approach is applied to value the facility. A greens fee multiplier is used as the unit of comparison.

TABLE 5.8

Calculation of Public Benefit		
	Public	**Private**
Annual rounds played	70,000	50,000
Average greens fee per round	× $15	× $30
Annual greens fees	$1,050,000	$1,500,000
Greens fee multiplier	× 4.0	× 4.0
Value	$4,200,000	$6,000,000
Public benefit ($6,000,000 − $4,200,000) =		$1,800,000

Operated as a municipal course, the property has a value of $4.2 million, based on its 70,000 annual rounds played and $15 average greens fee per round. If it were operated for profit as a privately owned, daily fee facility, a $30 fee could be charged, which would reduce the number of rounds to 50,000 but increase the value to $6 million. Therefore, the market value of the course is $6 million, while its value as a municipal course is $4.2 million. The municipality, in essence, has underwritten the $1.8 million difference as a public benefit. This benefit is realized by those who play the additional 20,000 rounds that would otherwise be denied them, presumably because they could not pay a $30 fee.

Thus, the highest and best use of the facility in the above example may be deemed its present use as a municipal course since the public believes the recreational benefits it receives are worth $1.8 million. The feasibility of the public use is further enhanced by the government's ability to borrow funds for the project at lower rates than are available to private developers. If the public and its officials believe the benefit is not worth the price, the course can be sold for its $6 million market value.

SPECIAL ASPECTS OF VALUATION

In some cases the appraisal assignment may be to estimate the value of a golf course based on its continued use as a publicly owned asset. Such an assignment could be undertaken for financing, for asset reporting, or for the lease or sale of the property to an entity that would continue to operate it on the same basis. In this instance, all three approaches can be employed.

In applying the cost approach, the difficulty is estimating the land value since there will be no sales of large parcels suitable for development as a golf course that are entitled on this basis and designated only for a municipal type of operation. If a government agency were going to acquire the land, it would have to pay a price based on its highest and best use, but once its use is limited to recreation as a public benefit, its value in the market may be vastly diminished. However, value would not be diminished if one employs the concept of value in use.

Except in extraordinary circumstances, such as in a rural environment where there are many tracts of agricultural land that could be considered for golf course use, the land component for a municipal golf course must be subsidized. This conclusion can easily be understood by reference to the national data shown in Table 5.6. Taking the most extreme example, consider a course in Region 8 where the average operating margin is 28%. Applying this rate to the total revenue of $2,397,000 produces a net operating income *(NOI)* of $671,160. Capitalizing *NOI* at a generally accepted rate of 11% produces a total value of $6,100,000 for the real property and business, an amount equivalent to about $340,000 per hole. This figure may approximate the cost to replace the facility's improvements in today's market. In such an instance, the cost approach may be the best method for estimating "value in use" since the concept of market value for a public sector property is irrelevant.

Many municipal courses have very high development costs because of government regulations regarding the contracting process and bureaucratic compliance to ambiguous regulations. This fact is undisputed. In regard to a public course, depreciation should be considered only on a physical and functional basis; economic considerations are irrelevant. The appraiser's main concern should be deferred maintenance, which is a common problem. Typically, government budgets get trimmed and maintaining public recreational amenities is not a priority.

PUBLIC-PRIVATE DEVELOPMENT AND GOLF COURSE PRIVATIZATION

Private participation in the operation of public courses has become common. A private entity may manage a municipal course and receive compensation from the profit left over after all expenses including rent are accounted for.

There are numerous opportunities for public-private ventures in the development of new golf courses. In these instances the golf course site is typically leased from an agency by a private development entity that constructs the golf facility and then operates it as an affordable daily fee course.

The ground lease is usually long enough to amortize the cost of the facility (say 25 to 40 years) and provide for a minimum, fixed, guaranteed rent, and/or for percentage rents specific to each revenue-producing department. (For an example of varied percentage rents for golf-related revenue and other department income, see Figure 8.2 on page 104.)

Public-private ventures have many benefits, including

- Available municipal bond financing at a lower, tax-exempt interest rate
- Eventual ownership of the golf facility by the public (at the end of the ground lease)
- The ability of the developer to amenitize the adjacent, residentially zoned land, which would be too small for a golf course
- The ability of the golf course operator to control and manage a golf facility with reduced financial investment
- Development of a community recreation asset with professional management and minimal fiscal outlay.

CHAPTER SIX

THE DAILY FEE COURSE

Golf courses operated as profit-oriented business enterprises are referred to as daily fee courses. This broad category includes courses owned and operated for and available to the general public. Daily fee courses can be very simple 9-hole or par-3 golf courses or complex enterprises of 18 holes or more providing a variety of services. Services may include a practice range, bar/grill, restaurant, and pro shop, where tee time reservations and instruction can be obtained and merchandise is sold.

The statistical data presented in this chapter assumes that the golf course is operated for profit by a private individual, a corporation, or a developer of a golf community for which the course serves as the primary amenity. It is also assumed that all of the revenue departments are operated by the owner of the course even though it is common to lease or contract out some of the business activities such as the merchandise sales in the pro shop and food and beverage sales. Both these operations require high levels of expertise that golf professionals commonly lack.

SUPPLY

There are nearly 10,000 daily fee courses of all types in the United States, representing the majority of golf courses in the nine regions. Most of these courses are regulation size (86%), with the balance divided between executive layouts (7.5%) and par-3 layouts (6.5%). A listing of the daily fee courses and hole supply for 2000 is included in the appendix.

CHARACTERISTICS

Daily fee, 18-hole regulation courses are fairly standard in size, typically averaging 155 acres, with 115 acres maintained as turf, of which 90 acres are irrigated. The remaining 40 acres are used for the clubhouse, parking lots, maintenance facilities, landscaping, other outdoor amenities, and access roads (see Table 6.1). Despite these standards, courses vary in size due to topography and layout. Some tight, core courses are as small as 125 acres, while rambling, single fairway courses can have as many as 200 acres. The total acreage maintained as turf is usually 70% to 75% and the total acreage maintained as irrigated land is two-thirds to five-sixths of the turfed area. The difference between the amount of turf and irrigated turf is mostly in rough areas at the edge of the fairways.

TABLE 6.1

Size, Operating, and Financial Data for Daily Fee Courses									
	Region 1	Region 2	Region 3	Region 4	Region 5	Region 6	Region 7	Region 8	Region 9	U.S.
Facility Characteristics									
Total median acreage	154	160	153	150	155	165	150	165	130	155
Acres maintained as turf	100	110	90	120	110	122	115	120	100	115
Acres maintained as irrigated	90	90	62	75	80	110	105	110	90	90

Sources: National Golf Foundation, Operating and Financial Performance Profiles, 2001.

The median age of daily fee courses is 19.5 years, but actual ages range from new to more than 40 years old. Age is not necessarily an indication of obsolescence because many courses, like fine wine, become more popular with age, as vegetation matures and playability is fine-tuned by course designers and greens management. Course age can be important in an appraisal as it relates to the deterioration of physical components over time. The useful life expectancies for golf course components are shown below.

Irrigation system	15–20 years
Tees and greens	15–20 years
Sand bunkers	5–8 years
Paving – asphalt	8–12 years
concrete	13–20 years
Maintenance building	30–40 years
Clubhouse	25–50 years
Maintenance equip.	5–15 years
Typical FF&E	5–15 years

A large percentage of new courses are associated with residential communities. Such courses make up only 14% of supply in Region 5, but 79% of supply in Region 1, which includes South Florida retirement communities. Few courses are associated with resorts, with the exception of a significant percentage (35%) in the mountain states (Region 7).

AMENITIES

Virtually all daily fee courses have some type of food and beverage service (see Table 6.2). This amenity is considered necessary to a successful operation, whether it is a small snack bar or an elaborate dining room with banquet facilities, a cocktail/entertainment lounge, and catering services. The median number of seats nationwide is 101, but Region 1 has an average of 164 seats while Region 2's average is 82.

TABLE 6.2

Size, Operating, and Financial Data for Daily Fee Courses									
	Region 1	Region 2	Region 3	Region 4	Region 5	Region 6	Region 7	Region 8	Region 9	U.S.
Facility Amenities										
Restaurant/lounge	100%	85%	91%	87%	85%	83%	88%	93%	85%	87%
Driving range	100%	89%	79%	73%	78%	87%	95%	100%	88%	84%
Golf school	57%	28%	44%	26%	22%	24%	45%	38%	30%	30%
Tennis court(s)	64%	8%	19%	5%	9%	18%	33%	27%	13%	17%
Swimming pool	64%	8%	13%	5%	6%	4%	25%	29%	18%	20%
Fitness facility	36%	8%	6%	2%	7%	0%	18%	26%	10%	9%

Sources: National Golf Foundation, Operating and Financial Performance Profiles, 2001.

The second most important amenity is the driving range. Considered a near-necessity, a driving range is a profitable adjunct for golfing practice and the operation of a golf school. More than five out of six daily fee courses have a driving range and, in Regions 1 and 8, all courses have this amenity. The average number of tee stations is 24, with a range of 19 to 31.

Other daily fee golf course amenities include a golf school (found at 30% of U.S. courses), tennis courts (16%), swimming pool (20%) and a health club/gym/spa (9%). Tennis courts, swimming pools, and health clubs are most likely to be found in residential community facilities, especially those that are family-oriented.

CAPITAL INVESTMENT

The annual capital investment in a facility is known by many names in the appraisal industry. For tax purposes, it can be described as "the amount set aside for annual depreciation." For appraisal purposes it may be described as "an amount set aside in reserve for replacement of short-lived items." In the owner's view, it is the amount that must be spent periodically to maintain the course's integrity and market position.

More than 40% of U.S. courses incurred expenditures for capital investment in 1999. Among these courses the average annual capital investment, in addition to the original book costs, totaled approximately $459,000, allocated as follows: $102,445 to golf course renovation, $140,245 to clubhouse renovation, $38,181 for maintenance and building renovation, $49,143 for maintenance of equipment and golf cars, $51,934 for irrigation upgrading, and $76,832 for infrastructure improvements. This figure is 22% lower than the amount set aside by municipal courses in 1999, mostly because daily fee courses have a lower average age and are subject to less intensive play.

Nationwide, 59% of all facilities incurred a golf course renovation/reconstruction/expansion expense in 1999: 39% for clubhouse renovation/reconstruction, 23% for maintenance and building(s) renovation/reconstruction, 68% for maintenance of equipment and golf car purchases, 40% for irrigation installation and upgrading, and 38% for infrastructure improvements.

There is no accepted standard for the percentage of revenue to be set aside for reserves for replacements. A newer, well-maintained facility may require a low percentage of revenue, while an older one should have a reserve double that amount. Most analysts use a percentage that is less than 5% of gross revenue.

TOTAL ROUNDS PLAYED

The number of rounds varies substantially from one region to another (see Table 6.3). The median for the United States is 30,000, approximately 15,000 or one-third less than municipal courses. The range of rounds played is broad, from 18,500 for the bottom 25% of courses in Region 5 to 88,000 for the top 5% of courses in Region 8.

TABLE 6.3

Size, Operating, and Financial Data for Daily Fee Courses									
	Region 1	Region 2	Region 3	Region 4	Region 5	Region 6	Region 7	Region 8	Region 9	U.S.
Total Rounds Played										
Bottom 25%	40,000	23,000	28,000	23,000	18,500	27,000	25,000	38,000	26,000	23,000
Median	45,000	32,000	35,200	27,000	24,000	35,000	30,000	45,000	35,000	30,000
Top 25%	54,000	39,000	41,000	34,000	30,000	44,100	41,000	52,000	45,000	40,000
Top 5%	55,000	55,000	47,300	42,000	49,000	73,000	59,700	88,000	82,800	55,000

Sources: National Golf Foundation, Operating and Financial Performance Profiles, 2001.

Daily fee courses on average have fewer rounds played than municipal courses because they set fees to emphasize profits, and management wants to control the speed of play. On the other hand, many more rounds are played at daily fee courses than at private courses where the membership size is limited.

Nationwide, 22% of 1999 rounds played were nine-hole rounds, 19% were played by visitors, 64% were played during the peak season, and 42% were played on the weekend. Typically, actual rounds equal about 85% of the number of rounds the owner or operator desired to achieve.

STAFFING

Statistics are available on the distribution of staffing for each department by region and for the bottom 25%, median, top 25%, and top 5% of courses. Table 6.4 also shows full-time staff, part-time staff, total staff, and staff allocated for golf course maintenance.

TABLE 6.4

Size, Operating, and Financial Data for Daily Fee Courses										
	Region 1	Region 2	Region 3	Region 4	Region 5	Region 6	Region 7	Region 8	Region 9	U.S.
Staffing (Median Facility—All)										
Course maintenance	12	6	5	3	4	8	8	15	5	6
Golf shop	6	3	2	2	2	4	4	7	3	3
Food & beverage	4	2	2	1	1	1	1	6	2	2
Administrative	2	1	1	1	1	1	1	3	1	1
Other	1	2	1	1	1	1	1	1	2	1
Total staff	25	14	11	8	9	15	15	32	13	13
Employed year round	24	14	7	4	2	18	12	28	10	8

Sources: National Golf Foundation, Operating and Financial Performance Profiles, 2001.

Nationwide, the average full- and part-time staff totals 13, with six allocated to golf course maintenance, three to the golf shop and player services, two to food and beverage, one to administration, and one to other functions.

There are substantial differences in the amount of golf course maintenance personnel, ranging from a low of three in Region 4 to a high of 15 in Region 8. The difference is primarily a function of seasonality and the number of rounds. For the golf shop, the number ranges from two to seven, for food and beverage from one to six, for administration from one to three, and for total staff from eight to 32.

Most of the staffing budget goes to golf course maintenance. Nationwide, 38% of the budget is spent on maintenance by the bottom 25% courses, 48% by the median courses, 60% by the top

25%, and 68% by the top 5%, which again shows the relation-ship between revenue and the size of staff as well as the need to maintain the course's reputation.

The number of staff employed year-round is also a function of the zone, ranging from a low of 8% in Region 5 to a high of 78% in Region 1.

GREENS FEES

Combining greens and guest fees with annual dues from mem-bers produces the total revenue from golf only. Dividing that figure by the total number of rounds played provides the aver-age actual golf revenue per total rounds played (see Table 6.5).

TABLE 6.5

Size, Operating, and Financial Data for Daily Fee Courses									
	Region 1	Region 2	Region 3	Region 4	Region 5	Region 6	Region 7	Region 8	Region 9	U.S.
Greens Fees (Median Club)									
Average actual	$14	$13	$14	$15	$11	$10	$18	$27	$21	$15
Weekend rate	$45	$28	$35	$25	$28	$21	$28	$65	$33	$28
Golf Car Fees									
Average, all rounds	$10	$7	$6	$4	$5	$5	$5	$6	$4	$5
Weekend rate	$13	$12	$12	$11	$12	$10	$12	$12	$12	$12

Sources: National Golf Foundation, Operating and Financial Performance Profiles, 2001.

The data indicates that total golf revenue converted to a price per total round varies. For the median club, the price per round ranges from approximately $12.50 in Region 6 to approximately $29.25 in Region 8, with a nationwide average of $17.20. For newer clubs in urban locations where development costs are much higher, the averages indicated for the top 5% of courses may be more appropriate. These are $43.04 for Region 1, $36.35 for Region 2, $42.16 for Region 3, $35.07 for Region 4, $30.18 for Region 5, $28.04 for Region 6, $35.75 for Region 7, $25.86 for Region 8, and $26.47 for Region 9. The average price per round for the entire country is $37.50. Among the top 5% of courses, the highest greens fees/guest fees and annual dues for mem-bers are found in Region 1 (south Florida); the lowest fees are in Southern California and Arizona.

The posted weekend rate for each region is also shown in Table 6.5. These rates range from $21 in Region 6 to $65 in Re-gion 8. Typical weekend rates are two to three times higher than the average weekday fees.

REVENUE

Total revenue sources by category include greens fees, guest fees, and annual dues from members; golf car rentals; golf range; pro shop (merchandise) sales; food and beverage sales; and other revenue. NGF provides data by region for the bottom 25%, median, top 25%, and top 5% of golf courses. The data in Table 6.6 is for a median daily fee course only and is presented as an example. The analyst should review information for the climate region in which the subject property is located and compare the reported data for the property being appraised to the performance of other courses of similar financial status.

Daily fee courses are, for the most part, managed for profit. Therefore the owner, through his own management or through management policies, attempts to maximize the revenue from the course by reaching a desired number of rounds. There is a wide variance in total revenue per course throughout the United States due to vast differences in the number of rounds played and greens fees. For example, the median club in Region 5 had total revenue of $689,000 compared to the median club in Region 8, which had $2,555,000, a difference of 270%.

The data can be understood best by converting the revenue by category into revenue per round. In this way the differences between the lowest revenue-performers and the highest is narrowed. Region 5, with much fewer rounds, had total revenue of $26.04 per round compared to Region 8, which had $46.40, a difference of 78%.

Revenue per round differentials are subject to numerous variables, but the key ones are course quality and playability. Table 6.7 shows that the gross revenue per round for the top 5% of U.S. courses ($92) is four times higher than the revenue for the bottom 25% of courses ($23).

Revenue per round should be as important as the greens fee schedule in comparing one course to another. Managers differ in the policy they pursue. Some may emphasize rounds at the expense of the daily fee charged, while others may prefer to have fewer rounds at higher greens fees. This latter policy seems more desirable since it results in less wear on the course and lower maintenance costs.

Analysts should study gross revenue for all seven categories on a per-round basis so that the subject property revenues can be compared with NGF's published benchmark percentages for the various categories. Individual analyses can be performed for each category. For example, food and beverage sales can be compared on a per-seat basis or such comparisons can be used to determine how golf car usage can be maximized through fee mechanisms or other

TABLE 6.6
Financial Performance of Daily Fee Courses (Median Data)

	Region 1	Region 2	Region 3	Region 4	Region 5	Region 6	Region 7	Region 8	Region 9	U.S.
Revenue by Category (in thousands)										
Greens & guest fees	$650.00	$424.00	$671.00	$371.00	$256.00	$366.00	$542.00	$1,199.00	$725.00	$444.00
Annual member dues	300.00	81.00	159.00	56.00	75.00	74.00	87.00	117.00	71.00	72.00
Golf car rentals	466.00	222.00	205.00	132.00	114.00	183.00	153.00	285.00	155.00	161.00
Golf range	14.00	20.00	27.00	13.00	11.00	21.00	27.00	31.00	31.00	19.00
Pro shop sales	91.00	80.00	74.00	80.00	53.00	122.00	159.00	120.00	119.00	78.00
Food & beverage sales	299.00	114.00	160.00	126.00	109.00	143.00	184.00	299.00	158.00	137.00
Other revenue	27.00	13.00	14.00	8.00	7.00	18.00	24.00	37.00	16.00	12.00
Total	$1,847.00	$954.00	$1,310.00	$786.00	$625.00	$927.00	$1,176.00	$2,088.00	$1,275.00	$923.00
Revenue per Round										
Greens & guest fees	$14.44	$13.25	$19.06	$13.74	$10.67	$10.46	$18.07	$26.64	$20.71	$14.80
Annual member dues	6.67	2.53	4.52	2.07	3.12	2.11	2.90	2.60	2.03	2.40
Golf car rentals	10.36	7.25	5.82	4.88	4.75	5.23	5.10	6.33	4.43	5.37
Golf range	0.31	0.62	0.77	0.48	0.46	0.60	0.90	0.69	0.89	0.63
Pro shop sales	2.02	2.50	2.10	2.96	2.21	3.49	5.30	2.67	3.40	2.60
Food & beverage sales	6.64	3.56	4.55	4.67	4.54	4.09	6.13	6.64	4.51	4.57
Other revenue	0.60	0.41	0.40	0.30	0.29	0.51	0.80	0.82	0.46	0.40
Total	$41.04	$30.12	$37.22	$29.10	$26.04	$26.49	$39.20	$46.39	$36.43	$30.77
Expenses per Round										
Payroll	$17.22	$10.94	$12.78	$8.70	$8.13	$12.46	$13.04	$22.22	$11.55	$10.83
General & administrative	3.89	1.28	2.47	1.26	0.79	1.29	1.60	3.33	2.06	1.60
Irrigation water	0.04	0.09	0.11	0.07	0.13	0.37	0.43	1.67	0.17	0.13
Fertilizers/chemicals	1.47	1.06	1.42	1.04	0.71	0.63	0.80	0.89	0.60	0.97
Lease expense/golf cars	1.38	1.44	1.82	1.48	1.21	1.66	1.33	1.60	0.97	1.43
Lease expense/equipment	0.82	0.97	1.22	0.85	0.88	0.83	0.77	1.64	0.66	0.97
Cost of merchandise sold	2.20	1.75	1.76	1.41	1.75	2.66	3.20	2.02	2.34	1.90
Cost of food & beverage	2.49	1.63	1.85	1.89	1.92	2.20	2.93	2.98	2.11	2.00
Advertising/marketing/promotion	0.42	0.47	0.31	0.33	0.42	0.26	0.33	0.93	0.46	0.37
Property tax	0.82	0.53	0.80	0.63	0.75	0.46	0.87	1.40	0.69	0.63
Facility insurance	0.53	0.50	0.57	0.48	0.46	0.40	0.47	0.80	0.37	0.47
Utilities	0.64	0.72	0.68	0.63	0.58	0.83	0.63	1.42	0.63	0.70
Other expense	0.82	0.66	1.14	0.70	0.67	0.49	0.80	1.29	0.60	0.70
Totals	$32.74	$22.04	$26.93	$19.47	$18.40	$24.54	$27.20	$42.19	$23.21	$22.70

TABLE 6.7

	Region 1	Region 2	Region 3	Region 4	Region 5	Region 6	Region 7	Region 8	Region 9	U.S.
Gross Revenue Per Round										
Bottom 5%	$28	$20	$32	$22	$18	$22	$22	$37	$29	$23
Median	$41	$33	$38	$30	$27	$26	$33	$50	$38	$32
Top 25%	$59	$49	$54	$43	$39	$45	$68	$89	$56	$55
Top 5%	$90	$80	$117	$75	$75	$91	$95	$120	$105	$92

programs. Such analyses may be performed in an appraisal assignment or a feasibility study such as a cost/benefit analysis.

Studying revenues by category and by percentage levels reveals the great disparity in business from course to course and from revenue department to revenue department. Data is available in published form from NGF for rough comparisons. Actual data obtained from the analyst's own local market research is the best measure of course performance.

EXPENSES

Golf course expenses may be analyzed on a percentage basis, on a per-round basis, or both. Individual categories should be examined and compared to published data such as the data shown in Table 6.6 or actual data from competing courses, if available. Most golf course financial statements contain many more line-item expense categories than are shown in the table.

The problem for the analyst making comparisons is the lack of conformity in the data and the need to combine many small items into the 13 categories used by NGF. Successful golf clubs keep detailed listing of expenses as shown in Figure 6.1.

Overall expense percentages should also be examined. The reciprocal of the average operating margin reported by NGF indicates the average expenses shown in Table 6.8.

This is a fairly tight range in total operating expenses (72% to 80%) and the overall average of 75% leaves little margin for poor management and few extra dollars for reserves for replacement. Obviously management needs to be highly efficient.

Experience shows that golf course operating expense ratios are highly variable, depending partially on the critical factors of course age, condition, maintenance policies, and environmental factors. Profitable businesses may have expense ratios between 60% and 70% and poorly run or older facilities that have not been properly maintained or updated may have expense ratios of 80% to 90% or higher. Some may lose money on paper, but provide a livelihood for the owner.

TABLE 6.8

Average Expenses	
Climate Region	Total Expenses as % of Revenue
1	72
2	76
3	72
4	74
5	79
6	80
7	75
8	74
9	80
U.S.	75

FIGURE 6.1

Detailed Revenue and Expense Statement for 12 Months of Operation

Revenues	YTD	Operating Expenses (cont.)	YTD
Course	$2,098,974.06	Landscaping	$599.53
Driving range	180,439.37	Laundry	40,827.31
Restaurant–banquet	551,604.13	Legal	12,560.01
Snack bar–HWH	138,102.89	Licenses & permits	3,040.46
Bar	419,479.72	Meetings & seminars	1,232.34
Pro shop	92,302.76	Miscellaneous expenses	7,539.73
Total sales	$3,480,902.93	Office expense	4,251.44
Cost of Goods Sold		Outside labor	12,354.53
Driving range–food/soda	$1,351.58	Range balls	13,125.00
Driving range–clubs	23,649.58	Professional fees	6,339.89
Restaurant/banquet	200,471.68	Rent	35,400.00
Half way house	44,968.84	Rental of equipment	41,596.89
Bar	113,390.62	Printing	542.21
Pro shop	56,202.05	Promotion expense	35,048.70
Inventory adjustment	1,684.96	Replacement expense	1,370.63
Total cost of goods sold	$441,719.31	Repairs & maintenance–general	71,422.63
Gross profit	$3,039,183.62	Repairs & maintenance–auto/truck	719.88
Operating Expenses		Repairs & maintenance–carts	11,248.72
Salaries–officers	$121,148.94	Repairs & maintenance–course	22,629.68
Salaries–employee	868,439.42	Repairs & maintenance–equipment	27,372.33
Salaries–employee–OT premium	8,009.84	Repairs & maintenance–irr. system	23,118.63
Employee benefits	10,582.25	Repairs & maintenance–greens	4,228.31
Accrued vacation	52,935.52	Repairs & maintenance–tees	583.92
Accounting	22,753.25	Sand & gravel	11,754.21
Advertising	26,232.34	Seeds–greens	550.39
Amortization	249.96	Seeds–tees & fairways	15,815.30
Bacteria injections	7,437.71	Shop supplies	37,427.41
Bad debt expense	1,088.71	Supplies	10,477.52
Bank service charge	26,258.86	Banquet supplies	767.23
Chemicals	8,266.01	Taxes–payroll	101,133.29
Computer support expense	4,472.19	Taxes–property	50,621.25
Contributions	7,135.94	Taxes–other	1,371.43
D.G.	1,120.60	Travel	4,039.12
Depreciation	115,742.41	Training/in house	736.38
Dues and subscriptions	3,683.36	Utilities & telephone	109,153.14
Fertilizer–fairways/greens/tees	40,809.29	Total operating expenses	$2,190,269.94
Fungicides	10,702.27	Operating profit (loss)	$848,913.68
Insurance		**Other Income**	
Freight	2,543.53	Gain (loss) on sale of assets	$108,500.00
Gas & oil auto & equipment	9,480.30	Other income	3,251.80
Gypsum–fairways	6,281.76	Total other income	$111,751.80
Insecticides	179.44	**Other Expense**	
Insurance–general	35,362.42	Interest expense	12,046.38
Insurance–health	43,045.80	Total other expenses	$12,046.38
Insurance–w/comp	26,529.29	Net income	$948,619.10
Janitorial supplies	8,779.09		

Notes: Cost of goods sold and operating expenses, excluding depreciation and amortization, are 72% of revenues.

A difficult problem for the analyst arises when a facility has a recent history of high operating expenses that leave a net operating income that is inadequate to support the sale prices being paid for competitive or comparable courses. In these circumstances it will generally take several years for the new owners to retool the business to increase profits to a normal level. The financial gap between normal net operating income and the actual net operating income is a penalty against the stabilized value estimate.

EXPENSE CATEGORIES

Payroll. A major expense for any golf course, payroll for a course ranges from $8.70 to $22.22 per round and from a low of 44% of total expenses (in Region 5) to a high of 53% (in Region 8). Payroll averages 48% of total expenses nationwide. The lowest percentage for payroll is 23% (bottom 25% in Region 5) and the highest is 55% (top 25% in Regions 2 and 6).

General and Administrative. This category includes general manager expenses, office expense, liability and other non-property insurance, accounting fees, and legal costs. It is the second highest expense item, after payroll, not including the cost of merchandise sold and the cost of food and beverage. The cost per round for a typical course ranges from $0.79 in Region 5 to $3.89 in Region 1.

Cost of Goods Sold. Both categories of cost of goods sold (merchandise and food and beverage items) account for 17% of all expenses. Individually, the cost of merchandise sold represents 73% of pro shop sales, while the cost of food and beverage is 44% of departmental sales. When one considers a proper allocation of undistributed or nondepartmental operating expenses, the pro shop business can easily be unprofitable. Therefore, the size and design of the pro shop and the selection of merchandise should be carefully analyzed and, possibly, even operated by a third-party lessee.

Total Operating Expenses. Total operating expenses for a typical golf club range from $20.57 per round in Region 5 to $34.34 in Region 8.

OPERATING MARGINS

The operating margin, or percentage of total revenue, is the reciprocal of the total operating expenses as a percentage of revenue. Daily fee golf courses that are below average in terms of gross revenue may be operating at a profit that is slim or nonexistent. Nationwide, the bottom 25% of courses showed a 9% operating margin. The average operating margin by region for the median golf course, top 25% and top 5% of courses are shown in Table 9.1 on page 132. The U.S. average is 25% for the median, 43% for the top 25% (or 75th percentile), and 51% for the top 5% (or 95th percentile).

UNIQUE ASPECTS OF HIGHEST AND BEST USE

The highest and best use analysis of a daily fee golf course can embrace everything from the way the course is operated, to how it is designed, to whether it should be redeveloped. This analysis requires a high degree of skill on the part of the analyst.

In general, an owner of a daily fee golf course has more flexibility in possible highest and best uses than operators of municipal courses, which are highly politicized, and private courses, which are often encumbered by membership agreements.

Information on how the course is operated and its profitability can be derived from outside the property by interviewing managers of competing properties, talking with golfers, and assessing the facility's reputation in the community. Data from within the property includes comparative operating statistics, the observable condition of the property, personnel input, and other information. The appraiser can analyze the various possibilities available by looking at the golf course through a buyer's eyes and attempting to determine how the golf course can achieve its best potential and how much this process might cost.

In terms of design, a golf course is like many other real estate investments, especially those like shopping malls that are used by the public. These properties require major renovations on a periodic basis. Typically, parts of a golf course will be renovated every five to 10 years. The appraiser should always consult a course designer when changes in fairways, hazards, routing, and other course elements are being considered to determine how the changes will influence the facility's competitiveness, market dynamics, and pricing. An assignment involving a proposed capital expenditure program requires a cost/benefit study or internal rate of return analysis.

The highest and best use study may result in a recommendation for an alternative re-use of the golf course. Such a recommendation is fairly rare, except in circumstances involving older rural courses that are now subject to the pressures of suburban development. Surrounding land uses may support much greater unit prices for an alternative use of the land.

Consider two alternative uses, each with an *IRR* of 15%. One investment has a 95% probability of meeting or exceeding this

IRR, while the other has an 85% probability. The first use, which is more certain, would most likely represent the highest and best use. If, however, the first project requires an investment of $8,000,000 and the second requires only $3,000,000, the situation becomes more complicated. The relative uncertainty of the investments remains the same, but the risk is different, so the choice of highest and best use is less clear. Probabilistic forecasting and risk analysis, which address such situations, are beyond the scope of most appraisal assignments and of this text. Uncertainty and risk are relevant to the appraisal process, however, so the appraiser should be familiar with the concepts.

At a minimum, the income and expenses of all alternative uses must be forecast with the same level of certainty to facilitate comparison. If the most likely income level is determined for one alternative, and the income of another is projected conservatively, the basis for effective comparison is eroded.

In conclusion, the highest and best use determination serves as a bridge between the factual data on the subject property and its environment and the valuation process. A highest and best use determination is made based on the characteristics of the subject and its environment, and the property is valued at that use.

SPECIAL ASPECTS OF VALUATION

When the highest and best use analysis indicates that the daily fee course should continue to be operated in the manner for which it was designed, the course should be considered an investment-type property in which financial results are emphasized. This means that the income capitalization approach is most important. The sales comparison approach will primarily be employed as a check on the value indicated by the income capitalization approach and, in most cases, indicate a range in value for the subject property.

CHAPTER SEVEN

THE PRIVATE COURSE

Private courses are either owned by members, which is referred to as *equity ownership,* or by a separate entity that has sold non-equity memberships. The latter type of enterprise is usually operated for a profit. Clubs with equity ownership are nonprofit operations. About one-half of the private golf clubs in the United States reflect equity ownerships while the other half are operated for profit. Most of the statistical data presented in this chapter applies to both categories of ownership.

SUPPLY

There are about 4,800 private courses in the United States, accounting for about 28% of the golf courses in the nine climate regions. Virtually all of these courses are regulation size (95%) with the balance divided evenly between the executive and par-3 layouts.

CHARACTERISTICS

Private courses tend to be the most expensive. Commonly referred to as *country clubs,* the majority are stand-alone courses not associated with a real estate development. The percentage of facilities associated with a real estate development range from 25% in Region 4 to 80% in Region 1. A private course is the primary amenity of a retiree golf community. When a private club is associated with a real estate development, the course is laid out to be visible from residential lots along the perimeter.

Because country clubs market their exclusivity, these courses are often slightly larger than daily fee and municipal courses and are more likely to be designed by a name architect. They also tend to have more land that is irrigated and maintained as turf (see Table 7.1).

TABLE 7.1

				Size, Operating, and Financial Data for Private Courses						
	Region 1	Region 2	Region 3	Region 4	Region 5	Region 6	Region 7	Region 8	Region 9	U.S.
Facility Characteristics										
Total median acreage	151	175	160	160	210	175	170	150	150	160
Acres maintained as turf	100	125	110	130	140	140	125	110	140	120
Acres maintained as irrigated	120	110	90	100	125	120	125	105	130	102
Affiliation										
Equity ownership	64%	45%	44%	43%	25%	58%	45%	66%	81%	50%
Non-equity membership	36%	55%	56%	57%	75%	42%	55%	34%	19%	50%

Most of the early golf courses were developed as private clubs so the median age for a private club is quite high (approximately 37 years) and many courses (48%) are 40 years old or older. Private clubs have become less popular in recent decades because developers have recognized that daily fee and semi-private courses built as part of a real estate community can be profitable, rather than a loss leader. Only 8% of the private clubs in the United States are less than five years old.

AMENITIES

Country clubs are family-oriented and most provide a full range of amenities, such as a restaurant/lounge, a driving range, tennis courts, and a swimming pool. Fitness facilities have become more popular in recent years and about one-third of courses have golf schools (see Table 7.2). All of these amenities contribute to higher development costs.

TABLE 7.2

				Size, Operating, and Financial Data for Private Courses						
	Region 1	Region 2	Region 3	Region 4	Region 5	Region 6	Region 7	Region 8	Region 9	U.S.
Facility Amenities										
Restaurant/lounge	100%	95%	93%	99%	100%	100%	100%	100%	100%	97%
Driving range	100%	93%	98%	94%	100%	92%	100%	97%	94%	96%
Golf school	25%	35%	41%	25%	38%	23%	28%	30%	47%	33%
Tennis court(s)	64%	70%	61%	56%	50%	85%	70%	69%	47%	64%
Swimming pool	57%	84%	52%	76%	63%	85%	70%	59%	53%	70%
Fitness facility	50%	22%	18%	21%	0%	62%	42%	42%	20%	27%

High costs are also associated with the size and design of the clubhouse because newer clubs are driven to outdo the older competition. Table 11.2 in Chapter Eleven shows actual statistics for eight golf courses developed in private residential communities. These clubs are of country-club quality although they were designed to operate at a profit. The clubhouses in these communities range in size up to 42,000 square feet; the average size is approximately 28,000 square feet.

Country club facility amenities are rated in order of importance below. The percentage of clubs that contain each amenity is indicated.

- Restaurant/lounge   97%
- Driving range   96%
- Swimming pool   70%
- Tennis courts   64%
- Golf school   33%
- Fitness facility   27%

One amenity that has gained importance in recent years is the community recreation center, which is commonly developed as a separate building. These centers are important to golf course community projects, which are discussed in Chapter Eleven. Center amenities include swimming pools, basketball and volleyball courts, exercise rooms, weight rooms, aerobics rooms, and spas.

The restaurant/lounge is a key gathering place in a country club where members and guests socialize on a daily basis whether or not they play golf. The average number of seats ranges from 129 in Region 7 to 269 in Region 6, with a national average of 176 seats. Data presented later in the chapter indicates that the food and beverage department of a typical club is unprofitable.

CAPITAL INVESTMENT

Private facilities require ongoing capital expenditures. In 1999, two-thirds of the reporting facilities indicated an investment in golf course renovation, reconstruction, or expansion. Clubhouse renovation or reconstruction was reported by 50% of the facilities, 39% of facilities reported an irrigation system installation or upgrade, 31% of the facilities reported infrastructure improvements, and 24% of the facilities reported an expenditure for maintenance renovation or reconstruction.

TOTAL ROUNDS PLAYED

The number of rounds varies substantially by climate region (see Table 7.3). The median for private U.S. courses is only 25,000 rounds, but total rounds played range from 20,000 rounds in

TABLE 7.3

	Size, Operating, and Financial Data for Private Courses									
	Region 1	Region 2	Region 3	Region 4	Region 5	Region 6	Region 7	Region 8	Region 9	U.S.
Total Rounds Played										
Bottom 25%	28,900	20,000	20,000	17,000	18,100	24,000	24,000	31,500	30,000	20,000
Median	30,000	26,500	23,000	20,000	22,000	30,000	25,000	39,000	35,000	25,000
Top 25%	34,000	32,000	28,000	24,000	26,000	38,000	32,500	47,300	39,200	33,000
Top 5%	55,252	43,000	34,000	30,000	32,000	55,000	45,000	72,000	65,000	47,300

Region 4 to 39,000 rounds in Region 8. Private facilities do not receive intensive play because membership is costly and limited. The number of members per club averages 445 nationwide, with a fairly tight range of 358 to 513. Memberships are typically allocated as follows: 25% single/individual memberships, 66% family memberships, and the remaining 9% other/corporate memberships.

Nationally, the bottom 25% of the clubs surveyed experienced 20,000 rounds and the top 25% had 33,000 rounds; the most rounds (47,000) were played at the top 5% of clubs. A club with 45,000+ rounds played will be very busy and may lack the aura of exclusivity. It is likely that clubs with a high number of rounds have efficient course layouts and relatively short starting intervals.

About 15% of rounds played at private clubs were 9-hole rounds, 16% were played by visitors, 66% were played during the peak season, and 39% were played on the weekend. Typically, actual rounds played average about 92% of the rounds desired by management.

STAFFING

Statistics on the staffing of each department are available by climate region and for the bottom 25%, median, top 25% and top 5% of courses (see Table 7.4) for full-time facility staff, part-time facility staff, and total facility staff.

TABLE 7.4

	Size, Operating, and Financial Data for Private Courses									
	Region 1	Region 2	Region 3	Region 4	Region 5	Region 6	Region 7	Region 8	Region 9	U.S.
Staffing (Median Facility— Full Time)										
Course maintenance	10	10	8	6	6	13	9	20	12	10
Golf shop	9	4	3	3	2	5	3	6	5	4
Food & beverage	13	8	8	8	7	15	10	12	14	9
Administrative	4	3	3	3	4	4	4	5	5	4
Other	2	2	2	0	0	0	5	3	3	3
Total staff	38	27	24	20	19	37	31	46	39	30
Employed year round	37	27	16	19	10	33	19	46	39	24

The total full- and part-time staff for the median club is 30, allocated 10 to golf course maintenance, four to golf shop and player services, nine to food and beverage, four to administration, and three to other services.

There are substantial differences in the number of golf course maintenance personnel, ranging from six in Regions 4 and 5 to 20 in Region 8. This difference is primarily a function of seasonality and the number of rounds played. The staffing of the golf shop ranges from two to nine and for food and beverage from eight to 15. More staff is needed in the food and beverage department when the club serves as a social center for a community that lacks social and cultural activities. Administrative staff ranges from three to five and total full-time staff from 19 to 46. For a typical private club, 32% of expenses are allocated to golf course maintenance staffing as compared to 44% of expenses for the median municipal course. This difference is due to the greater emphasis on food and beverage functions and services at a private club, but does not necessarily reflect a difference in dollars spent. The dollars spent on golf course maintenance staffing can be as high as 52% (for the top 5% of courses).

The percentage of staff members employed year-round is also a function of the climate zone, ranging from a low of 7% in Region 5 to a high of 70% in Region 6. Nationwide, only 32% of staff members at a typical course are employed year round.

MEMBERSHIPS

Private facilities involve initiation fees and membership agreements, which can be extremely complicated. Every club has a different way of handling the bundle of services received for this one category of operating revenue. Initiation fees average $9,500 nationwide, ranging from $4,000 in Region 2 to $45,000

TABLE 7.5

Size, Operating, and Financial Data for Private Courses									
	Region 1	Region 2	Region 3	Region 4	Region 5	Region 6	Region 7	Region 8	Region 9	U.S.
Memberships									
Initiation fees (single individual)									
Median	$42,500	$4,000	$12,500	$8,000	$8,000	$45,000	$15,000	$25,000	$32,000	$9,500
Top 25%	$110,000	$15,000	$25,000	$20,000	$27,500	$10,000	$18,000	$40,000	$44,000	$25,000
Annual dues									
Median	$5,200	$1,860	$3,680	$2,580	$2,950	$2,580	$2,400	$3,900	$2,040	$2,784
Top 25%	$6,859	$3,000	$5,200	$3,660	$6,042	$3,540	$3,060	$4,580	$4,212	$4,000
Annual food minimum									
Median	$400	$4400	$600	$600	$300	$300	$550	$600	$480	$540
Top 25%	$1,000	$600	$900	$650	$675	$300	$600	$1,000	$600	$700

in Region 6 (see Table 7.5). For the top 25% of private golf clubs, the median is $25,000, with a range of $10,000 in Region 6 to $110,000 in Region 1. For the top 5% of clubs, the average is $56,000, ranging from $35,000 in Region 7 to $125,000 in Region 1. However, it should be noted that extremely exclusive clubs have reported fees as high as $300,000 to $600,000. It is unclear whether turnover fees are reflected in any of these numbers.

Annual dues average $2,784, ranging upward to $4,000 for the top 25% and $6,859 for the top 5%. On average, the range spans a low of $1,860 per year in Region 2 to a high of $5,200 per year in Region 1.

Most private clubs have an annual minimum food/beverage expenditure requirement. For the median club, the requirement is $540 per year, with a range of $300 in Regions 5 and 6 to $600 in Regions 3, 4, and 8. The minimum expenditure can be quite high; for the top 5% of clubs, the nationwide average is $1,250, or more than $100 per month.

REVENUE BY CATEGORY

In addition to initiation fees and annual dues, private clubs also charge greens fees, mostly for guests. As Table 7.6 shows, this is a relatively minor source of revenue, about 7% of total revenue for the median club.

Total golf revenue, a combination of greens fees, guest fees, and annual member dues is high for a private course. Revenue averages $46.68 per round on a national basis, or 52.5% of total revenue.

Total revenue by category per round and for each climate region is set forth in Table 7.6. Total revenue per round for the average private course is far greater than for municipal and daily fee courses. Revenue per round totals $88.92 for the median U.S. courses, ranging from $65.09 in Region 2 to $117.43 in Region 3. The categories that account for the major differences are annual member dues and food and beverage sales, which make up close to 75% of all revenue per round.

Revenues for private facilities are quite high, reaching an average of $3,761,000 for the top 25% of courses, and $6,624,000 for the top 5%. As is true for all golf courses, the facilities with the greatest number of rounds do not necessarily achieve the highest total revenue per round. For example, the median club in Region 3 had total revenue of $2,701,000 and revenue per round of $117.43 compared to the median club in Region 8, with total revenue of $3,460,000 and revenue per round of $88.72.

Another source of up-to-date financial information for private country clubs is *Clubs in Town & Country,* an annual publication by PKF North America. This publication is a statistical

TABLE 7.6
Financial Performance—Private Courses (Median Data)

	Region 1	Region 2	Region 3	Region 4	Region 5	Region 6	Region 7	Region 8	Region 9	U.S.
Revenue by Category (in thousands)										
Greens & guest fees	$149.00	$125.00	$177.00	$131.00	$175.00	$125.00	$149.00	$279.00	$125.00	$153.00
Annual member dues	1,583.00	815.00	1,292.00	862.00	799.00	1,437.00	966.00	1,600.00	1,125.00	1,014.00
Golf car rentals	299.00	158.00	191.00	140.00	125.00	199.00	131.00	222.00	125.00	164.00
Golf range	14.00	15.00	27.00	11.00	14.00	29.00	20.00	40.00	26.00	20.00
Pro shop sales	199.00	125.00	217.00	137.00	199.00	250.00	217.00	333.00	237.00	180.00
Food & beverage sales	500.00	431.00	716.00	692.00	549.00	999.00	599.00	914.00	719.00	624.00
Other revenue	56.00	56.00	81.00	74.00	35.00	74.00	70.00	72.00	74.00	68.00
Total	$2,800.00	$1,725.00	$2,701.00	$2,047.00	$1,896.00	$3,113.00	$2,152.00	$3,460.00	$2,431.00	$2,223.00
Revenue per Round										
Greens & guest fees	$4.97	$4.72	$7.70	$6.55	$7.95	$4.17	$5.96	$7.15	$3.57	$6.12
Annual member dues	52.77	30.75	56.17	43.10	36.32	47.90	38.64	41.03	32.14	40.56
Golf car rentals	9.97	5.96	8.30	7.00	5.68	6.63	5.24	5.69	3.57	6.56
Golf range	0.47	0.57	1.17	0.55	0.64	0.97	0.80	1.03	0.74	0.80
Pro shop sales	6.63	4.72	9.43	6.85	9.05	8.33	8.68	8.54	6.77	7.20
Food & beverage sales	16.67	16.26	31.13	34.60	24.95	33.30	23.96	23.44	20.54	24.96
Other revenue	1.87	2.11	3.52	3.70	1.59	2.47	2.80	1.85	2.11	2.72
Total	$93.33	$65.09	$117.43	$102.35	$86.18	$103.77	$86.08	$88.73	$69.44	$88.92
Expenses per Round										
Payroll	$49.67	$29.62	$39.35	$42.45	$32.64	$46.67	$45.20	$40.18	$28.57	$39.80
General & administrative	11.10	6.19	7.87	7.75	8.50	7.50	5.80	7.67	9.06	7.28
Irrigation water	0.60	0.11	0.30	0.20	0.09	0.83	0.32	1.26	0.71	0.28
Fertilizers/chemicals	2.47	2.26	3.43	2.30	1.41	1.33	1.00	1.64	1.11	2.32
Lease expense/golf cars	1.63	1.47	2.26	2.15	1.50	1.93	1.64	1.26	0.89	1.68
Lease expense/equipment	2.47	1.28	1.48	1.05	0.91	0.80	1.48	0.95	1.40	1.24
Cost of merchandise sold	4.97	3.47	6.26	4.45	6.05	5.40	5.96	5.54	4.03	5.08
Cost of food & beverage	4.97	7.66	12.17	14.40	11.36	9.97	7.96	8.97	8.26	10.24
Advertising/marketing/promotion	0.70	0.34	0.39	0.45	0.41	0.30	0.36	0.33	0.23	0.36
Facility insurance	1.47	0.87	1.87	1.30	0.50	1.70	0.92	1.38	0.89	1.20
Utilities	1.63	1.25	2.04	2.10	1.91	2.07	1.84	1.23	1.31	1.72
Other expense	4.17	3.43	5.57	3.80	2.23	2.50	4.48	3.03	1.66	3.68
Totals	$85.85	$57.95	$82.99	$82.40	$67.51	$81.00	$76.96	$73.44	$58.12	$74.88

review of selected clubs in the United States, with separate figures for clubs in the eastern, central, and western portions of the country. While this material is helpful, PKF notes that it is not set forth as a standard for private clubs.

Among the various categories of information gathered and analyzed by PKF, one of the most interesting is a recent history of sources and disposition of income per member. Table 7.7 indicates that member income from dues, for example, has increased from an average (in the United States) of $1,021 in 1983 to $4,429 in 2002. The increase from $3,063 in 2000 to $4,429 in 2002 probably reflects the need for clubs to combat rapidly rising expenses. Total cost per member in 2000 was $7,999, but by 2002 had risen to $9,994, an increase of 24.9% in three years. Between 2001 and 2002, payroll and related expenses increased from $3,937 to $5,373. In terms of the bottom line, the average club had $215 per member in excess income over expenses, but in 2002 that figure declined to -$626.

Many clubs are looking to income from nonmember use of club facilities to enhance revenue. While 87% of the clubs reporting in 2002 are tax-exempt, 82% allowed nonmember use.

TABLE 7.7

Source and Disposition of Member Income (1983 to 2002)

——— Source of Income per Member ———   ——— Disposition of Income per Member ———

Year	Membership Dues	Food and Beverage Sales	All Other Sales and Income	Total Revenue	Payroll and Related Costs	All Other Operating Expenses	Total Costs and Expenses	Available for Debt Service, Capital Improvements, etc.
1983	$1,020	$854	$333	$2,208	$937	$1,045	$1,982	$226
1984	$1,129	$945	$370	$2,444	$1,036	$1,152	$2,188	$256
1985	$1,230	$1,007	$409	$2,646	$1,119	$1,242	$2,361	$285
1986	$1,349	$1,049	$441	$2,839	$1,207	$1,335	$2,542	$297
1987	$1,443	$1,100	$479	$3,022	$1,300	$1,407	$2,707	$315
1988	$1,465	$1,161	$520	$3,146	$1,378	$1,504	$2,882	$264
1989	$1,569	$1,211	$561	$3,341	$1,475	$1,602	$3,077	$264
1990	$1,718	$1,269	$600	$3,587	$1,580	$1,732	$3,312	$275
1991	$1,735	$1,348	$647	$3,730	$1,728	$1,853	$3,581	$149
1992	$1,847	$1,497	$785	$4,129	$1,942	$2,095	$4,037	$92
1993	$1,963	$1,485	$800	$4,248	$2,031	$2,156	$4,187	$61
1994	$2,230	$1,526	$1,095	$4,851	$2,496	$2.289	$4,785	$66
1995	$2,312	$1,713	$1,135	$5,160	$2,513	$2,441	$4,954	$206
1996	$2,360	$1,737	$1,164	$5,261	$2,430	$2,725	$5,155	$106
1997	$2,299	$1,769	$1,087	$5,155	$2,554	$2,481	$5,035	$120
1998	$2,704	$1,823	$1,373	$5,900	$3,048	$2,852	$5,900	$0
1999	$3,445	$1,959	$1,503	$6,907	$3,198	$3,118	$6,316	$591
2000	$3,063	$2,444	$2,964	$8,471	$3,833	$4,166	$7,999	$472
2001	$3,787	$2,784	$2,104	$8,675	$3,937	$4,523	$8,460	$215
2002	$4,429	$3,043	$1,895	$9,368	$5,373	$4,621	$9,994	−$626

About 11.75% of gross revenue for these clubs came from outside, nonmember use.

The figures in Table 7.7 are not applicable to every club's experience, but they do indicate the struggle clubs have experienced from 2000 to 2002. Many clubs ceased to grow during this period and, as of 2002, only 40% of clubs had a waiting list, with an average of 29 names.

EXPENSES

Due to the high costs of operating a private club, especially payroll expenses and the cost of food and beverage, the total expenses as a percentage of revenue are much higher for a private club than for daily fee and municipal courses. Obviously, good management is important. Total expenses represent 84% of total revenue for the median U.S. club. Expenses range from slightly more than 71% for the median club in Region 3 to 92% for the median club in Region 1.

OPERATING MARGINS

Private golf courses and country clubs are less profitable than municipal courses, which have an average operating margin of 22%, and daily fee courses, which have an average operating margin of 25%. Of course, a private club is managed for the benefit of members, not for its profitability as an investment. Nevertheless, a positive operating margin is needed to meet the club's debt service and reserve requirements. The average operating margins for private clubs are shown in Table 7.8.

As Table 7.8 shows, operating margins are tight. When capital expenditures are included (but not real estate taxes which are not shown as a line item expense) private clubs tend to operate at close to zero cash flow or even negative cash flow. Clubs with severe problems will need to charge assessments to members if there are no reserves to cover such contingencies.

CASH FLOW STATEMENT

Figure 7.1 is a statement of actual and projected revenues, costs of goods sold, expenses, and cash flows from a highly regarded country club. The club has 12 categories of revenue, five categories of cost of goods sold, and 18 categories of expenses. With so many categories, it is difficult and time-consuming to analyze each revenue, cost of goods sold, and expense item. This club also had seven categories of golf memberships and four categories of social membership to complicate the analysis. Given the negative cash flows and actual costs in excess of $23 million, this is an extremely difficult appraisal problem. In this case it seems obvious that the club was developed as an ame-

TABLE 7.8

Average Operating Margins	
Region	Percent
1	13
2	14
3	14
4	8
5	15
6	7
7	15
8	12
9	6
U.S.	12

FIGURE 7.1

Statement of Actual and Projected Cash Flows for Private Golf and Country Club

Item	1998 Actual	12 Mo. Ended 8/31/99	2000 Budget	2001 Budget
Revenues				
Golf shop	$1,062,364	$1,145,627	$1,573,909	$1,627,688
Restaurant	784,177	845,098	950,412	991,220
Beverage	354,191	392,194	430,080	487,168
Tennis	13,361	5,051	3,300	3,578
Pool	2,500	1,960	2,000	2,168
General and administrative (+ charges & int.)	568,259	633,544	803,916	869,328
Membership (nonrefundable)	427,209	146,000	0	261,469
Locker room	35,350	36,925	39,808	45,533
Tournament	515,984	522,128	550,190	597,600
Tournament maint., subsidy	184,487	313,674	71,007	74,557
Miscellaneous	32,704	28,778	37,811	39,900
Interest income	0	0	0	8,143
Total revenues	$3,980,586	$4,070,979	$4,462,433	$5,008,352
Cost of Goods Sold				
Golf shop (67%)	$210,698	$222,360	$280,800	$303,075
Restaurant (31%)	241,750	262,354	301,534	307,278
Beverage (21%)	72,186	84,193	89,700	151,022
Tennis (N/A)	9,348	2,262	0	0
Tournament (44%)	146,701	145,831	137,250	139,062
Total cost of goods sold	$680,683	$717,000	$809,284	$900,437
Gross margin	$3,299,903	$3,353,979	$3,653,149	$4,107,915
Expenses				
Golf shop	$376,985	$394,066	$409,923	$420,000
Restaurant	572,986	593,957	629,398	675,000
Beverage	120,156	129,444	156,610	162,000
Tennis	56,675	62,110	71,406	73,500
Pool	21,679	23,425	28,820	26,250
General & administrative	663,829	745,835	778,920	813,750
Real estate taxes	144,052	151,359	150,000	168,000
Management fees	148,321	123,415	218,721	150,251
Membership	99,880	103,888	87,026	89,250
Locker room	50,966	48,419	43,457	42,000
Maint./janitor/laundry	153,476	161,268	194,605	183,750
Golf course maintenance	667,578	660,255	701,142	735,000
Golf course construction	41,174	35,830	0	0
Club grounds maintenance	88,251	101,491	118,992	110,250
Tournament expenses	228,059	242,721	159,902	167,897
Golf course capital imp.	0	0	0	42,000
Clubhouse capital imp.	0	0	0	157,500
Other	39,050	31,953	0	0
Total expenses	$3,473,117	$3,609,436	$3,748,922	$4,016,398
Net operating income	-$173,214	-$255,457	-$95,773	$91,517

nity to increase the sale of lots in the residential community. It was not expected to be profitable although it might possibly be able to support itself.

Unique Aspect of Highest and Best Use

Private courses are rarely converted from their original purpose even if it is physically possible to do so. Membership rights can be legally enforced and land use restrictions typically limit the property to park, open space, or recreation activities.

Special Aspects of Valuation

A distinction should be made between equity and non-equity golf clubs for appraisal purposes. The concept of fee simple ownership is a hypothetical one as far as equity clubs are concerned, except in rare circumstances. A fee simple appraisal may be sought in an assignment for a lender when membership interests may be pledged to obtain a loan. In the case of foreclosure, however, all of the membership interests would be dissolved. When the fee simple property rights are appraised, the income capitalization approach may reflect a daily fee valuation assumption. Alternatively, a new, private non-equity club may be operated on a for-profit basis with revenues derived primarily from the sale of memberships (initiation fees) and monthly or periodic dues and service changes.

CHAPTER EIGHT

COST APPROACH

The cost approach is uniquely applicable to the appraisal of golf facilities. The cost estimate represents the cost to develop or replace a property and, when applied to a golf course, this estimate can include the value of all of the elements of the enterprise listed below.

- Land (entitled, but unimproved)
- Course improvements such as irrigation and drainage systems, trees, greens, tees, fairways, service roads, golf car paths, bridges, and lakes
- Buildings such as the clubhouse, maintenance buildings, and miscellaneous structures
- Personal property such as maintenance equipment, office equipment, clubhouse furniture, pro shop fixtures, and golf cars
- Liquor license
- Intangibles (or *business value*) attributed to factors such as the facility's reputation or name, trained staff and management, unique design, and membership list

APPLICABILITY OF COST APPROACH

Traditionally, the cost approach has been accorded great weight in the valuation of a golf course because golf courses are considered special-purpose properties that were not frequently exchanged in the market. Potential buyers, therefore, are assumed to focus on the cost of replacing the facility minus an allowance for recognized depreciation. As will be demonstrated, the appraisal of a golf course is extremely complicated and open to error. An understanding of the entire process is needed to guide the analyst.

Some golf facilities, such as country clubs, are not profit-oriented ventures and, therefore, income capitalization techniques may have limited applicability. The absence of a profit motive and the scarcity of golf course transactions also limit the sales comparison approach, which further indicates that the cost approach must be emphasized. The cost approach is especially important when a project is new and a market feasibility study supports the objectives of the investment. Investment objectives rather than economics or projected cash flows are considered because many golf courses are created to support or amenitize the investment in the surrounding project by boosting residential subdivision sales or resort revenues.

Specialized appraisal assignments often rely on the cost approach. A purchase price segregation and remaining life study, which is typically performed for tax purposes, is based entirely on depreciated cost estimates of the physical assets. Similarly, an appraisal for insurance purposes is derived from a separate valuation of the insurable components of the golf course. A study of costs is also essential to the determination of financial feasibility. In a feasibility study the analyst estimates the internal rate of return *(IRR)* of a proposed golf course or an addition to an existing facility. Financial feasibility is indicated when the golf course's net present value exceeds its development costs.

In applying the cost approach, the appraiser assumes that the project is complete, but the definition of *complete* is subject to misinterpretation. There is a difference between a physically complete project and a financially, operationally complete project. Failure to recognize this distinction can result in a market value estimate that does not include consideration of certain development costs. Such costs may include fill-up or membership sales costs and fees, negative cash flows during the development and marketing phases, and higher-than-normal interest rates for a construction loan or related holding costs until permanent financing is achieved.

The cost approach assumes that the project is physically complete, but not stabilized. Stabilization is the point in a property's life when it has reached a level of utility commensurate with supply and demand. Stabilization occurs when the optimum level of income and utility are achieved.

The determination of economic feasibility requires a market value estimate of the property as it currently exists ("as is" value) and a value estimate at a prospective time–i.e., upon completion of a certain phase of construction, achievement of a stabilized condition, or both. Stabilization indicates that the property has reached the level of utility for which it was designed or planned.

The appraiser must recognize that the values of a property as is, upon completion of construction, and upon stabilization are not concurrent; they occur at different points on the development timeline. An appraiser who fails to remember this may lose sight of predictable changes in market conditions and make erroneous assumptions in feasibility analysis and value estimation.

SPECIAL SITUATIONS

Investors rarely use the cost approach to estimate an acquisition price; sellers of these properties rarely apply the approach either, although some may. When a golf course is slated for redevelopment, however, the cost approach may be applicable because an accurate land appraisal based on various highest and best use scenarios is the primary determinant of value. The appraiser valuing a course for redevelopment need not have golf course experience unless parts of the existing course – i.e., the land, improvements, or a combination of both – are to be retained and incorporated into an adaptive reuse plan.

Transactions involving the sale of land approved or expected to be used solely for a golf course are extremely rare. They require a complicated adjustment process and a land value estimate derived by the cost approach is normally quite difficult to derive and somewhat speculative. When market data is plentiful, the cost approach may be considered only as a check on the other approaches to value. Deriving cost and depreciation estimates for most physical assets should not present a problem, but compiling a complete, valid estimate of the value of intangibles is a task that requires special training.

Appraisers should recognize that a golf course is a business enterprise operating in a real property environment. Many appraisers of golf facilities overlook the business enterprise component or confuse it with the value of the real estate, making the land residual to the value indicated by the economics of the project. It is essential that all the contributing elements of the golf course be properly identified, especially in an appraisal for mortgage lending or real property taxation purposes. In both of these cases, the business enterprise element should receive special attention. The lender is primarily interested in the security provided by the physical assets; the local assessing body is prohibited from taxing the intangibles.

APPRAISING A GOLF COURSE SITE

When the continued operation of the golf course or country club is the highest and best use of the property, land value would ideally be derived from sales of land that is specifically approved or designated only for golf course use. This can be difficult because such transactions are scarce. Sometimes it is appropriate to consider sales of undeveloped land zoned or planned for low-density residential use or mixed residential use as comparables, but extra care must be taken to quantify the proper adjustments. When a golf course is slated for redevelopment to an alternative land use, the assignment is not golf-related and the comparables can be derived from other sources.

In most appraisals, the problem is finding an adequate number of applicable transactions. The problem is compounded by the fact that many golf course land transactions involve a combination of proposed land uses (usually residential and golf), so the analyst may need to separate the components through a use allocation process. The use allocation would be made using a residual process, with the golf course land identified as the remainder after the appraised value of the residential land has been deducted.

The first step in appraising the golf course site is understanding and categorizing the site characteristics. The critical factors are surrounding land uses; topography; the availability of utilities, especially water; access and location; and site shape. Less important factors include easements, zoning (if golf is an allowed use), views, and vegetation. An adjustment grid should be used for listing site characteristics and making comparisons.

Land prices are usually expressed on a per-acre basis, but they may also be compared based on the value or price of the whole site. A number of estimates should be made, if possible, to arrive at a land value conclusion. Sometimes rules of thumb or tests are applied. Using one rule of thumb, the greens fee multiplier, the golf course land is valued by multiplying the typical or average greens fee by a factor derived from sales of golf course sites for which greens fees are known. This calculation is illustrated below.

Average greens fee for subject	$20.00
Factor derived from golf course sales in region	× 100,000
	$2,000,000

In this example, the factor of 100,000 was derived by analyzing three sales of golf course sites. The average price of these sites was $1,808,000 and the average greens fee was $18.00 at the time of sale ($1,808,000/$18.00 = 100,444, or 100,000). Because the subject course has an average greens fee of $20.00 on the date of the appraisal, the land is assumed to be more valuable than the comparable sites. Sole reliance on this value estimation technique is inadvisable; other adjustments should always be considered. A detailed analysis of comparable land sales is recommended (see Figure 8.1).

In analyzing sales of land that were eventually used for golf course or country club projects, it is important to determine the state of project approvals at the time of purchase. In many jurisdictions the approval process can take years and involve legal and consultant fees, holding costs, management time, and overhead expenses. The purchase prices of unapproved raw land (i.e., sites without proper zoning or entitlements) can be misleading and must be adjusted. The many costs that separate raw land prices from the prices of land approved for a golf project can be quantified on an itemized basis, but the total still may not represent the difference in value between a parcel of land without entitlements and a parcel with a tentative map or building permit.

Acreage that has all the necessary approvals often increases in unit value by hundreds of percentage points (i.e., it becomes two or three times more valuable) especially in communities where developable land is scarce or growth restraints are common. The adjustment grids prepared by appraisers should account for the significant differences in the stages of development or approvals that separate raw land sales from sales of golf course sites. Rules of thumb or land adjustment factors (e.g., approvals increase raw land acreage by a factor of 1.6) may be applicable if they are derived from an analysis of actual developments and supporting sales data is available.

In some markets golf course land prices may be expressed on the basis of price or value per hole. This system is appropriate when land sales of 9-hole, 18-hole, 27-hole, and larger projects are analyzed. Comparing per-acre prices for smaller and larger projects may require adjustment because prices often vary based on size factors alone. Other factors that can significantly affect land prices include open-space dedications, land use restrictions, utility easements or lines, and topography.

Restrictive land use designations, covenants, or deed restrictions may be significant to the appraisal if market participants are considering possible alternative uses for the golf course in the future. Such considerations might arise in the appraisal of an urban course surrounded by high-priced residential and commercial land. However, for a golf course with no likely alternative use, comparison with golf course land sales subject to re-

FIGURE 8.1

Summary and Adjustment of Golf Course Land Sales

	Property Characteristics	Location	Sale Date	Acres	Holes	Price/Acre	Time*	Topography†	Location‡	Other§	Total Adjustment	Adjusted Price/Acre
Subject	Developing area; completed in 1988	Semi-private course on the outskirts of town	4/02	139	18	-	-	-	-	-	-	$4,100
Comparable 1	Superior demographics; sold with all approvals	Newly completed course in adjacent community	2/99	126	18	$5,200	$6,188	-	-35%	-	0.65	$4,022
Comparable 2	Same influences as subject, but older; sold without entitlements	Nearby course on crowded site	3/96	91	18	$2,500	$3,412	-	-	+20%	1.20	$4,094
Comparable 3	Small course near apartment projects; had other potential land uses; sold without entitlements	Par-3 course in developed area	7/99	27	9	$4,900	$5,708	+5%	-25%	-	0.80	$4,566
Comparable 4	Slightly less desirable location; buyers thought golf land as valuable as land for other uses	Land that is part of mixed-use project	2/99	380	27	$2,950	$3,510	-	+5%	+20%	1.25	$4,388
Comparable 5	Good comparable, but old transaction; sold without entitlements	Major course in same community	6/96	160	18	$2,300	$3,105	0	+20%	+20%	1.40	$4,347

Value Conclusion Sale 3 was disregarded due to its small size and differences in the financial aspects of the operation. The other sales range in value from $4,022 to $4,388 per acre. The best comparable is Comparable 2. The value conclusion is $4,100 per acre, or $570,000.

Adjustment Notes

* Time adjustment is 6% per year or 0.5% per month, compounded

† No adjustment for level or rolling land, varied adjustments for steeper topography or elongated shape based on site preparation cost differential

‡ Location or market adjustments reflect qualitative difference in sites as reflected by demographics and fee structure.

§ Other adjustments reflect various stages of entitlements at date of sale (a typical cost for 18 holes converted to a percentage basis). Transactions with positive adjustments lacked various approvals at time of sale.

strictive planning or other zoning regulations may be entirely proper.

Easements for underground cables or overhead utility lines may be a significant problem for residential or commercial projects, but they mostly appear to pose no problem for golf courses. The routing of fairways and the placement of tees and greens can be adjusted to accommodate these unattractive, but necessary features of our environment. Surface uses, landscaping, paths, and other site improvements are typically allowed within utility rights of way. A talented architect can conceal or work around utility lines so they do not detract from the course design or represent a hazard to golfers.

Golf course land value can also be estimated by capitalizing projected land rental income. The income should be discounted if the income stream is irregular or the project is in a growth stage. The appraiser may capitalize land rental income in valuing public or municipal courses by studying the leases of operators who have developed golf projects on publicly owned sites. Land rents are typically based on a percentage of the gross incomes generated by the course's revenue-producing departments. The capitalized value of the annual estimated land rental income can be used as evidence of the site or acreage value of the golf course in the appraisal process. This type of analysis is shown in Figure 8.2.

Estimating the land value component of a golf course is difficult, and the appraiser may need to consider a variety of techniques when comparable sales are unavailable. Land sales for golf course developments in distant locations may be considered if the market dynamics are similar and they can be adjusted without applying unreasonable assumptions. It may also be proper to consider older sales in locations closer to the subject property.

Cost Estimates: Sources and Techniques

The most difficult task in applying the cost approach to unique properties is typically the estimation of replacement cost. This problem is magnified by the technical nature of golf course improvements. Because most appraisers are unfamiliar with golf terminology and data sources, a glossary and a bibliography with additional information are provided at the end of this manual.

Sources of information on golf course replacement costs include published construction cost manuals, computer cost services, course builders and architects, and trade publications. The *Marshall Valuation Service*, published by Marshall & Swift, con-

FIGURE 8.2

Land Value Estimate Derived by Capitalizing Income From Ground Lease (18-Hole Public Course)

Revenue Estimates at Stabilization

Category	
Greens fees	
Weekdays	$420,000
Weekends & holidays	340,000
Discount play	110,000
Subtotal	$870,000
Other fees	
Golf car rental	$192,000
Driving range	23,000
Subtotal	$215,000
Total golf income	$1,085,000
Departmental income	
Food sales	$115,000
Beverage sales	70,000
Shop sales	130,000
Total departmental income	$315,000
Gross income	$1,400,000
Estimated land rents	
Golf-related revenues @ 20% of $1,085,000	$217,000
Departmental revenues @ 4% of $315,000	12,600
Total annual land rent	$229,600
Value of golf course site	
$229,600 capitalized @ 11% (rounded)	$2,087,000

tains golf course cost information. Appraisers may also have access to special valuation monographs prepared by state agencies for use by assessors and boards of equalization.

UNIT COSTS

Most replacement cost figures are reported in typical ranges for golf courses of various quality classifications. For example, *Marshall Valuation Service* lists unadjusted costs for the four classes of regulation courses described below:[1]

Class I. Minimal quality, simply developed, budget courses on open natural or flat terrain, few bunkers, small tees and greens
Cost per hole: $46,250–$62,500

Class II. Simply designed course on relatively flat terrain, natural rough, few bunkers, small built-up tees and greens, some small trees
Cost per hole: $64,750–$89,000

Class III. Typical private-type club on undulating terrain, bunkers at most greens, average elevated tees and greens, some

1. *Marshall Valuation Service* (Los Angeles: Marshall & Swift, 2001), December 2001.

large trees moved or clearing of wooded areas. Driving range included

Cost per hole: $91,000–$126,000

Class IV. Better championship-type course on good undulating terrain, fairway and greens sprinklered and contoured, large tees and greens, large trees transplanted, driving range, may have name architect

Cost per hole: $127,500–$180,000

The cost manual warns users that individual course costs can vary substantially from the stated ranges and that it may be appropriate to adjust items included in the cost per hole after analyzing individual unit costs. It states

> Primary variables in golf course costs are type of terrain, size and layout, amount and quality. Excluded from these ranges are extensive grading, such as required for canyon and hillside courses, special drainage problems, and all structures including bridges, and lakes. Included in the cost per hole are normal clearing of land including incidental grading, complete irrigation and drainage systems, planting of trees in open land, greens, tees, fairways, service roads and cart paths, financing during construction, and architect's fees.[2]

More accurate golf course cost estimates can be derived by applying unit costs or segregated costs rather than cost-per-hole figures.

DETAILED COST ESTIMATES

In many valuation assignments, except those in which only preliminary recommendations are made, it is wise to use itemized unit costs or contractor's estimates. Unit costs may be difficult to obtain because sources of published data on golf course reproduction and replacement costs are limited. Appraisers should consult golf course maintenance superintendents, golf course architects, and contractors who specialize in the development of golf courses to obtain actual cost data and specifications for improvements such as irrigation lines, which are underground and cannot be measured accurately in the field. Figure 8.3 is an example of a typical cost estimate that might be used by a developer. Such an estimate shows direct costs only.

The direct costs of a project can be obtained from golf course contractors or subcontractors. Indirect costs, however, are usually unique to each project and do not fall into standard categories. Indirect costs may include financing costs, fees, or points; interim interest; utility costs; and special community fees for utility connections, traffic improvements, and schools. Building permit fees are generally included in direct costs.

2.   Ibid.

FIGURE 8.3

Cost Estimate for Proposed 18-Hole Project

Code	Description/Unit Costs		Total Cost
10	Engineering and surveying	$26,000	
	Design fee—golf course architect	227,500	
	Architect's expenses	19,500	
	Irrigation design fee	33,800	
	Construction management	78,000	
	General and administrative	26,000	
	Subtotal for consultants		$410,800
20	Utilities (electrical power installation to operate wells, pump station, and office)	$65,000	
	Utility installation (to pumphouse and maintenance facility)	26,000	
	Water source (fee for water rights)	32,500	
	Pump station	130,000	
	Intake and enclosure (intake value and pipe: $10,000; pump station enclosure: $35,000	58,500	
	Irrigation system (100 acres with 3 parallel lines, sprinkler head, outlets, connections, etc.)	1,248,000	
	Irrigation repairs (repairs and parts for irrigation system following installation)	13,000	
	Subtotal utilities and irrigation		$1,573,000
	Finish grading (final grading: greens, tees, and bunker construction)	$650,000	
	Cleaning/trash removal	13,000	
	Lake construction		
	Stage 1	93,600	
	Stage 2	78,000	
	Stage 3	131,300	
	Stage 4	55,900	
	Subtotal major site work		$1,021,800
30	Lake transfer lines (10-in. pipe, fittings, valves and installation)	$32,500	
	Car paths (4-ft. wide; 1½-in. asphalt over gravel base)	109,200	
	Sand bunkers	52,000	
	Parking lot	55,250	
	Drainage	195,000	
	Subtotal for course and land improvements		$443,950
40	Seed (cost of fairway seed @ $18,000 and costs of greens seed @ $2,000)	$26,000	
	Fertilizer/chemicals	122,200	
	Stolons (estimated for 50 acres of fairways and 3.5 acres of tees; stolons plus hydromulch)	152,750	
	Trees	260,000	
	Plants	52,000	
	Fumigation (dependent on greens design; use methyl bromide)	26,650	
	Greens material (estimated @ 9,100 tons of sand and 2,570 tons of gravel)	165,100	
	Subtotal for ground cover/landscaping		$804,700
50	Labor/wages (18 months of development)		
	Laborers	$774,800	
	Mechanics	45,500	
	Irrigators	68,900	
	Foremen	97,500	
	Leadmen	44,200	
	Subtotal for labor and wages		$1,030,900
60	Equipment rental	$39,000	
	Equipment repair	32,500	
	Small tools and supplies	26,000	
	Fuel	19,500	
	Golf course accessories (e.g., flags, poles, cups, trash cans, ball washers, benches, tee markers, trap rakes, etc.)	32,500	
	Subtotal for equipment, etc.		$149,500
	Total golf course costs		$5,434,650

DEVELOPER'S OVERHEAD AND PROFIT

In the cost approach an allocation must be made for entrepreneurial incentive. Depending on the type of operation, the developer's overhead and profit may be as important in a golf course valuation as it is in the appraisal of a commercial property. An allowance for entrepreneurial incentive may not be applicable in the development of nonprofit courses when a suitable allowance is made for management expense in the development process.

A theoretical discussion of entrepreneurial compensation is beyond the scope of this text. Nevertheless, appraisers should attempt to estimate an appropriate amount for developer's overhead and profit by investigating the practices of golf course development organizations.

ESTIMATING DEPRECIATION

To derive a market value estimate using the cost approach, depreciation is deducted from the replacement or reproduction cost of the improvements. The depreciation attributable to a golf course may be physical, functional, or external and result from a variety of conditions (see Figure 8.4).

Some types of depreciation are unique to golf courses because of their constant exposure to the elements, use of chemicals (e.g., pesticides, fertilizers), and extensive physical contact (e.g., golf cars on fairways, divots on tees and fairways, players trampling on vegetation). Many components of a golf course have much shorter useful lives than components of commercial property (see the table on page 72 of Chapter Six). Land improvements generally depreciate at more than twice the rate of building improvements.

METHODS

Formulas can be used to calculate total golf course depreciation, but techniques such as the economic age-life method are rarely appropriate and their results can be problematic. A sales comparison analysis to derive depreciation estimates from other courses may be conducted if suitable golf course sales transactions are available, but this is unlikely. Income capitalization techniques may be applicable. Although these techniques are sometimes oversimplified, they may provide guidance as to the amount of investment required to maximize the financial potential of a course.

Because the physical components and useful lives of golf courses can vary widely, the breakdown method of estimating accrued depreciation is recommended. To apply this method the appraiser measures each cause of depreciation separately. This analysis is useful to both the preparer and the user of an

FIGURE 8.4

Factors Illustrating Various Types of Golf Course Depreciation

Tees

- Area is too small.
- Surface is uneven or poorly sloped.
- Sides are so steep that hand maintenance is required.
- Soil is too heavy, making compaction a major problem.
- Vegetation and trees provide too much shade and restrict air movement.
- Poor access for golfers creates adverse traffic patterns and paths or worn turf.
- Location of tees is hazardous; golfers risk being hit by errant golf shots.
- Poor drainage impedes play and causes compaction.

Roughs

- Pasture-like surface may be bumpy and full of holes and weeds.
- An abundance of trees, brush, or rocks complicates maintenance.
- Undrained wet areas cause play and maintenance problems.
- Clumpy and thin turf results from an unsuitable seed mix.

Hazards

- Positioning requires a long "carry" over the water or short lay-up shots.
- Weeds and algae create eyesores.
- Bunkers are too tall, too steep, and weed-infested, making them hard to maintain.
- Traps are too flat and not visible.
- Poor drainage causes traps to hold water.
- Difficult shape impedes maintenance.
- Location is handicap for average golfer.
- Sand is hard-packed or contains stones.

Greens

- Greens not elevated for visibility; merely a closely mowed area.
- Slope is improper, either too steep or allowing pockets that trap water.
- Soil structure is incorrect. Too much clay causes compaction problems; too much sand causes leaching problems; rock in the subsoil interferes with cup placement; improper soil mix depth causes localized dry spots.
- Landscaping or trees block sunlight and hinder air movement.
- Steep side banks cause maintenance problems.
- Poor approaches create traffic wear.
- Putting area is too large or too small.

Fairways

- Improper drainage hinders playability.
- Lack of width makes play overly difficult.
- Excessive roughness causes difficult lies, bumps, or unpredictable bounces of the ball.
- Soil is too hard, so a divot cannot be taken.
- Boundaries are poorly defined, confusing the golfer about direction of play.
- Poor bridges or steep hills make movement difficult or hazardous.
- Outcroppings of rocks damage clubs and mowing equipment.
- Poor turf increases maintenance requirements and impedes play.

appraisal because it provides a detailed study of the condition of all physical elements of the facility. The process can be conducted using a checklist of common defects (see Figure 8.4) and should result in separate estimates for curable and incurable physical deterioration and curable functional obsolescence. Incurable functional obsolescence is rarely found in golf courses and usually considered a minor item. External obsolescence may be attributable to excess competition, economic conditions, and neighborhood changes.

CURABLE PHYSICAL DEPRECIATION

Items of deferred maintenance can be identified through consultation with the golf course superintendent. Curable physical depreciation is measured as the cost of replacement. For example, the appraiser may need to estimate the cost to replace worn and leaking irrigation lines or the cost of reseeding fairways. For buildings, the cost of roof repairs and a paint job may be estimated. Observed conditions are considered curable if the cost of correcting the problem would be offset by an equal or greater increase in value. Minor items of physical deterioration do not always require individual treatment and may be provided for in a lump-sum deduction.

INCURABLE PHYSICAL DETERIORATION

As a general rule, all physical defects in golf course improvements can be corrected. Depreciation due to incurable physical deterioration typically applies only to the structural elements of the clubhouse and related buildings after the cost to cure deferred maintenance items has been deducted. A detailed explanation of the treatment of long-lived and short-lived building components is beyond the scope of this text. Typically, incurable physical deterioration is calculated with the physical age-life method, applying the ratio of effective age to estimated total physical life separately to the reproduction or replacement cost of each short-lived and long-lived building component affected.

CURABLE FUNCTIONAL OBSOLESCENCE

An obsolete golf course design results in a loss of value. Problems in routing, hole lengths, and the placement of hazards, tees, or holes can hurt the image of a facility and have a negative impact on its potential revenue. Courses can be redesigned to eliminate undesirable features or to attract a different type of player. Many older courses have been altered a number of times to increase their competitiveness and renew their reputation. The principles governing curable functional obsolescence in site improvements also apply to the clubhouse and other buildings.

Input from technical experts is needed to analyze and quantify golf course design deficiencies. Usually the golf course superintendent is aware of the curable problems of the course and may already have a budget for corrections. Determining the economic benefits of correcting deficiencies is difficult and will involve projecting future revenues and operating expenses. For a discussion and examples of curable functional obsolescence in buildings, readers should consult general valuation texts such as *The Appraisal of Real Estate*.[3]

Many golf course appraisal assignments relate to the valuation of an existing golf course or country club after an expansion and modernization program has been completed. In these

3. *The Appraisal of Real Estate*, 12th ed. (Chicago: Appraisal Institute, 2001).

cases the design defects of the property are being corrected and the added value of the investment is reflected in the appraisal of the completed facility. No estimate of functional depreciation is needed unless other deficiencies remain.

If a course is being appraised "as is," an appropriate allowance for depreciation attributable to design problems must be made. To be curable, the cost of replacing the outmoded or unacceptable aspect must be the same or less than the anticipated increase in value."[4] The two steps required in estimating curable functional obsolescence are determination of feasibility and estimation of the loss in value.

Estimating depreciation due to functional obsolescence is illustrated in the following example, which relates to a golf course that has badly designed holes. In the example, the golf course is being penalized for the immediate cost of improving the three holes plus the detrimental influence on the total course income attributed to the undesirable features. This oversimplified analysis is presented for illustration only. In the real world, individual improvements to the golf course and buildings would be scheduled as part of a major renovation project.

Determination of Feasibility	
Cost to eliminate undesirable features of three holes	$450,000
Salvage value of irrigation lines and attachments	− 50,000
Net cost	$400,000
Potential increase in annual rounds: 3,500	
Potential gain in annual revenue	
(3,500 rounds × $30/round)	$105,000
Less increase in maintenance costs and taxes	− 50,000
Gain in net operating income	$55,000
Increase in course value ($55,000 capitalized at 12%)	$458,333

Estimation of Depreciation	
Total replacement cost of golf course improvements	
($185,000/hole × 3 holes)	$555,000
Less physical deterioration already deducted	− 375,000
Subtotal	$180,000
Plus net cost to improve	$400,000
Loss in value	$580,000

EXTERNAL OBSOLESCENCE

External obsolescence is identified as the underperformance of a golf course in comparison with more successful facilities in the market area. Externalities that can detract from a golf course's income-producing potential generally relate to

4. Ibid.

locational factors such as poor demographics or an inadequate number of golfers within the appropriate income categories. In some areas, notably in Sunbelt communities, excess competition can cause external obsolescence.

Although external obsolescence attributable to market dynamics is largely incurable on the part of the owner or operator, it may diminish over time as the target population grows or golf participation and frequency of play increase due to other factors.

External obsolescence attributed to existing neighborhood conditions is almost always found in declining communities. Except in an undeveloped market that is in a growth stage, the depreciation attributed to outside forces is usually reflected in the land value estimate. If a golf course is badly located relative to potential and existing golfers, a full cost approach analysis should probably not be undertaken.

A deduction for external obsolescence due to slow market absorption is calculated in Figure 8.5.

FIGURE 8.5

Calculating Depreciation Due to Loss in Income During Absorption Period						
Year	Desired Rounds	Projected Rounds	Difference	Average Greens Fees	Lost Income	Discounted at 15%
1	30,000	25,000	5,000	$20	$100,000	$86,957
2	45,000	37,000	8,000	$22	$176,000	133,081
3	50,000	48,000	2,000	$24	$48,000	31,561
						$251,599
Rounded						$250,000

FURNITURE, FIXTURES, AND EQUIPMENT

To prepare a detailed cost approach analysis, a specialist may analyze the depreciated replacement cost of each item of furniture, fixtures, and equipment (FF&E). Such a detailed analysis might be excessive, however, because of the time required to prepare an inventory, inspect each item, contact suppliers for cost information, and determine an appropriate deduction for each form of depreciation. Since FF&E generally accounts for just 3% to 9% of total golf course property value and its analysis is essential only in the cost approach, the appraiser should instead apply one of the procedures described below to arrive at a reasonably accurate estimate of value for all personal property.

BOOK VALUE METHOD

The value imputed to FF&E can be taken from the balance sheet for the golf course operation. This method is quick and easy, but it produces doubtful results when the FF&E is older. It is most applicable when the personal property is new because the prices paid for the FF&E are current.

MODIFIED BOOK VALUE METHOD

The first step in the modified book value method is to analyze the average age of the FF&E. Then the original cost of the entire group of assets is adjusted upward to approximate the current replacement cost. Finally, an average rate of depreciation is applied to the entire category of FF&E to arrive at an estimate of current market value.

COMPARABLE COURSE METHOD

To apply the comparable course method, cost information from newly developed courses with similar characteristics is analyzed to estimate the total replacement cost for the course being appraised. An estimated percentage of depreciation is then applied to this total cost figure to derive the current value of all items of FF&E. The overall depreciation percentage applied is a function of the average life expectancy and condition of the personal property and its effective age, which is determined by studying asset acquisition dates and maintenance records.

ASSET GROUPING METHOD

As an alternative, an average cost of replacement can be derived for each revenue and expense department through consultation with department managers and the head accountant. These department costs can then be individually depreciated and used to compile an accurate estimate of the depreciated market value of the personal property.

Of the four techniques just described, the asset grouping method is most accurate, followed by the comparable course method, the modified book value method, and the book value method. The method applied depends on the purpose of the appraisal assignment and the requirements of the client. Most appraisals can be completed in a satisfactory manner using one or more of these four techniques as long as the required cost data is adequately supported and the depreciation study is based on sound reasoning.

A detailed, item-by-item replacement cost and depreciation estimate for FF&E is beyond the scope of most golf course appraisals unless the client requires this information for asset management or tax purposes. If a detailed estimate is required, the real estate appraiser may find it necessary to consult a golf course equipment specialist. Several principles must be considered in appraising FF&E. The analyst must

1. Choose a method appropriate to the degree of accuracy required for the assignment at hand.
2. Recognize that an overhead or installation cost factor should be added to most items to account for assembly.
3. Apply a separate estimate of external obsolescence to the total depreciated replacement cost if external obsolescence affects the value of the golf course as a going concern.
4. Recognize the need for outside assistance from suppliers or other specialists if the available data is inadequate.

A sample inventory of FF&E by department with estimated acquisition costs is included in the appendix to this text.

APPRAISING THE BUSINESS COMPONENT

The intangible value of a real estate development operated as a business is, at times, ignored by real estate appraisers. Even when intangible value exists and can be independently quantified, real estate appraisers often combine this element of value with the real property or tangible assets of the project and include it as part of the value derived in the income capitalization approach. When comparable sales that include an intangible asset component are used for comparison, the business value of each sale price is often not segregated or separately identified, but is included as part of the value of the physical assets. These practices may be unacceptable and in violation of accepted standards.

In applying the cost approach to a golf course facility, the appraiser must investigate and identify financial factors that create intangible value in addition to real and personal property values. It may not be sufficient to conclude that the difference between the values estimated with the cost approach and the income capitalization approach can be attributed to business value or goodwill. Instead, the appraiser might provide a separate estimate of the value of intangible factors so that the cost approach conclusion can be independently compared to the conclusion derived in the income capitalization approach and the business value component can be isolated in the comparable sales analysis.

Obviously, a recreational facility that gets its operating revenues from golfers is a business activity operating within a real estate environment. A golf course's business value component can include a variety of intangible assets and, if possible, these assets should *not* be aggregated into a single unit referred to as *goodwill.* Intangible assets can include permits and licenses, the golf course's name or reputation, customer lists, management systems, management contracts and covenants not to compete, staff in place, supplier relationships, golf professional agreements, and tournament contracts.

Analyzing and separately valuing a complicated group of individual intangible assets is beyond the scope of virtually all golf course appraisal assignments. Nevertheless, an accurate technique must be available to the valuer. Intangible assets can be valued separately through use of the excess profits technique, analysis of sales of golf course business opportunities, the residual/segregated value technique, or the management fee technique.

EXCESS PROFITS TECHNIQUE

The excess profits technique is a modified income capitalization process in which a stabilized net income figure is allocated between the real, personal, and intangible assets. The stabilized net income excludes annual cost factors that are not related to operations such as depreciation, amortization, and interest expense. This income does include an appropriate annual allowance for *all* management functions, including the activities of the owner. Appropriate returns on all assets and the recapture of depreciating assets are estimated on an annual basis. This amount is then deducted from the stabilized net income to yield the excess income attributed to the business. The calculation of net income attributed to the business is illustrated in Figures 8.6 and 8.7.

The final step in the analysis is to capitalize the excess profit of $168,300 into a value conclusion. The capitalization rate applied to intangible assets is typically higher than the percentage returns on tangible assets. Assuming that a rate of 20% is indicated, the appraised value of the subject's business component would be $841,500 ($168,300/0.20). The full value of the golf course entity is summarized in Figure 8.8.

SALES OF GOLF COURSE BUSINESS OPPORTUNITIES

Some golf course operations are leased from a local municipality. Sales of the leasehold interest in these courses can be used to determine the business value of another golf course by developing multipliers that can be applied to total revenue or net income.

Returning to the property described in the previous example, assume that the rental expense for the real property asset is 20% of gross annual revenues, which total $2,200,000. Assume also

FIGURE 8.6
Calculation of Stabilized Net Income

Income Adjustments			Summary of Asset Value	
Taxable income		$322,500	Land	$500,000
Plus:			Golf course	$1,725,000
Depreciation	$167,500		Buildings	$1,200,000
Interest	300,000		Equipment	$350,000
Inventory adjustment	22,000		Inventory	$80,000
Less:			Operating capital	$120,000
Owner's salary	72,000		Liquor license	$30,000
Retirement plan	21,000			
Car expense	6,000			
Other personal	3,000			
Total adjustments		$387,500		
Stabilized net income		$710,000		

FIGURE 8.7
Determination of Asset Returns and Recapture Requirements

Asset	Values	Return	Recapture	Portion of Net Income
Land:	$500,000	10%		$50,000
Golf course:	$1,725,000	10%	4%	241,500
Buildings:	$1,200,000	10%	2.5%	150,000
Equipment:	$350,000	12%	10%	77,000
Inventory:	$80,000	14%		11,200
Operating capital and liquor license:	$150,000	8%		12,000
Total required net income				$541,700
Stabilized net income				$710,000
Difference—net income attributed to business				$168,300

that other golf course leasehold transactions indicate that buyers are acquiring golf course business opportunities for 50% of their annual gross revenues, or four times their adjusted net incomes. Multipliers such as the total revenue multiplier (*TRM*) or the net income multiplier, which is the reciprocal of the capitalization rate, can be derived from actual sales transactions. If sales are not available, survey data may be used. Using the values of the equipment, inventory, and license given in Figure 8.8, a valuation range of $620,000 to $640,000 is indicated for the intangible assets. The calculations are shown in Figure 8.9.

FIGURE 8.8
Value Conclusion

Asset	Value
Land	$500,000
Golf course	1,725,000
Buildings	1,200,000
Equipment	350,000
Inventory	80,000
Liquor license	30,000
Business enterprise	841,500
Total value	$4,726,500

RESIDUAL/SEGREGATED VALUE TECHNIQUE

If an appraiser has an assignment to appraise a golf course that has been recently acquired and the valuation analyses for the whole enterprise support the indicated price, the appraiser can value the components of the property by the cost approach and assume that any residual amount is attributed to intangible factors or the business enterprise.

FIGURE 8.9

Valuation of Intangibles	
Using annual income multiplier: 0.5 × $2,200,000	$1,100,000
Less value of equipment, inventory & license ($350,000 + $80,000 + $30,000)	460,000
Net value of intangibles	$640,000
Using net income multiplier:	
Net income	$710,000
Less rent of 20% × $2,200,000	440,000
Net to leasehold operator	$270,000
Net income multiplier	× 4
Total business value	$1,080,000
Less value of equipment, inventory & license	460,000
Net value of intangibles	$620,000

MANAGEMENT FEE TECHNIQUE

A simplified technique that is sometimes appropriate involves capitalizing all or part of the management fee. Obviously, some management expense is incurred in operating any golf facility. In some circumstances, however, a particular management organization may produce operating returns that result in excess profits. The incentive fees paid to management for extraordinary performance are, in essence, a return on intangible services such as the organization of personnel, management systems, public relations, and promotion. In other words, paying a management fee may result in a higher level of performance than is found at similar golf courses. Calculating intangible value based on a management fee is problematic, however, due to the ill-defined relationship between the amount of the management fee and the extent of intangible asset value.

In some valuation assignments the appraiser does not need to isolate or separately quantify the business component of the golf facility. The total value of the facility as a going concern is usually sought when the assignment involves transfer of ownership, gift or inheritance tax matters, or investment counseling and decision making. In assignments for mortgage financing and other purposes, however, each individual asset of the golf course or country club must be identified and valued.

CHAPTER NINE

INCOME CAPITALIZATION APPROACH

The income capitalization approach to value is based on the economic principle that the value of an income-producing property is the present worth of anticipated future benefits. The annual cash flow, or net income projection, is converted into a present value indication using discounting and capitalization. Methods of capitalization are based on inherent assumptions concerning the quality, durability, and pattern of the income stream. Depending on the circumstances, appraisers apply direct capitalization or yield capitalization techniques such as discounted cash flow analysis.

Direct capitalization is performed by applying an overall capitalization rate to a single year's net operating income. This technique is appropriate for valuing an existing property when its current revenue and income equal or approximate the stabilized income level at market rates.

Sometimes the pattern of projected income is irregular, as it is during the absorption period of a new or modified facility. An existing facility that has not reached stabilization or is not stable due to internal or external causes may also have an irregular income pattern. In these cases a yield capitalization technique like discounted cash flow (DCF) analysis is most appropriate. To apply this method, the present worth of future cash flow expectations is calculated by individually discounting each anticipated, periodic future cash receipt at an appropriate discount rate. The market value derived is the accumulation of the present worth of each year's projected net income plus the present worth of the reversion, or terminal value. The estimated reversion, which is the anticipated property value at the end of the projected holding period, is usually based on direct capitalization of the projected net income in the reversion year.

In performing appraisals or feasibility studies, appraisers should not estimate golf course income and expenses based solely on industry averages or medians for various expense categories. Rather, they must use data from a variety of sources, especially comparable golf courses. Median performance data is presented in Chapters Five, Six, and Seven for the purposes of illustration only.

APPLICATION TO GOLF FACILITIES

The theory of the income capitalization approach can be applied to most types of property, including golf facilities. The methodology of the approach is well documented in valuation literature and should be understood by any appraiser or consultant undertaking a golf course appraisal assignment.

The challenge to the appraiser lies in applying income capitalization approach techniques to a unique property type. It is difficult to obtain the data required to make sound income and expense projections and to determine appropriate discount and capitalization rates for a golf facility. To obtain current, specific information that corresponds to the unique characteristics of the subject facility, the appraiser must find and verify primary data. Fortunately, such data is generally available to appraisers who have developed professional networks and successful interview techniques. Facility managers for private and public courses are often willing to share their data in exchange for other market data. Although gathering primary data may seem difficult at first, with experience an appraiser can develop the contacts, database, and interview skills needed.

There are several excellent sources for secondary data, including the National Golf Foundation (NGF) and the Korpacz Real Estate Investor Survey. At least one accounting firm (PKF North America) publishes operating statistics for country clubs. Because no single publication or source provides sufficient data to meet all the requirements of the income capitalization approach, appraisers will need to consult several sources to accumulate data. The data available may be general, outdated, or unsuitable as the sole basis for valuation, but it can be valuable in specific instances and as a general indicator of industry trends.

NGF regularly conducts national surveys of the income and expenses of golf facilities and publishes the findings in separate reports for municipal, daily fee, and private facilities. Detailed data on each of the income and expense categories discussed later in this chapter is available from these sources and some of this data will be used for illustration and discussion.

VALIDITY OF APPROACH

The income capitalization approach is the most commonly applied and typically provides the most accurate measure of value for golf facilities. It reduces the differences between courses to the least common denominator–i.e., net income or cash flow–which is quantified in the market and converted into value using a capitalization rate derived from market data and/or investor surveys. A golf facility is typically acquired for its income-producing capacity, and the income capitalization approach directly measures this important attribute.

Some appraisers maintain that the approach is not entirely appropriate for facilities that are not profit- or income-oriented. Such facilities include both publicly owned facilities and non-profit private clubs that provide golf as an amenity to the surrounding real estate development. The nonprofit orientation of a golf course, however, is only the structure elected by the current owner. The facility's future income potential may still be measured with a profit-oriented analysis to produce an accurate and appropriate value indication. In this case, the valuation produced would be based on an extraordinary assumption and should be employed primarily for informational purposes or to assess feasibility.

STEPS IN THE APPROACH

The income capitalization approach consists of five basic steps:

1. Select an appropriate projection period.
2. Forecast gross revenues.
3. Forecast annual operating expenses.
4. Select appropriate discount and/or capitalization rates.
5. Apply proper discounting and capitalization procedures.

PROJECTION PERIOD

Projection periods may range up to 10 years but a projection period of four to six years is typical. The period should extend until the property's net income stream is expected to stabilize, which will occur when demand (rounds played), prices, and expenses reflect a stable level of performance. In projecting future revenues and expenses, past results should be carefully considered; negotiations among potential purchasers typically focus on the seller's most recent operating statement.

One-year projection periods are appropriate for existing facilities that have achieved stabilized income. In these cases direct capitalization is applied to the stabilized net income to arrive at an estimate of value (see Figure 9.1). The formula is:

net income/capitalization rate = indicated market value

Projection periods for proposed facilities and existing facilities with unstable income patterns typically range from three to 10 years after the completion of construction. This period may reflect the typical holding period for golf facilities, an investor's requirements, or a business cycle. A project with an absorption period of more than five years is frequently infeasible unless it is a phased development for which slower absorption and a longer projection period are warranted.

FIGURE 9.1

Stabilized Golf Course: Direct Capitalization Approach	
Item	Year 1
Gross revenue	
Greens fee rounds	40,000
Fee/round	× $45
Total greens fee	$1,800,000
Golf car rental	460,000
Driving range	125,000
Food and beverage	580,000
Merchandise sales	260,000
Other revenue	25,000
Total gross revenue	$3,250,000
Expenses	
Fixed operating:	
Maintenance	$690,000
Personnel	255,000
General & administrative*	325,000
Golf car	58,000
Driving range	32,000
Total fixed	$1,360,000
Variable operating:	
Merchandise	$117,000
Food & beverage – cost of goods	277,000
Food & beverage personnel	100,000
Total variable	$494,000
Total operating expenses	$1,854,000
Capital expenses (reserves)	165,000
Management	195,000
Total expenses	$2,214,000
Net operating income	$1,036,000
Capitalization rate	12.00%
Value indication	$8,633,333
Rounded to	$8,635,000

* In this model, certain expenses such as taxes and insurance are embedded in the general and administrative category.

The projection period should extend no more than one year beyond stabilization. If, for example, a project has a three-year absorption period after construction is completed and stabilization is expected in Year 4, Year 5 will also be projected. The premise is that Year 5 will serve as the basis for determining the reversion value of the facility. The reversion value is presumed to be realized at the end of Year 4 in the form of proceeds from a hypothetical sale of the facility. The value of the project at completion of construction is, therefore, the present value of the cash flow benefits (and deficits) realized over the three-year absorption period, plus the fourth year's stabilized operating cash flows and the proceeds of reversion (less costs of sale). A detailed DCF analysis is shown later in this chapter.

Projection periods of more than 10 years are rarely used in the valuation of golf facilities. Nevertheless, they may be necessary if the facility is subject to a ground lease that is due to expire or is influenced by other factors that will change the expected income within the foreseeable future. The use of the appraisal may make it necessary to employ a longer projection period, particularly when the payment of debt service is critical.

Projecting absorption periods for golf facilities is difficult and imprecise. Because the absorption period extends until stabilized income is achieved and this point almost always coincides with stabilized demand, market analysis forms the basis for determining the absorption and projection period. (When stabilization is affected by factors other than demand, such as changes in price or operating expenses, the duration and effect of these factors are usually well known.) In estimating the absorption period for a facility, the appraiser should consider the following indicators:

- The absorption periods of comparable projects
- The results of the market analysis
- The subject's competitive position
- Specific primary data on absorption such as information from market or investor surveys
- Extent of the marketing campaign
- The golf-related experience of the developer and facility management

Market trends show that absorption is not constant. Demand tends to increase fastest in the project's early years and tapers off as the facility nears stabilization.

THE FINANCIAL STATEMENT

The revenue and expense categories shown in golf course facility income and expense statements are not uniform. Since the income capitalization approach requires an analysis of financial statements, the analyst must have sufficient accounting or related experience to determine which income and expense categories are to be included and which are to be excluded. A nonrecurring capital expenditure, for example, would not be a proper expense item.

NGF publishes operating and financial profiles in a standardized format using the following typical revenue and expense categories:

- Revenue
    - Greens fees/guest fees
    - Annual dues from members
    - Golf car rentals
    - Golf range charges
    - Total merchandise sales
    - All food and beverage sales
    - Other revenue
    - Total revenue
- Expenses
    - General/administrative
    - Irrigation water
    - Fertilizers/chemicals
    - Lease expense/golf cars
    - Lease expense/equipment
    - Cost of merchandise sold
    - Cost of food and beverages
    - Advertising/marketing/promo
    - Facility insurance
    - Property taxes
    - Utilities
    - Other nonpayroll expenses
    - Full-time payroll
    - Part-time payroll
    - Total expenses
- Net operating expense

These categories are very helpful in assignments involving proposed golf courses. They can also be useful when the accounting categories of an existing club can be grouped in a manner that facilitates comparison with NGF's categories of the bottom 25%, median, top 25%, and top 5% of golf facilities nationwide.

GROSS REVENUE

Gross revenue can be derived from a number of sources depending on the services and products offered by the specific facility. These sources can be grouped into two general categories: course utilization income and ancillary income.

COURSE UTILIZATION INCOME

Course utilization income represents all revenues received from the use of the golf course. This income may be generated through daily fees or course memberships. These two fee structures may operate separately or simultaneously.

The term *daily fee* typically refers to the payment of a prescribed fee for use of the course once. Within this general structure there are usually several fee categories, including general use, weekend and weekday play, twilight hours play, seniors, juniors, shoulder seasons, local residents, or others. These fees may be set at different rates and are commonly grouped together as *greens fees.*

A course membership purchased by a golfer entitles the member to certain privileges, which typically include unlimited use of the course with no greens fee or a reduced greens fee for all rounds played over a prescribed time period. This time period varies and may cover a year, a summer, the member's lifetime, the period of residence in the neighborhood or at an on-site hotel, or until the grantor of the membership (the course owner) sells the course.

In exchange for membership, the member will typically pay both a membership fee and dues. The membership fee is a one-time entry charge; member dues are periodic payments, usually monthly or quarterly. Occasionally other payments are also required. One common type of fee is a minimum food and beverage charge. If the member spends less than a set amount on food and beverages at the facility during a prescribed period, he or she is billed for the difference.

There are typically two types of memberships: proprietary and nonproprietary. A proprietary membership grants the member a partial ownership interest in the facility. Although this is usually permanent, it may be some other type of interest such as a lifetime estate. A proprietary membership may be revocable. With some exceptions, the membership fee generated through the sale of proprietary memberships should not be considered a source of revenue in the income capitalization approach because it does not constitute income to the owner; rather, it is a sale of a portion of the ownership interest in the property. Note, however, that in the determination of highest and best use, the analyst may find that maximum productivity would be realized by selling individual or other interests in the facility under a proprietary membership structure. Revenue from this sales program may assist in establishing financial feasibility.

A nonproprietary membership grants the member certain privileges and use of the facility, but no ownership interest.

Treatment of Course Utilization Income. The gross income forecast typically begins with a forecast of course utilization income. First, the income structure to be used by the course must be determined. This determination is typically based on the highest and best use and represents the structure that will be most productive. For example, the highest and best use of an existing facility operated on a daily fee basis may be conversion to a nonproprietary private club. In this case, the course utilization income structure analyzed must be that of the subject as a private club.

Alternatively, to apply the income capitalization approach to a proprietary facility that does not have a profit objective, one must first assume that the proprietary members sell their interests in the facility. (This type of assumption may be required to obtain a loan). Then highest and best use analysis is performed to determine the course utilization income structure that yields maximum productivity, and the facility is valued under that optimal structure to find the income it will generate for a buyer.

Utilization income from all sources must be recognized and various categories of income must be considered. For example, a private club may generate utilization income not only from membership fees and dues, but also from guests or reciprocal privileges that generate greens fee revenue.

To demonstrate the preparation of a gross income forecast, a simple daily fee course utilization structure will be assumed in the following discussion. If a specific membership structure is indicated, three special factors should be considered.

1. *Nonrecurring income.* Nonrecurring income should not be capitalized unless the membership is nonproprietary. Specifically, initiation fees are a one-time revenue item that must be excluded from direct capitalization. (For exceptions, see *turnover fees* below.)

2. *Turnover fees.* Turnover initiation fees are generated when memberships are resold. These fees are commonly recurring and may be capitalized. A membership club usually limits the number of memberships it will sell. Once this capacity is

reached, no new membership sales will occur. When an existing membership is discontinued, it may be resold but this may or may not generate revenue for the facility. If the membership is fully transferable with no transfer fee, the member may sell the membership personally and retain the proceeds. If the membership is nontransferable or there is a transfer fee, however, revenue will be realized by the facility upon transfer. There is usually some turnover of memberships, which generates recurring annual revenues that must be included in the projection. Often a regular turnover rate, representing a certain percentage of the membership base, may be determined based on the subject's history, the experience of comparable facilities, and demographic and market trends.

3. *Services included.* The services included in membership must be considered. For example, members may be entitled to free lockers and shoe service, while daily fee golfers pay full price. These services must be factored into ancillary income projections.

Course Utilization Income Projection. The course utilization income projection is calculated as the forecast demand or annual rounds times the price per round. Briefly stated, the analyst estimates a greens fee and measures the number of rounds played at this price to produce the forecast revenue (see Figure 9.2).

To demonstrate the projection of course utilization income and ancillary revenue in a discounted cash flow procedure, a hypothetical, partially completed daily fee course is presented in Figure 9.3. This resort facility is an 18-hole daily fee course which will offer full services. The value to be determined is the value at completion of construction, assumed to be current at the date of the appraisal report.

It is estimated that stable operations will be achieved in the fifth year of operation, after a one- year completion and grow-in period and four years of increasing business. Demand is measured in annual rounds played, and greens fees and dollar forecasts are expressed in estimated inflated dollars.

FIGURE 9.2

Greens Fee Income Forecast			
Year	Annual Rounds	Greens Fee	Annual Revenue
1	$0	$0	$0
2	36,000	$61.50	$2,214,000
3	40,000	$64.25	$2,570,000
4	44,000	$67.00	$2,948,000
5	48,000	$69.75	$3,348,000
6	50,000	$70.50	$3,525,000

FIGURE 9.3

Partially Completed Golf Course DCF Summary						
	Year 1	Year 2	Year 3	Year 4	Year 5	Year 6
Total rounds		36,000	40,000	44,000	48,000	50,000
Revenue						
Greens fees		$2,214,000	$2,570,000	$2,948,000	$3,348,000	$3,525,000
Golf car rental		432,000	520,000	616,000	720,000	800,000
Driving range		90,000	110,000	132,000	156,000	175,000
Food & beverage		252,000	300,000	352,000	408,000	468,000
Golf shop		180,000	220,000	264,000	312,000	364,000
Other		36,000	50,000	66,000	84,000	104,000
Subtotal		$3,204,000	$3,770,000	$4,378,000	$5,028,000	$5,436,000
Less cost of sales:						
Golf shop (65%)		$117,000	$143,000	$171,600	$202,800	$236,600
Food & beverage (42%)		105,840	126,000	147,840	171,360	196,560
Total revenue		$2,981,160	$3,501,000	$4,058,560	$4,653,840	$5,002,840
Expenses						
Course maintenance		$1,250,000	$1,275,000	$1,300,000	$1,326,510	$1,353,040
Golf operations		300,000	318,000	337,080	357,304	378,743
Golf car lease		100,000	102,000	104,040	106,120	108,243
Food & beverage		130,000	133,900	137,917	142,054	146,316
General & administrative	$50,000	150,000	157,500	165,375	173,643	182,325
Fixed		95,000	96,900	98,838	100,814	102,831
Management fee (3%)		89,434	105,030	121,756	139,615	160,165
Reserves (3%)		89,434	105,030	121,756	139,615	160,165
Other (3%)	150,000	59,623	70,020	81,171	93,076	106,766
Complete construction	1,900,000					
Total expense	$2,100,000	$2,263,491	$2,363,380	$2,467,933	$2,578,751	$2,698,594
Net operating income	−$2,100,000	$717,669	$1,137,620	$1,590,627	$2,075,089	$2,304,246
Reversion cap rate:						10.50%
Stabilized value						$21,945,200
Less sales cost (2%)						$438,902
Reversion value						$21,506,202
Net cash flow	−$2,100,000	$717,669	$1,137,620	$1,590,627	$2,075,089	
Discount rate: (14%)		0.769468	0.674972	0.59208	0.519369	
Present value	−$2,100,000	$552,216	$767,861	$941,778	$1,077,736	
Present value cash flow	$1,239,591					
Present value reversion	$11,169,654					
Net present value	$12,409,245					
Rounded to :	$12,400,000 (as completed)					
	$10,300,000 (as is—$12,400,000 less $2,100,000)					

ANCILLARY REVENUE

The second major category of revenues is ancillary revenue, which includes income from all sources other than course utilization. Some analysts group together all categories related to golf play (e.g., revenue from greens fees, golf cars, and driving range) because this is a commonly accepted measure of the recreational function of a facility. Ancillary revenues, which are derived from a number of sources, may exceed course utilization income. Ancillary revenues may come from all or some of the following sources: golf car rental, driving range, food and beverage sales, golf shop sales, and other sources–e.g., tournament fees, instruction, locker and equipment rental, miscellaneous. These categories represent common sources of ancillary revenue and each is addressed below.

Golf Car Rental. Golf cars are rented by the seat (i.e., one or two riders per car) or by the car. The appraiser must be aware of the rental basis when surveying comparables and forecasting revenues. The simplest and often most appropriate unit of measure and comparison is to express car rental revenue in terms of the rounds played. It is sometimes appropriate to estimate the actual percentage or number of rounds to be played with a rental car and multiply that estimate by the rental price.

Golf car utilization can vary substantially and has been increasing as the player population ages. Less than 25% of golfers may use cars on short, inexpensive courses in moderate climates, but more than 75% may use them on long, expensive courses in hot climates. A large and growing number of facilities require the use of golf cars at all times.

In the example shown in Figure 9.3, it is assumed that all golfers at this 18-hole resort facility must use a golf car. The beginning rental rate is $12 per round, increased to $16 per round in Year 6.

Driving Range Revenue. Driving range revenues are affected not only by the number of rounds played on a course, but also by factors such as range quality (e.g., mat or grass surface, level or sloped range), price, and proximity to population centers. When data is available from competitive courses, the estimate is based on revenue per round.

In Figure 9.3 driving range revenue begins at $2.50 per round in Year 2 and reaches $3.50 per round in Year 6.

Food and Beverage Revenue. Virtually all golf courses offer some food and beverage service, ranging from vending machines or a snack bar to top-quality restaurants, cocktail lounges, and catering service. Food and beverage sales may constitute a major portion of total revenues, more than 50% at some facilities. The unit of comparison for daily fee facilities is usually dollars per round, while for private country clubs it is usually dollars per member. According to the national data available, food and beverage revenue averages about $5 per round for daily fee courses and many times higher ($25 per round) for private facilities. A consumer price index (CPI) factor should be used to inflate these figures in the projection.

The food and beverage revenue shown in Figure 9.3 is relatively modest (beginning at an estimated $7 per round) since the course is at a resort where there are several other restaurants and lounges available.

Golf Shop. Merchandise sales are generated through the sale of goods such as golf clubs, balls, and accessories. With rare exceptions, customers have come to play a round of golf and the purchase of merchandise, especially golf balls, is incidental to this purpose. Therefore, golf shop revenue is usually directly related to the number of rounds played and is expressed as merchandise sales per round in comparison with other facilities.

As a retail business, golf shop sales are influenced by factors such as the disposable income of the patrons, competition, management skill, and the character of the golf facility. Although the national mean is $5 to $7 per round, this figure can be misleading. Certain high-profile courses with strong name recognition can generate substantial revenue, sometimes more than $12 per round, through the sale of products carrying the course name or logo. In Figure 9.3 golf shop sales are estimated at $5.00 per round and increase to $7.28 per round over a five-year period.

Other Revenue. Other revenue is often generated through vending machine sales, lessons, club rental and repair, pro shop services, tournament fees, and miscellaneous sources such as telephone and locker rentals. Although each of these categories is relatively minor, collectively they may be substantial. Each of these categories, with the exception of tournament fees, is closely related to the volume of play and therefore revenues are projected on a per-round basis.

OPERATING EXPENSES

Most operating expenses are routine expenditures required to produce the facility's gross income. Operating expenses are estimated on a cash basis and do not include expenses unique to a particular type of management, the cost of debt service, a depreciation deduction, amortization, or income taxes. When the direct capitalization technique is used, one-time costs and capital expenditures are excluded; these are reflected in the reserves for replacement account. When discounted cash flow analysis is used, capital and one-time expenditures may be shown in the period in which they are budgeted or an estimate for annual replacement reserves can be applied.

Operating expenses have three components: fixed expenses, variable expenses, and reserves for replacements, which include capital and one-time expenses.

Fixed Expenses

Fixed expenses are expenses that vary little, if at all, with the volume of demand for, or use of, the revenue department they support. Major categories of fixed expenses include course maintenance, personnel, general and administrative, golf car, and driving range expenses.

Course Maintenance. Course maintenance costs are nearly always one of the largest expense categories of a golf facility. NGF's 2001 report for the top 25% of private facilities indicated an average cost of $875,000 to maintain an 18-hole facility. However, maintenance costs vary greatly, so generalizations are unreliable. Maintenance costs depend on factors such as the course location and topography, climate, length of season, intensity of play, age of installation, type of facility, size, and indicated quality of maintenance. This last factor is especially significant because any amount of money can be spent to keep a course immaculately groomed and maintained. Management must determine an appropriate level of maintenance – i.e., the level at which an additional dollar spent will not generate an equivalent return. An experienced appraiser with good judgment should be able to forecast a reasonable expenditure for course maintenance. The best source of information is the golf course superintendent.

Personnel. Personnel costs are usually the second largest fixed expense. This category typically includes the cost of all personnel required for facility operations except maintenance and food and beverage personnel costs, which are shown in their respective departmental accounts. The personnel account covers payroll, payroll taxes, and employee benefits. Personnel costs are affected by factors such as local labor rates, the level of service, facility size, the length of the season, and management skill.

General and Administrative. The general and administrative account typically includes administrative expenses for office operations, insurance, utilities (except utilities for course maintenance such as irrigation), phone, postage, travel, accounting, legal consultation, dues, subscriptions, automobile use, and miscellaneous other costs. Taxes are sometimes included here.

Golf Car. Expenses related directly to golf car rental operations include lease payments, energy, maintenance, and cleaning. These expenses vary somewhat with car use, but experience demonstrates that costs are generally stable and reflect routine maintenance requirements.

Driving Range. Driving range expenses are generally fixed. The most variable part of this expense is the cost of replacement golf balls, which amounts to approximately 10% of total revenue.

VARIABLE EXPENSES

Variable expenses are those that vary significantly with the volume of demand. There are two major categories for a typical facility: golf shop merchandise and food and beverage expenses.

Golf Shop Merchandise. Merchandise expense consists of the actual cost of the goods sold. This category usually excludes personnel who perform other services in addition to selling the merchandise. Although the merchandise expense at the median daily fee facility is 73% of sales, this percentage may vary widely, especially for high-profile courses that sell products with course identification or logos at a substantial profit.

Food and Beverage. Food and beverage expense may be divided into two components: the cost of goods (food consumed) and personnel. Together these components usually equal 85% to 100% of sales or more. Although food and beverage profit margins are low, the service is usually necessary. Management may not be skilled in this aspect of the business and sales volume is low by restaurant standards. Nonetheless, prices cannot be set too high or they will create feelings of ill will among the users of the facility.

Often it is necessary to forecast the cost of goods sold and personnel expenses separately, especially during the absorption period of a proposed facility. A certain number of staff is required to provide the basic level of service desired, regardless of volume. The personnel expense is often estimated based on the actual number of employees required for each projection period and their wage rates. The cost of goods sold, on the other hand, is directly variable and can be forecast as a percentage of sales.

REPLACEMENT RESERVES AND CAPITAL EXPENDITURES

In addition to normal operating expenses, a golf facility will frequently incur capital expenses and other one-time charges. Capital expenses usually relate to the repair or replacement of capital improvements with economic lives shorter than that of the facility, such as irrigation systems, golf cars, and the clubhouse carpet, paint, and roof. One-time expenses may be incurred for unusual legal fees or promotional programs. A thorough discussion of how these expenses are treated in the income capitalization approach can be found in the Appraisal Institute's textbook *The Appraisal of Real Estate*. The size of the account for replacement reserves and capital expenditures depends on the size, quality, and condition of the facility. In a discounted cash flow analysis, these expenses may be estimated separately and projected for each future period in which they will be incurred if sufficient data is available. In direct capitalization (and sometimes in the reversion year of a DCF analysis), they are shown as a single payment in a reserves account.

EXPENSE FORECASTING

Itemized expense forecasts should be prepared for each major category of fixed and variable expense. The expenses are forecast to estimate a reasonable level of expense necessary for the subject to operate at its highest and best use under competent management. When the actual expense history of the subject is available, it usually serves as the basis for this forecast. It may be adjusted for indicated changes in management, highest and best use, and market conditions.

Expense estimates can be based on the actual cost of labor, materials, and outside services; the expenses incurred by comparable facilities; the opinions of knowledgeable professionals such as club management personnel or golf course consultants; or information in NGF reports. Expense estimates serve as the basis for expense projections when the expense history of the subject is unavailable and when the appraisal is of a proposed facility or one that is under construction.

The appraiser must exercise care when comparing the subject's expenses to expense data from other sources to ensure that consistent accounting practices have been followed. Accounting practices at different facilities can vary considerably. For example, the food and beverage expense reported for one facility may include related personnel expenses, while another facility may include these expenses in the personnel expense for the total facility. The appraiser must carefully analyze every component of each expense category to prevent double counting or the omission of any expense items.

The expense forecast shown in Figure 9.3 was prepared using internal figures, NGF data, and the procedures described in this chapter. Since the property in the example is a partially completed facility, a one-year delay in revenue production was assumed to allow time for the remaining 30% of the course to be completed and become operational.

NET OPERATING INCOME, CAPITALIZATION RATES, AND DISCOUNT RATES

A facility's net operating income or cash flow is the annual gross revenue minus all expenses and capital improvements (replacement reserves) and excluding debt service. Once a net operating income estimate is derived, capitalization and discount rates are applied to reach a final value estimate.

Average operating margins for daily fee courses representing the median, 75th percentile, and 95th percentile, as reported by NGF, are summarized in Table 9.1.

Discount and capitalization rates are factors that reflect the relationship between annual cash flows and present value. Again, the reader is referred to *The Appraisal of Real Estate,* 12th edition, for a thorough discussion of related concepts and procedures.

CAPITALIZATION RATES

A capitalization rate reflects the relationship between one year's net income and the property's present value. The capitalization rate, expressed as a decimal, is divided into the net income to produce an estimate of value by direct income capitalization.

Capitalization rates can be derived from studying comparable sales, analyzing the nature of golf facilities in relation to other property types, or using a band-of-investment technique. They can also be obtained from investment surveys (see Figure 9.4 derived from the *Korpacz Real Estate Investor Survey*) and interviews with owners, managers, developers, brokers, and lenders familiar with golf facilities.

Ideally, the capitalization rate applied in the appraisal of a golf facility is derived from sales of comparable projects. Although capitalization rates generally range from 10% to 15%, rates are affected by time, location, and the type and condition of the facility.

The band-of-investment technique is based on the assumption that most properties are purchased with debt and equity capital and that each investment position requires a market-determined return of and on its investment. The return on investment includes a competitive interest rate for the debt holder or lender and a competitive equity yield for the equity investor or developer.

Because the typical loan-to-value ratio for a golf course is 65%, capitalization rates are sensitive to mortgage conditions. When the mortgage market is active and information is available, it may be difficult to estimate an equity dividend rate that reflects the risks and intensive management associated with golf investments. Again, this information should ideally come from

TABLE 9.1

Average Operating Margins (Profitability Ratios)

Climate Regions	Median	Top 25%	Top 5%
1	28%	32%	41%
2	24%	30%	49%
3	28%	33%	65%
4	26%	35%	47%
5	21%	30%	62%
6	20%	44%	66%
7	25%	34%	46%
8	26%	32%	57%
9	20%	39%	64%
U.S.	25%	43%	51%

Source: National Golf Foundation

FIGURE 9.4

Key Golf Indicators[a] (Spring 2002)			
	Spring 2002	**Fall 2001**	**Year Ago**
Discount rate (IRR)[b]			
Range	10.5%–26.5%	11.0%–28.0%	10.0%–30.0%
Average	14.40%	14.30%	14.20%
Change (basis points)	–	+10	+20
Overall cap rate (*OAR*)[b]			
Range	6.0%–22.0%	5.0%–20.0%	5.0%–26.0%
Average	11.00%	11.10%	10.85%
Change (basis points)	–	–10	+15
Net income multiplier (*NIM*)[b,c]			
Range	5.5–13.5	5.0–13.0	6.0–26.0
Average	8.9	88	9.0
Change (%)	–	1.1%	–1.1%
Residual cap rate[d]			
Range	9.0%–14.0%	9.50%–15.0%	9.0%–16.0%
Average	11.20%	11.25%	11.10%
Change (basis points)	–	–5	+ 10
Revenue cap rate[e]			
Typical range	1.0%–4.5%	1.0%–5.0%	1.0%–5.0%
Average	3.0%	2.9%	3.0%
Change (basis points)	–	+10	0
Expense change rate[e]			
Typical range	1.0%–5.0%	1.0%–5.0%	1.0%–5.0%
Average	3.1%	3.0%	3.0%
Change (basis points)	–	+10	+10

a. Includes daily-fee, semi-private & private and various property rights (fee simple, leases & leasehold).

b. Rate on unleveraged all-cash transactions.

c. The *NIM* commonly used in golf. *OAR* is the reciprocal.

d. Also referred to as the *terminal rate*. Typical holding period 5–10 years.

e. Some respondents indicated higher rates than the typical initial rate of change presented.

Source: *Korpacz Real Estate Investor Survey*

comparable sales or from knowledgeable market participants. The best information is obtained by analyzing comparable sales.

Finally, the appraiser must assess the advantages and disadvantages of the subject property and the duration and risks of its income stream. The subject's income stream is compared to market-indicated rates to determine the appropriate capitalization rate or range of rates for the subject property.

DISCOUNT RATE

A discount rate is a rate of return on capital used to convert future payments or receipts into present value. It can also be derived from investor surveys (see Figure 9.4), but the primary method of derivation is to add an inflation rate or annual compounded growth rate to the capitalization rate. This technique assumes that cash flow and the reversionary value will increase at the projected inflation rate.

A discount rate cannot be estimated until all inflationary assumptions have been determined and the cash flow model has been completed. If no adjustments for inflation are included in the projection, the discount rate may be the same as the capitalization rate. In a typical DCF analysis in today's market, discount rates range from 13% to 18%. Because of their greater risk, proposed facilities may have higher discount rates than existing courses.

INVESTOR SURVEY DATA

The *Korpacz Real Estate Investor Survey*, available on-line by subscription, is published quarterly. The *Golf Financing and Investor Survey* is issued twice a year and shows trends and investor criteria specific to the golf industry.

Figure 9.4, Key Golf Indicators, indicates the typical discount rate, overall cap rate, net income multiplier, residual cap rate, revenue cap rate, and expense change rate for a golf facility. Figure 9.5 sets forth survey indicators for selling expense, marketing time (in months), capital reserve, and management fees. Investor surveys are also published by other entities.

BUSINESS VALUE COMPONENT

As applied to the operations of a golf facility, the income capitalization approach includes an allowance for the contribution of the business component. In applying income capitalization, the appraiser should consider the unique risk, liquidity, and yield requirements of the intangibles that comprise the entire entity. The methodology for deriving the business value of a golf course is presented in Chapter Eight. The income capitalization approach can be used to appraise the assets of the entire facility as well as individual components such as intangibles.

FIGURE 9.5

National Golf Market* (Spring 2002)			
	Spring 2002	Fall 2001	Year Ago
Selling expense[a]			
Range	0.50% to 6.00%	0.50% to 6.00%	0.50% to 6.25%
Average	3.00%	3.10%	3.00%
Change (basis points)	–	−10	0
Marketing time (in months)			
Range	2.00 to 18.00	2.00 to 26.00	2.00 to 32.00
Average	8.70	9.00	9.20
Change (%)	–	−3.33%	−5.43%
Capital reserve[b]			
Range	1.00% to 10.00%	1.00% to 10.00%	1.00% to 10.00%
Average	3.20%	3.00%	3.10%
Change (basis points)	–	+20	+10
Management fee			
Base fee			
Range	$36,000 to $400,000	$40,100 to $380,000	$32,000 to $625,00
Average	$88,700	$89,100	$88,500
Change ($)	–	−$400	+$200
Incentive (%) of *NOI*[c]			
Range	2.00% to 35.00%	2.50% to 30.00%	1.00% to 40.00%
Average	10.60%	11.00%	11.00%
Change (basis points)	–	−40	−40
Incentive (% of gross income)			
Range	2.00% to 7.00%	2.00% to 8.00%	1.50% to 10.00%
Average	3.85%	3.90%	3.80%
Change (basis points)	–	−5	5

* Data relating to discount, overall, and residual cap rates and changes rates are published every second and fourth quarters only.

a. Some respondents reported an initial flat fee. Selling expenses are generally inversely related to the price of the golf course.

b. As a % of gross income; upper end of the range typical of private clubs that own the majority of their own equipment. Courses or clubs that lease equipment have lower reserves.

c. Some respondents reported a base management fee as a percentage of gross income plus an incentive fee based on a percentage of net income as contractually defined.

Source: *Korpacz Real Estate Investor Survey*

CHAPTER TEN

SALES COMPARISON APPROACH

A golf course, like a resort or a hotel, is a unique grouping of facilities, amenities, and revenue-producing departments. No two courses are alike in terms of their physical characteristics, playability, reputation, social atmosphere, and other attributes. Because of these many differences, estimating the value of a course by comparing the prices paid for other properties is very difficult. Unlike the other two valuation approaches, the sales comparison approach depends on the availability of sales of competitive golf courses. Data may be obtained through other means, however, such as interviews with market participants. Many insights and secondary data can also be gained from investigating historical sales.

Except in unusual circumstances or when absolutely required, the results of a sales comparison analysis of a golf course should be expressed as a value range, not a single point estimate. This is accepted methodology in the appraisal of special-purpose property and a realistic course of action considering the number of variables for which adjustments may be required. The following list identifies variables that could be considered in the sales comparison analysis of a golf course.

Location site relationships
- Distance from player population
- Demographics of market
- Surrounding land uses
- Access and parking

Climate

- Length of playing season
- Wind direction and velocity
- Frequency of inclement weather

Playability

- Course challenge
- Player appeal, steep fairways, aesthetic design, surface drainage, size of greens, width of fairways
- Shrub and tree maturity
- Course condition
- Rounds played annually

Irrigation system

- Reliability of water source
- Water cost (pumping cost or vendor charges)
- Water quality, system type (e.g., fully automatic)
- Other (treated effluent, water rights, etc.)

Soil type and texture

- Intrinsic drainage, water-holding capacity
- Salinity or alkalinity

Furniture, fixtures, and equipment

- Type and condition
- Rental versus ownership
- Adequacy

Practice range

- Width and length
- Number of tee stations

Size

- Acreage
- Number of holes
- Turf versus rough

Improvements

- Size and condition
- Clubhouse
- Bar
- Restaurant
- Club room
- Locker rooms
- Pro shop
- Swimming pool
- Tennis courts

Financial factors

- Greens fees
- Monthly dues
- Initiation fee
- Number of members
- Minimum to be spent at bar/restaurant
- History of special assessments
- Annual operating costs
- Profitability

Sales terms and conditions

- Sale price
- Trust deeds or mortgages including chattels, interest rates, terms of loans, leases (especially lease-back), options, mineral rights, or liquor license included in the sale price or financing.

Analysis of golf course sales transactions may require creativity, but appraisers should remember to think about pricing and value in the same way buyers, sellers, and brokers do. The rules of thumb applied by knowledgeable market participants and the more precise units of comparison used by appraisers are both derived from experience and investigation.

RECENT SALES OF GOLF COURSES AND COUNTRY CLUBS

There is no national database of golf course transactions available to appraisers and other market participants or analysts in either online or print form. This has been a major problem for the industry. Much of the data that has been gathered is jealously guarded due to the high cost of gathering information and organizing it into analytical components.

News articles, industry publications, brokers, and participants are typical data sources. In 2002 Crittenden Magazines, Inc. and an associated entity, Golf, Inc. produced *The Golf Course Sales Report*, which contains information on 109 transactions that took place in 2001 and 2002 (see Figure 10.1). The report is available from Crittenden Magazines, Inc. for a fee. The reporting template for a transaction involving the Inverrary Country Club is set forth in Figure 10.2.

Summary of Golf Course Sales

No.	Course name/location	Facilites	Date	Holes	Price (000)	Price/Hole
1	Osprey Cove Golf Club, St. Marys, GA	a). b)	January 2002	18	$11,000	$611.11
2	Valencia Country Club, Valencia, CA	a), c)	January 2002	18	$12,000	$666.67*
3	Fox Squirrel Country Club, The Lakes, NC	a), b)	March 2001	18	$862.50	$47.92
4	White Columns Golf Club, Alpharetta, GA	a), b)	2000	18	$20,000	$1,111.11*
5	Chesapeake Hills Country Club, Lusby, MD	a), g)	February 2002	18	$3,000	$166.67*
6	Heron Creek Golf Course, LaGrange, IN	a), b)	March 2001	18	$1,000	$55.55
7	Wading River Gold Course, Norton, MA	a), b)	March 2001	18	$1,200	$66.67
8	Big Oaks Golf Club, Saltillo, MS	a), b)	late 2000	18	$1,200	$66.67
9	Oak Haven Golf Club, Macon, GA	a), b)	November 2001	18	$1,500	$83.33
10	Carolina Pines Golf & Country Club, New Bern, NC	a), b)	April 2001	18	$1,600	$88.89
11	Drake Creek Golf Course, Ledbetter, KY	d)	January 2002	18	$1,700	$94.44
12	Wedgefield Golf & Country Club, Orlando, FL	a)	March 2002	18	$1,700	$94.44
13	Rio Rancho Country Club, Albuquerque, NM	a), c)	March 2002	27	$1,800	$66.67
14	Iron Horse Golf Club, Tuscola, IL	a), d)	January 2002	18	$1,850	$102.78
15	Topsail Greens Golf & Country Club, Hampstead, NC	a), b)	September 2001	18	$1,900	$105.56
16	Shattuck Golf Course, Jaffrey, NH	a), b)	July 2002	18	$1,950	$108.33
17	Franklin Greens Golf Club, Franklin, NH	a), g)	December 2001	18	$1,975	$109.72
18	Cherokee Valley Golf Club, Tigerville, SC	a), b)	April 2002	18	$1,980	$110.00
19	Southland Country Club, Stone Mountain, GA	a), b)	December 2001	18	$2,000	$111.11
20	Belle Terre Country Club, La Place, LA	a), b)	March 2001	18	$2,200	$122.22
21	Barrington Golf Club, Aurora, OH	a), e)	February 2002	18	$2,400	$133.33
22	Brentwood Golf & Country Club, White Lake, MI	a), b)	March 2001	18	$2,600	$144.44
23	Club of the Country, Louisburg, KS	a), c)	March 2001	18	$2,655	$147.50
24	Los Rios Country Club, Plano, TX	a), d)	October 2001	18	$2,750	$152.78*
25	Kiahuna Golf Club, Kauai, HI	Resort	January 2002	18	$2,800	$155.56
26	Sabal Trace Golf & Country Club, North Port, FL	g)	January 2002	18	$3,000	$166.67*
27	River Downs Golfers' Club, Finksburg, MD	a), b)	February 2002	18	$3,250	$180.56*
28	Sweetwater Golf & Country Club, Apopka, FL	a), c)	September 2002	18	$3,250	$180.56
29	Dub's Dread Golf Club, Kansas City, KS	a), b)	April 2002	18	$3,300	$183.33
30	Tregaron Golf Course, Bellevue, NE	a), b)	March 2001	18	$3,300	$183.33
31	Auburn University Club, Auburn, AL	a), c)	October 2001	18	$3,410	$189.44
32	Baymeadows Golf Club, Jacksonville, FL	a), b)	August 2001	18	$3,600	$200.00*
33	Saints Golf Course, Port St. Lucie, FL	a), g)	August 2001	18	$3,600	$200.00
34	Oakridge Country Club, Garland, TX	a), c)	February 2002	18	$4,000	$222.22
35	Palm Desert Country Club, Palm Desert, CA	a), b)	May 2001	27	$4,075	$150.93
36	Cypress Creek Country Club, Boynton Beach, FL	a), b)	November 2001	18	$4,100	$227.78
37	Red Mountain Ranch Country Club, Mesa, AZ	a), c)	March 2002	18	$4,150	$230.56
38	Silverthorn Country Club, Brookville, FL	a) b)	May 2001	18	$4,250	$236.11
39	Creekside Golf Course, Salem, OR	a), c)	February 2002	18	$4,300	$238.89
40	Pukulani Country Club, Maui, HI	a), b)	January 2002	18	$4,300	$238.89
41	Lone Pine Country Club, Shakopee, MN	a), b)	February 2001	18	$4,500	$250.00
42	The Rail Golf Course, Springfield, IL	a), d)	March 2001	18	$4,500	$250.00
43	Metamora Golf & Country Club, Metamora, MI	a), c)	April 2001	18	$4,930	$273.89
44	Houndslake Country Club, Aiken, SC	a), b)	December, 2000	27	$5,050	$187.04
45	Mililani Golf Course, Honolulu, HI	a), d)	January 2002	18	$5,300	$294.44
46	Interbay Golf Center, Seattle, WA	h)	February 2001	9	$5,650	$627.78
47	Eagle Watch Golf Club, Woodstock, GA	a), b)	July 2001	18	$5,850	$325.00
48	Meadowlands Golf Course, Winston Salem, NC	a), d)	March 2002	18	$6,000	$333.33

FIGURE 10.1

Summary of Golf Course Sales *(continued)*

No.	Course name/location	Facilites	Date	Holes	Price (000)	Price/Hole
49	Island Green Country Club, Philadelphia, PA	a), d)	September, 2001	18	$6,000	$333.33*
50	Woodlands Golf Course at Craft Farms, Gulf Shores, AL	a), d)	May 2001	18	$6,400	$355.56
51	Rotonda Golf & Country Club, Rotonda, FL	a)	November 2001	54	$6,500	$120.37
52	Chesapeake Golf Club, Chesapeake, VA	a), b)	June 2001	18	$3,375	$187.50**
53	Honey Bee Golf Club, Virginia Beach, VA	a)	June 2001	18	$3,375	$187.50**
54	Olde Atlanta Golf Club, Suwanee, GA	a), b)	July 2001	18	$7,800	$433.33
55	Inverrary Country Club, Lauderville, FL	a), b)	May 2001	54	$7,965	$147.50*
56	Big Island Country Club, Kailua, HI	a), c), d)	January 2002	18	$8,000	$444.44*
57	Polo Trace Golf & Country Club, Delray Beach, FL	a), b)	October 2001	18	$8,350	$463.89
58	Stonebridge Golf Course, West Valley, Ut	a), b)	April 2001	18	$9,300	$516.67
59	Raintree Golf Course, Uniontown, OH	a), c)	January 2001	18	$5,325	$295.83**
60	Ohio Prestwick Country Club, Uniontown, OH	a), c)	January 2001	18	$5,325	$295.83**
61	Legends at Stonehouse, Toano, VA	a) d)	June 2001	18	$5,400	$300.00**
62	Royal New Kent, Providence Forge, VA	a), d)	June 2001	18	$5,375	$300.00**
63	Clear Lake Golf Course, Houston, TX	a), d)	January 2002	18	$6,000	$333.33*
64	Quail Valley Country Club, Missouri City, TX	a), c)	January 2002	54	$6,000	$111.11*
65	Rancho San Marcos Golf Club, Santa Barbara, CA	a), d)	November 2001	18	$12,000	$666.67
66	Pete Dye Golf Club, Bridgeport, WY	a), c)	December 2001	18	$13,432	$746.22
67	Emerald Dunes Golf Club, W. Palm Beach, FL	a), d)	September 2001	18	$16,900	$938.89
68	Due Process Golf Course, Colts Neck, NJ	a), c)	January 2002	18	$20,000	$1,111.11
69	The Owners Club at Telluride, Telluride, CO	a), c)	April 2002	18	$22,200	$1,233.33
70	Hamilton Farm Golf Club, Gladstone, NJ	a), c)	July 2001	36	$51,000	$1,416.67
71	The Golf Club at Genoa Lakes, Genoa Lakes, NV	a), d)	Late 2000	18	$7,500	$416.67*
72	Parkland, Myrtle Beach, NC	a), b)	July 2001	18	$13,538	$752.14**
73	Moorland, Myrtle Beach, NC	a), b)	July 2001	18	$13,538	$752.14**
74	Heathland, Myrtle Beach, NC	a), b)	August 2001	18	$13,538	$752.14**
75	Heritage Golf Club, Pawley's Island, SC	a), b)	July 2001	18	$13,538	$752.14**
76	Oyster Bay Golf Links, Sunset Beach, NC	a), b)	July 2001	18	$13,538	$752.14**
77	Tiburon Golf Course, Omaha, NE	b)	July 2001	27	$20,308	$752.14**
78	Loch Lloyd Country Club, Belton, MO	a), c)	April 2002	18	$6,750	$375.00*
79	The Links of North Dakota at Red Mike Resort	a), b)	February 2002	18	$467.5	$25.97
80	Clydesdale Meadows, Colquitt, GA	a), d)	June 2001	18	$700	$38.89
81	Arbor Springs Plantation Golf Club, Newman, GA	a), b)	October 2001	18	$850	$47.22

*	Exact figure not given
**	Allocated price due to multiple course acquisition.
a)	Clubhouse
b)	Semi-private
c)	Private
d)	Daily fee
e)	Residential land
f)	Resort complex
g)	Municipal course
h)	Other

Source: Crittenden Golf, Inc.

FIGURE 10.2

Inverrary Country Club

3840 Inverrary Blvd.
Lauderhill, FL 33319
(954) 733-7550

Course Information		Buyer:	Fore Golf Services
Number of holes: 54		Address:	10688 C Crestwood Drive
Annual rounds:	140,000	City/state/zip:	Manassas, VA 20109
Greens fees:		Phone:	(703)367-7237 Fax: (703)367-8911
Land size:		Contact:	Charlie Staples, member manager
Year built:		Seller:	ClubCorp.
Amenities:	Clubhouse with banquet	Address:	3030 LBJ Parkway
Driving range:		City/state/zip:	Dallas, TX 75234
# Tees:		Phone:	(972)243-6191 Fax:(972) 888-6209
Course type:	Semi-private	Contact:	Jim Hinkley, president and CEO
Building sizes:	Clubhouse: 44,000 sq. ft.	Sale date:	May 31, 2001
		Sale price:	$7,965 million plus closing
		Financing utilized:	Heller Financial Golf Lending Group, $6.6
		Gross income:	$5.7 million
		Net operating income:	
		Cap rate:	

General Information:

Sold as part of ClubCorp's liquidation of non-strategic assets.

Property includes three courses, all designed by Robert Trent Jones, Sr. The east course measures 7,040 yards from the back tees and plays to a par 72. The west course measures 6,621 yards from the championship tees and plays to a par 71. The par-61 executive course measuers 3,314 yards from the back tees.

The club has 270 members at the east and west courses and 250 members at the executive course. Fore Golf Services would like to increase the number of members but sees more potential in public play.

The company has bought and sold nearly a dozen Florida golf courses over the years and is a partner in two Virginia courses.

The prices of the golf courses in the Crittenden report are summarized and allocated below:

% of Total	Total Price Range ($000)	Price Per Hole Range ($000)
14	Under $1,000	Under $100
35	$1,800 – $3,582	$100 – $199
26	$3,600 – $7,182	$200 – $399
9	$7,200 – $11,888	$400 – $666
12	$12,000 – $18,000	$667 – $1,000
4	Over $18,000	Over $1,000

Examination of the details of the transactions indicates that nearly one-half of the sales, and virtually all of the sales transacted at prices below $3,600,000, involved financial problems. In these cases, an auction sale, bankruptcy, foreclosure, or other event resulted in an orderly liquidation of a poorly performing operation by a major national golf management or investment organization.

The data in Figure 10.1 indicates a mean price of $5,920,000 for an 18-hole property and a median price of $4,300,000. Many of the transactions were resales of acquisitions made in the late 1990s and sold for about one-half of the 1990s price.

The data is expressed on a price-per-hole basis, which is a starting point for most appraisals and analyses. This is a commonly accepted reporting unit because a size adjustment is built into the indicated price.

UNITS OF COMPARISON AND ANALYSIS

Golf courses with the same number of holes may have very different land areas due to a number of factors such as unusable topography, the configuration of fairways, the amount of natural vegetation, and the presence of natural waterways. These variables may not affect revenue, but they could increase maintenance expenses if the course needs excessive watering or mowing. Thus, a value comparison based on price per acre is not recommended in appraising any golf course, whether existing or proposed.

Obviously, if the assignment is the appraisal of a parcel of land that is presently improved with a golf facility but has another highest and best, the size of the land parcel is very important. In this case, the price per developable unit or price per square foot derived from appropriate comparable sales would be a proper unit of comparison. These units of comparison could also be applied to the excess land of a golf course that can be developed separately.

In most cases, however, units of comparison that relate to the financial aspects of a golf course transaction are preferred. When a substantial amount of data on recent golf course sales is available, the following value indicators may be considered:

- Total revenue multiplier
- Golf revenue multiplier
- Price per round
- Price per membership
- Greens fee and rounds multiplier

The derivation, application, and validity of these indicators should be understood because they can produce varying results. These calculations are illustrated in Figure 10.3.

TOTAL REVENUE MULTIPLIER (*TRM*)

Most real estate professionals are familiar with the gross income multiplier (*GIM*). Gross income multipliers are used to compare the income-producing characteristics of comparable

FIGURE 10.3

Deriving Units of Comparison from a Golf Course Sale

Available Data

Type:	18-hole, semi-private regulation course
Price:	$4,500,000
Rounds:	38,000
Average greens fee:	$32
No. of members:	220

Income (most recent 12-month reporting period)

Greens fees	$1,216,000
Car fees	427,500
Driving range	128,000
Food & beverage sales	402,000
Pro shop sales	190,000
Total revenue	$2,363,500

Units of Comparison

1. Total revenue multiplier (*TRM*)
   $4,500,000 divided by $2,363,500 =   1.904
2. Golf revenue multiplier (*GRM*)
   $4,500,000 divided by ($1,216,000 + $427,500 + $128,000) =   2.54
3. Price per round (*PPR*)
   $4,500,000 divided by 38,000 = $118.42
4. Price per membership (*PPM*)
   $4,500,000 divided by 220 = $20,455
5. Greens fee and rounds multiplier
   $4,500,000 divided by 38,000 = $118.42 divided by $32 =   3.70

properties with the characteristics of the subject. Although the conversion of income into a value estimate is a capitalization process, multipliers are commonly applied in the sales comparison approach.

A total revenue multiplier, or *TRM*, can be applied to value a golf facility. The multiplier is typically derived by dividing the sale price of a golf course by the total income produced by the facility during the most recent 12-month operating period. It is important to know whether the multiplier is derived from the 12-month period before or after the date of sale so that the multiplier can be applied consistently to the total income of the subject facility.

The advantage of the *TRM* is that revenue production is directly related to the sale price. The multipliers vary from property to property depending on the mix of departmental revenues and the relative profitability of each revenue source. If a facility's food and beverage operation is large, the multiplier will tend to be lower because the net income from these facilities is usually small. When the food and beverage operation of a facility is leased to a third party, the income component for this department declines greatly and, if all other revenues remain equal, the multiplier will be substantially higher. If, in the example shown in Figure 10.3, the food and beverage operation were leased to a third party for 6.5% of the sales, the total property income would be $1,987,630 (reflecting $26,130, not $402,000, in food and beverage income) and the total revenue multiplier would jump from 1.904 to 2.264.

Careful application of a total revenue multiplier can be very useful, but accurate revenue or income data is needed to derive the multiplier. If information about profitability is unrealistic, or uneven, the value indication will be unreliable.

GOLF REVENUE MULTIPLIER (*GRM*)

The amount of non-golf revenue generated by individual golf courses varies greatly and non-golf operations (e.g., food and beverage service, pro shop, concession sales) generally contribute relatively little to a facility's bottom line. Therefore, a multiplier derived solely from golf activities such as greens fees, membership dues, car rental fees, and driving range fees is often appropriate.

*GRM*s should exclude initiation fees if they vary greatly from year to year; if they are a predictable source of annual revenue (such as annual turnover fees), they should be included. Food and beverage sales should always be excluded from the measure, but pro shop sales may be included if the property has a significant pro shop operation. The advantages and disadvantages of using a golf revenue multiplier are the same as those associated with the total revenue multiplier.

PRICE PER ROUND (*PPR*)

It is often difficult to obtain financial statements for golf courses that have been sold. However, other statistics may be readily available from data-gathering organizations and information may be obtained through investigation and interviews with knowledgeable parties such as club managers and golf pros. The annual number of rounds played at a golf course must be known to analyze the sale of the property.

The applicability of a price per round *(PPR)* valuation indicator depends on other factors involved in the operation of a golf course. If a golf course is not realizing its maximum rounds potential because of poor management and marketing policies, the value estimate will be understated. Similarly, if greens fees at the comparable courses differ significantly from fees at the subject property, a problem will arise in the interpretation of the data. A refinement that the analyst can use to adjust for differences in greens fees and annual rounds played is described later.

Sometimes a price per round figure can be estimated for a group of golf course transactions that involve similar properties with slightly different greens fees, but very different restaurant and shop facilities. Normally, if data are available to compute golf revenue multipliers (*GRMs*), a reasonably accurate value range can be estimated. However, if financial data are not available, some type of extra adjustment must be made to derive the valuation indicator. Valid adjustments for differences in building square footage can be made and their use is accepted in contemporary appraisal practice.

The advantage of using a *PPR* estimate is that it can be derived from data that are readily available to experienced golf course analysts. The weakness of this indicator is that it does not account for differences in the non-golf components of a course or the size and quality of amenities. It is most reliable when the comparables are very similar to the subject property in terms of fees and property characteristics.

PRICE PER MEMBERSHIP (*PPM*)

This valuation indicator is only applicable when the subject property and the comparables are also private or semi-private golf clubs. Price per membership is commonly used in the appraisal of health and fitness facilities because in these properties there is a direct relationship between the number of members, gross revenues, and net profit.

On the whole, private golf and country clubs are large, complicated investments and maintenance costs for the facilities are extremely high. Most have various classes of membership, which make comparisons difficult, and many are marginally profitable or unprofitable, which diminishes the applicability of multipliers.

In the late 1980s when it was believed that new memberships in exclusive golf clubs could be sold at very high fees, trophy golf course prices reached unheard-of levels. Price per membership was used as the rationale for these transactions. This market phenomenon is past and the low resale prices for those properties indicate that the earlier prices were unrealistic.

GREENS FEE MULTIPLIER (*GFM*)

The greens fee (and rounds) multiplier is a refinement of the price per round unit of comparison. A variation of this methodology was described in Chapter Eight as a technique for valuing raw land for a golf course. For a profit-oriented golf course, the *GFM* can be a highly effective valuation tool. It provides a common denominator in the comparison of golf course sales, and it can be derived without access to financial statements.

The *GFM* is calculated by dividing a price per round, or *PPR*, by the average greens fee. This multiplier can be extremely important because it automatically accounts for variations in annual rounds attributed to the different pricing policies of courses that appear to be comparable. For example, consider two courses in the same market area that vary in the number of annual rounds played by 30%. Sale 1 had 41,000 rounds and average greens fee of $24 and Sale 2 had 28,940 rounds and an average greens fee of $34. Their *PPR*s would vary by about 30%, but their *GFM*s would be identical because both courses had total revenues from greens fees of $984,000.

To derive a *GFM*, the analyst needs accurate data on average greens fees. Obviously, the most accurate figures come from financial statements, but these may be difficult to obtain. However, careful questioning of club personnel and analysis of the various rates charged for weekdays, weekends, seniors, and juniors will allow the appraiser to derive a reasonably accurate figure.

It is recommended that the *GFM* be used in all appraisals of profit-oriented golf course operations if possible, but this is contingent on having proper comparables. The *GFM* accounts for pricing and qualitative differences between properties and is based on data that can be obtained by an experienced analyst.

ADJUSTING GOLF COURSE SALES

When sufficient units of comparison can be derived from sales or obtained from a golf course database, the appraiser should be able to estimate a reasonable value range. Up to four separate valuations and calculations can usually be made under detailed research circumstances.

Typically, an appraiser may find evidence of only a few recent, arm's-length transactions involving golf courses over a large region; detailed information may be available on only one or two transactions involving courses reasonably similar to the subject.

When sales are scarce, the appraiser must conduct in-depth analyses of the few good sales available to construct a convincing argument and account for all significant differences between the comparable sales and the subject property. The major physical differences between golf courses of a similar type can be identified using the golf course rating data described in Chapter One.

A thoughtful study of a comparable golf course may reveal positive and negative cost factors that will account for property differences. For example, an estimate of the cost to improve fairways and greens, reconfigure the sprinkler system, or renovate the clubhouse of a comparable property could account for part of the difference in value or price between this course and the subject. Adjustments for deferred maintenance are common in all real estate appraisals and should always be considered in the appraisal of golf projects.

Functional problems in golf facilities can also explain price differences between properties. Excessive or penal fairway layouts and hazards that are very difficult for the casual golfer may cause a facility to lose business from this market segment. The appraiser can account for factors such as these with an adjustment in annual rounds.

Differences in the operating costs of golf courses may be revealed by studying their financial statements. These differences can explain why golf course prices vary significantly when other factors indicate that they should not. High operating costs may be attributed to inept management, which is a curable item, or to more serious factors such as the quantity and quality of the water supply or an inefficient course layout that results in excessive maintenance expenses.

Any number of factors can account for differences in golf courses. While the appraiser should look for major items that can be explained and quantified, it is fruitless to try to account for everything. Construction of a market data grid facilitates the visual presentation of data and the analytical process. A sample golf course sales analysis is shown in Figure 10.4.

In many appraisal assignments, the real estate must be separated from the non-real estate components of the property. This situation arises in valuations for lending purposes in which the real property alone represents the security for the loan. (One might think of the physical assets as the security for the loan with the furniture, fixtures, and equipment secured through a chattel arrangement.) The cost approach can be used to derive a separate value estimate for the FF&E. The business component can be quantified using the techniques described in Chapter Eight or by using comparative analyses.

In valuation assignments in which the appraiser must separate the physical assets (i.e., real estate and FF&E) from the intangible aspects or business value of the golf course, another step must be added to the analytical process.

VALUING THE BUSINESS COMPONENT

If properly applied, the sales comparison approach automatically allows for the intangible assets of the golf facility being appraised. A separate value estimate or adjustment for this factor is made in the cost approach but is often unnecessary in sales comparison. However, separate consideration of the business component is necessary when

- The comparable sales are underperforming golf courses.
- The transactions were made under duress
- The transactions involved sales of property subject to an operating lease.

FIGURE 10.4

Golf Course Sales Analysis				
	Subject	**Sale 1**	**Sale 2**	**Sale 3**
Physical Characteristics				
No. of holes	18	18	18	18
Clubhouse	5,500 sq. ft.	4,200 sq. ft.	8,100 sq. ft.	5,800 sq. ft.
Practice greens	Yes	Yes	Yes	No
Driving range	Yes	Yes	Yes	No
Car storage	Good	Average	Excellent	Good
Course rating*	35 (good)	32 (average)	39 (good)	27 (average)
Food & beverage	Average	Average	Excellent	Good
Condition	Average	Average	Good	Good
Other amenities†	L,R,B,T	L,R	L,R,B,S	B,T,S
Financial Data				
Price	TBD	$4,500,000	$6,900,000	$3,400,000
Date	10/02	11/01	8/02	11/98
Rounds	41,000	44,000	52,000	29,000
Total revenue	$2,350,000	$2,227,700	$2,782,300	$1,405,000
Golf revenue	$1,711,000	$1,630,400	$2,269,700	$780,000
Average greens fee	$37.57	$27.65	$38.80	$23.90
Value Indicators				
Total revenue multiplier (*TRM*)	2.31 (est.)	2.02	2.48	2.42
Golf revenue multiplier (*GRM*)	3.39 (est.)	2.76	3.04	4.36
Price per round (*PPR*)	$130.00 (est.)	$102.27	$132.69	$117.24
Greens fee and rounds multiplier (*GFM*)	3.97 (est.)	3.70	3.42	4.91

* From golf course rating data (See Chapter One)

† L = lockers, R = rain shelters, B = bag storage, T = tennis courts, S = swimming pool

Note: Value indicators (multipliers) for the subject property were estimated and used to derive a range of value estimates.

By total revenue multiplier (*TRM*): 2.31 × $2,350,000 = $5,428,500

By golf revenue multiplier (*GRM*): 3.39 × $1,711,000 = $5,800,290

By price per round (*PPR*): $130 × 41,000 = $5,330,000

By greens fee and rounds multiplier (*GFM*): 3.70 × $37.57 × 41,000 = $5,699,369

Conclusion: A value range of $5,300,000 to $5,800,000 is indicated.

A separate analysis of the business component is indicated if such factors are revealed in the investigative process. Needless to say, the analyst must understand the typical aspects of a real estate transaction and the unique considerations involved in the sale of a business. It is generally beyond the scope of a golf course appraisal assignment to appraise a comparable golf course business operation, except in extraordinary circumstances. It is proper for the appraiser to allocate a sale price for buyers, sellers, and their representatives as long as a realistic value is placed on the components of the total assets involved in the transaction.

If the appraiser only applies the sales comparison and income capitalization approaches to value and the assignment requires segregation of various value components, a distinct and separate analysis must be conducted to appraise the business.

This work can be accomplished as another aspect of the sales comparison approach or by application of other techniques.

Golf course business opportunities exist when facilities are leased, typically by municipalities, to operators. Sales of leaseholds usually involve the personal property or FF&E and the intangible assets or business enterprise, but they may also include an interest in the improvements made to the golf course or clubhouse by the lessee.

The following example illustrates the financial aspects of a leasehold transaction and important analytical data that can be useful to the appraiser. Consider a local municipal course subject to a 25-year lease. It was leased five years ago by an experienced golf pro who improved the greens and fairways, renovated the clubhouse, added new cars, and vastly upgraded the image of the facility. The rent schedule has a guaranteed step-up clause and includes a percentage formula that allows the lessee to recapture his investment in the improvements and the lessor to share in the success of the operation.

The golf course produces a net income of $725,000 after management compensation, but before rent payments of $350,000; the golf pro just sold his leasehold for $1,700,000. Investigation of this sale reveals that the price was allocated as follows: $620,000 to the FF&E and $1,080,000 to intangibles such as the license to operate, favorable contracts, business systems in place, a short-term management contract, favorable terms of the lease, reputation, and the golfer list.

A nearby golf course with similar characteristics, but no lease, was sold for $6,500,000. Assuming that this figure represents the approximate total value of either course unencumbered, the two transactions indicate an allocation of $4,800,000 for the land and golf course improvements, $620,000 for FF&E, and $1,080,000 for the intangibles of the enterprise, which are sometimes inaccurately referred to as *goodwill*. The capitalization rates indicated are 11.15% for the overall property ($725,000/$6,500,000), 22.0% for the business ($375,000/$1,700,000), and 7.3% for the real property ($350,000/$4,800,000).

With this type of information and other statistics from the operating statement of the comparable golf course, comparative techniques can be used to appraise the business component of a going concern separately. When a course is successful, the intangible component of the total enterprise can be quite significant. In the example described, the intangibles amounted to about one-sixth of the value of the golf course. Unlike sales of retail or service businesses, transactions involving the sale of golf course leaseholds as business opportunities are quite rare.

Specialists in the field should keep a careful record of these sales when they do occur.

MIXED USES

A golf course or country club appraisal assignment can sometimes involve a combination of other land uses held in one ownership or security interest. For example, a resort or recreational golf facility may be combined with a surrounding single-family home or condominium development in a master project. See Chapter Eleven for more information on analyzing golf course community projects.

When the sales comparison approach is applied, other land uses can be separately valued with comparative techniques using appropriate multipliers and unit value indicators. The sum of the parts can produce an indication of the total project value if the analyst carefully considers the risk, appropriate returns, and yield requirements associated with mixed-use projects. Appraisers involved in such assignments should be familiar with the techniques employed in the valuation of lodging, racquet sport, health and fitness, restaurant, and retail facilities.

CHAPTER ELEVEN

ANALYZING GOLF COURSE COMMUNITY PROJECTS

More than 50% of all golf courses developed in recent years have been integral parts of resort-oriented real estate projects or residential communities. The primary reasons to develop a golf course as part of a project are

- To increase the value and rate of absorption of the surrounding real estate, typically in an upscale residential subdivision
- To enhance the economic performance of a hotel, typically in a resort setting
- To create a unique environment that will enhance the status and financial success of a master-planned project.

Real property is enhanced not only by having frontage on a golf course, but also by being situated near a golf course in a planned community.

Today about 12% of all golf courses are in master-planned communities and 46% of golf course construction is related to projects that include another real estate component. Many new courses are being built in retirement-oriented destination locations.

In the past developers used golf courses as marketing tools and gave little consideration to their long-term management and fiscal requirements. These golf courses with country club facilities were commonly known as *developer's clubs*. This term connoted a combination of unique problems pertaining to membership relations and the tendency to attract litigation. With the increased popularity of golf and recognition of the financial viability of golf projects, golf course investments are not treated so casually today. Now considerable attention is focused on the key issues of course design, membership structure, enhancement of frontage, achieving a premium through the amenity of a golf course, and the maximization of profits.

For golf course consultants, the issues to be considered depend on the timing of the development cycle and the purpose of the assignment. The planning stage of a golf community is the ideal time to consider specialized land use design issues as well as the type of equity infrastructure that will maximize the overall goals of the project and avoid unnecessary problems with the membership or the subdivision of adjacent land.

TYPES OF GOLF COURSE COMMUNITIES

Golf course communities, or GCCs, are typically differentiated by the operational category of the course, its size, and its layout. Three common types of communities are

- Residential subdivisions built around an existing golf course
- Residential developments around a new municipal golf course
- Well-designed courses developed within a master-planned community

Golf course premiums can vary greatly depending on the design or layout of the lots and the reputation of the golf course. A study of 27 master-planned golf communities published in *Sports Place* in 1992 showed premiums for lot values (as compared to base lot values outside the community) ranging from a low factor of 1.4 to a high factor of 5.3 (see Table 11.1).

GOLF COURSE DESIGN

Table 11.2 sets forth summary statistics provided by a merchant builder who has developed golf course communities throughout the United States. Each community has a signature course designed by a renowned, retired professional golfer. The clubs are operated on an equity, private, or daily fee basis, depending on the location, characteristics of the competitive market, and types of home buyers. Private clubs usually operate in exclusive or retirement locations, while daily fee clubs are part of family-oriented, commuter developments.

All the courses are regulation size except one, which is an 18-hole executive layout. Course length ranges from 4,461 (the executive course) to 7,213 yards, averaging 6,935 yards (without the executive course).

TABLE 11.1

Differentials in Lot Prices by Location

Class of Community	Golf Frontage Lot	Interior Lot
High-end	4.1	2.6
Medium	5.3	2.7
Low	2.4	1.4
Average	4.1	2.4

Source: *Sports Place*, Spring 1992

TABLE 11.2

Characteristics of Golf Courses and Facilities Developed in a Residential Community		
Golf Course Characteristics	**Size Range**	**Average Size**
Number of holes	18	18
Course length	4,461–7,213 yards	6,935 yards
Tee areas	108,000–275,000 sq. ft.	180,000 sq. ft.
Average tee size	6,255–9,000 sq. ft.	6,855 sq. ft.
Green areas	100,125–155,790 sq. ft.	137,185 sq. ft.
Average green size	5,560–8,483 sq. ft.	7,020 sq. ft.
Bunker areas	40,100–156,000 sq. ft.	114,715 sq. ft.
Fairway areas	28–49 acres	39.2 acres
Rough areas	12–112 acres	59.2 acres
Areas of sod	10–30 acres	21.1 acres
No. of sprinklers	750–1,603 heads	1,151 heads
Car path length	17,740–33,000 feet	27,655 feet
Facilities		
Clubhouse	10,000–42,000 sq. ft.	27,985 sq. ft.
Car barn	3,100–8,400 sq. ft.	5,345 sq. ft.
Cabana	900–2,000 sq. ft.	1,375 sq. ft.
Recreation center	3,500–7,536 sq. ft.	5,695 sq. ft.
Maintenance building	5,675–8,400 sq. ft.	7,010 sq. ft.
No. of shelters	1–3	2
No. of tennis courts	1–9	4.4

There is a wide range in the size of tee areas due to the variable number of tees as well as the distance between tees. The average total tee area is 180,000 square feet. The average tee size is less variable, with a mean of 6,855 square feet (equivalent to overall dimensions of 83 feet by 83 feet).

The size of the greens average 7,020 square feet and the average amount of green area per course is 137,185 square feet. The number of bunkers is not available, but the average total size is 114,715 square feet. If the average bunker is 1,000 square feet, this indicates approximately 115 bunkers per course or an average of 6.4 per hole.

The total area of the fairways averages 39.2 acres; rough areas average 59.2 acres; and the area of sod averages 21.1 acres. When the tee, green, and bunker areas are added to the fairway, rough, and sod areas, the total land area of the typical golf course is approximately 129.5 acres, excluding the land area around the clubhouse, car barn, cabana, recreation center, and maintenance buildings.

The typical number of sprinklers is 1,151 sprinkler heads or 63.9 per fairway/green/tee; the car path length averages 27,655 feet, which is slightly more than 5.2 miles. Where car paths are continuous, the length will be greater than the course length, which is measured on a straight-line basis.

Statistics for golf course amenities and other facilities show averages of 27,985 square feet for the clubhouse, 5,345 square feet for the car barn, 1,375 square feet for the cabana, and 7,010 square feet for the maintenance buildings. Recreation centers are developed on only 50% of the courses and the typical size is 6,595 square feet.. There are usually two shelters on a golf course and the mean number of tennis courts is 4.4.

GOLF COURSE DESIGN OPTIONS

Considerable research has been done on the optimum size and layout of courses to maximize the value of adjacent real estate. In the past "sausage-link" courses–i.e., a single fairway with returning nines or a single fairway continuous–were emphasized because this design provides greater frontage for residential lots or other land use development along the course. Studies have shown that a sausage link course can theoretically achieve a 275% value premium over a comparable parallel-fairway course.

Today developers favor a modified "core" course, which provides for a better golfing experience as well as large consolidated blocks of open space, a significant amount of frontage for residential lots and other land development, and a superior marketing concept. Many professionals in the golf industry believe that courses with narrow fairways flanked with houses are currently out of favor.

The actual acreage required for a GCC varies greatly. A regulation golf course, by itself, will generally require between 150 and 200 acres; smaller executive courses may require less than 100 acres. The data set forth in Table 11.2 indicates 129.5 acres are needed for the course by itself. Adding another 20 acres for the clubhouse and other facilities results in an efficient minimum requirement of 150 acres for the golf course. When residential development is combined with a golf course, the minimum project size is 400 acres (half golf and half residential), but many consider such a project to be only marginally feasible. Larger projects of 800 to 1,500 acres or more allow the developer to spread the cost of the golf course over a larger number of potential residential units and other land uses and permit greater flexibility in project phasing.

Land planning and design are beyond the scope of this book and many other texts can provide detailed design and planning guidelines. Analysts do need to understand the difference between good and bad planning, however, and be familiar with lot dimensions, acceptable development densities, neighborhood configurations, phasing of developments (including infrastructure), and acceptable ratios for the combination of golf, housing, parks, community amenities, and resort components within a well-integrated GCC. For current information, readers are advised to consult *Golf Course Development and Residential Communities* published by the Urban Land Institute.

LOT PLANNING AND PREMIUMS

In the past many believed that the residential site premiums derived from a GCC could offset the cost of the land required for the course or even subsidize the entire golf course development. However, there are so many variables involved in these projects that a generalization such as this should not be given serious consideration. The size of the GCC is important, and small projects are at a disadvantage. Large projects have problems too and may incur compounded holding costs if they have extensive absorption periods. One key to success is a project's ability to support increasing lot values throughout the initial marketing program. Offering a wide range of amenities at the country club can broaden the potential market for lots by appealing to a wide range of demographic groups, but providing more amenities requires a greater initial investment.

As Table 11.1 shows, lot premiums are highly variable and depend on the attractiveness of the course design and layout. The golf experience or playability of the course should not be shortchanged to maximize the profits from land development. The golf course should be considered a profit center, not a loss leader that cannot pay for its own maintenance and capital improvements.

Through careful design, architects and land planners can extend golf course premiums to nonfrontage lots. View premiums can be emphasized if the elevations of the fairways and the adjacent residential land are different.

One advantageous land planning technique developed by David Jensen Associates is shown in Figure 11.1. Golf course premiums are created for nonfrontage lots through open space "windows," which allow residents to see the golf course. Higher lot prices are produced by increasing the number of focal points or visual "hot spots" on the course. In this example, local interior roads and cul-de-sacs pass through these windows and into the interior lots, giving many of the homes on the cul-de-sac views of the golf course. Lots situated across the road are considered to have secondary frontage on the course.

Lots with golf views do not command prices equal to those obtained for lots with frontage on the course, and all course frontage is not uniform in value. The most desirable lots overlook the greens, tees, lakes, bunkers, and first-shot landing areas. A water view is considered to have the highest value. Creative planning is cost-effective if it is based on sound design principles.

FIGURE 11.1

Traditional Lot Pattern

In the typical layout of golf course communities, interior lots can be walled off from the course.

Windows

Creating windows with views of the course and developing roads through them gives residents the feel of truly living in a golf community.

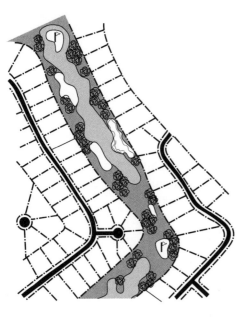

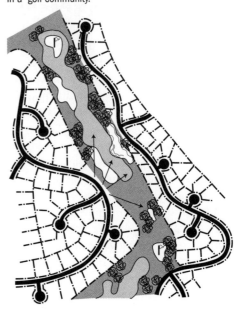

Create Hot Spots

Greens, tees, lakes, traps, and first-shot landing areas are the typical hot spots of a golf course. More prime lots can be created by placing additional attractive views—of ponds, streams, dramatic sand traps, and wooded areas—in dead fairway areas.

Hot Spot Orientation

Good lot configuration and home siting can maximize golf course views and thereby yield higher prices for lots. Tees, like the ones at the top and bottom, can be improved in appearance with sculpturing and flower beds.

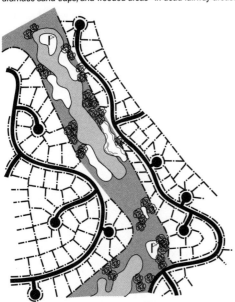

Source: David Jensen Associates

The quality of the course design will have a major impact on the project's financial feasibility. According to David Jensen, windows and focal points that maximize the exposure of lots to the golf course can improve project performance by 25% to 35%.

MEMBERSHIP ARRANGEMENTS

The types of membership established and the rights to which members are entitled are just as important as the design and layout of the GCC. There are no clearly recognized principles for evaluating membership structures. A structure that is successful in one location may be unacceptable in another. Some analysts believe that the popular trend is moving away from private clubs and toward partial daily fee or semi-private arrangements because of the large underserved demand for golf participation and the substantial greens fees that can be charged. Others believe that a social stigma is attached to public daily fee courses and this is a major reason so many real estate developers decide to establish private clubs.

Control of the investment is important. A developer will want to maintain ownership of the golf course if it produces a healthy cash flow. As a stand-alone investment, a golf project can add equity to a balance sheet and prestige to the owner. On the other hand, course costs can be so high that earnings before interest barely support debt service. In this case, the developer may willingly pass title to a home owners' association after absorbing losses for an extended period of time.

The intricacies of membership arrangements will not be covered here. The main point for the analyst to understand is that the structure established should maximize the marketing of the GCC and not burden the golf course with an inadequate revenue stream.

Flexibility is desirable in membership arrangements. Initially a golf club or resort project may allow daily fee players to use the course to capitalize on the club's income-producing potential. Later it may choose to limit play to private members and guests. Some clubs provide for nonowning members, while others require that members be property owners. A prudent developer will retain the right to buy membership rights back from nonresident members. Many GCCs help residents to realize the full resale potential of their residences by automatically providing a membership opportunity in the country club to new buyers, even if the seller is not a member.

As few as 20% of GCC residents may play golf, but a much larger portion, say 40% to 80%, will want to be members of the country club. Therefore, a club must offer a variety of membership categories, such as full privilege membership, all sports except golf membership, and social membership, which usually means access to the swimming pool and clubhouse. Using market research and competitive pricing, a developer may be able to charge monthly or annual dues and greens fees in addition to an initiation fee. Obviously, specific fee amounts depend on the demographics of the target market area, traditional fee arrangements, and the competitiveness of GCCs in the market.

RESORTS AND BUSINESS PARK FACILITIES

Many signature golf projects are resort-oriented and play is limited to hotel guests and golf club members. Memberships are available to residents of the GCC and to nonresidents, who are occasional users of the course. The outdated practice of paying huge prices for certain trophy courses, which was described in Chapter Ten, rests on the dubious assumption that very expensive private club memberships can be sold to nonresident aliens who love the game and want the prestige of membership in an exclusive facility.

Clearly the developers of expensive golf courses in resort settings expect to increase the occupancy rate of the lodging facilities and capture more customers than competitive facilities that do not possess the golf amenity. In the late 1980s, many of these resorts, especially those in Hawaii, were sold at extremely low capitalization rates based on the assumption that future values or yields would grow higher, Asian travel would continue to increase, and that a limit would be placed on permits for new projects. This premise was proven to be false.

The economic feasibility of a golf project at a resort or business park can be quantified by comparing the net present values of the additional net revenues attributable to the course to the additional net costs of adding the golf amenity. In addition to the usual golf-related revenue sources, resorts will have higher revenues from the rooms and food and beverage departments and from pro shop sales. (Sales of logo products have especially attractive sales margins.) Business parks expect to capitalize on the golf amenity by achieving higher property values and floor area ratios, increased absorption rates, and, in some areas, lower impact fees and infrastructure costs.

RISK REDUCTION

From a planner's perspective, GCCs have many advantages, including the preservation of wetlands and open space, the enhancement of the community's image, the promotion of additional property tax and other taxes for the community, and the orderly development of large tracts of land in a systematic and attractive manner.

On the other hand, the development process for a GCC can be extremely long and expensive, resulting in excessive costs and marginal profitability. Community opposition centered on a number of issues can lead to litigation and delays. Community planners may be concerned about infrastructure extensions, traffic problems, water supply and quality, pesticides, and the use of gates and brick walls to create a sense of privacy. When a course is invisible to everyone except adjacent home owners, the open space argument has little impact.

From a developer's perspective, including a golf course provides a project with a pricing and sales advantage. It enlarges the potential market for a variety of residential unit types, ranging from luxury residences to townhouses and condominium apartments. Because of these advantages, a large number of projects were started in the latter half of the 1980s. A small number of these GCCs have failed and gone into foreclosure due to development errors such as inadequate market feasibility analysis and poor golf course design. Some GCCs have been involved in lawsuits, with the home owners' association bringing a class action suit against the developers. However, it is possible to avoid some of these pitfalls, even in a highly competitive atmosphere.

GCCs have unique design problems due to the close relationship between the golf course and adjacent housing. Golf balls can be considered small missiles, traveling at speeds of up to 250 miles per hour, or 365 feet per second. With this speed and long drives of up to 250 yards, the potential for property damage is readily apparent. Trespassing is another problem because golfers may enter the yards and grounds of adjacent houses searching for errant balls. While the courts have ruled that residents of GCCs may have to suffer some damage, annoyance, and inconvenience in exchange for the enjoyment of living near a country club, there are ways to minimize conflicts.

The owner of the golf course should retain the right to alter the landscaping that borders the course to prevent golf balls from striking homes or persons on the fairway. This right should be expressly preserved without regard for how such changes will impact the views from neighboring homes or lots.

Landscape architect William R. Firth suggests design guidelines featuring uphill housing, natural buffers, slanted view corridors, variable setbacks, and proper bunker placement and hole orientation.[1] Some of his recommendations are summarized below.

- Uphill housing is generally preferred because buildings are less likely to be struck by a ball. Moreover, views down into a

1. William R. Firth, "Can Golf and Housing Get Along?" *Urban Land* (February 1990), 16-19.

golf course are generally better than views looking up, and valley soils are better for fairways.

- Trees and tall shrubs provide a natural defense against errant golf balls. Dense evergreens provide the best year-round screen. Unfortunately, the more effective the screen of vegetation is, the less visible the golf course will be to the residents who paid a premium to see it. A buffer planting program should be an integral part of golf course construction.

- Careful orientation of houses helps to solve the problem of views versus protection. If a house looks toward the green rather than straight onto the fairway, trees should be cleared along an angled corridor facing away from the path of the golf ball (see Figure 11.1).

- Conditions along fairways vary immensely, and each fairway has edge characteristics that should be considered in determining setbacks. Recognized minimum setbacks are about 70 yards from the center of the fairway to the facades of buildings, about 35 yards around tees, and about 65 yards around greens. A deep setback will be needed at a fairway edge where the drive is downhill, winds are strong, or little buffering foliage exists. A shallower setback is needed along fairways framed by dense forest.

- Many golfers try to avoid bunkers and drive far to their left or right and off the fairway. Bunker placement must be planned along with setbacks and buffering.

- Golf course architects generally agree that a north-south alignment of fairways is preferable to an east-west alignment, which requires early golfers to play into the morning sun and afternoon golfers to play into the setting sun. The sun's glare can affect golfers' accuracy.

Safety is a critical concern in the layout of a course within a GCC, but the course architect must also be committed to golf values and playability. With the implementation of effective design principles, a golf course can be both highly rated and a good neighbor. Often the real estate component of the GCC is the cause of the failure of the overall development. Developers must find the right balance between the demand segment of golf pricing and the housing product that will maximize market penetration. Jeffrey Maza has concluded:

Like any niche product, GCCs involve elements of risk. The housing market is very sensitive to the general economy and quick to register a turn for the worse. Upper-end housing like that found in a golf course development is especially dependent on the trade-up market—one of the first segments to go soft in a housing slump. Should this occur, any oversupply of GCC product could take years to work off.

GCC VALUATION EXAMPLE

Figure 11.2 shows a financial comparison of plans to develop 500 acres of land with 1) no golf course, 2) a semi-private daily fee course, and 3) a private equity club. Assuming there is good market potential for golf, the population's income and other demographics are positive, and approvals can be secured, the two GCCs support higher residual land values than the subdivision project with no golf amenity.

Some key assumptions applicable to this analysis are stated below.

- On average, a daily fee course will enhance unit lot values by about 25%, while a private course will increase lot values by 37%.
- Fairway frontage lots will have a 25% to 30% premium over secondary golf view lots, a 36% to 48% premium over interior lots in the GCC, and a 50% to 70% premium over interior lots in the subdivision without golf.
- The GCCs will sell out at a faster rate than the project without a golf course.

Figure 11.2 is included only to illustrate a methodology for comparing various development scenarios. The analyst should investigate the wide variety of factors affecting golf courses that have been described in this text. A more sophisticated analytical model would be employed to prepare a comparative financial analysis and evaluate development alternatives on a net-present-value basis.

FIGURE 11.2

	No Golf	Semi-Private Daily Fee Golf	Private Equity Club
Residual Land Value Under Alternative Development Plans			
Development Parameters			
Land area (in acres)	500	500	500
Residential	340	250	250
Golf course	–	150	150
Roads/easements/open space	160	100	100
Lots (@ 3.5 lots/acre)	1,200	875	875
Interior	1,200	375	375
Golf view	–	200	200
Fairway frontage	–	300	300
Average improved lot value			
Interior	$50,000	$55,000	$57,500
Golf view	–	$60,000	$65,000
Fairway frontage	–	$75,000	$85,000
Average per-unit site improvement cost	$25,000	$28,000	$28,000
Average annual unit absorption	200	219	219
Interior	200	94	94
Golf view	–	50	50
Fairway frontage	–	75	75
Golf Parameters			
Memberships			
Golf (@ $30,000)	–	–	400
Social (@ $2,500)	–	–	250
Average memberships sold per year			
Golf	–	–	100
Social	–	–	50
Net operating income			
Year 1	–	$200,000	$400,000*
Year 2	–	$500,000	$200,000*
Year 3+	–	$750,000	–
Golf development cost (excluding land)	–	$6,000,000	$10,500,000
Course	–	$3,000,000	$4,000,000
Clubhouse	–	$800,000	$3,500,000
Other costs	–	$2,200,000	$3,000,000
Years to sell out	6.0	4.0	4.0
Cash Flow Projections (1990 dollars)			
Site sales	$60,000,000	$55,100,000	$60,100,000
Less: site improvement costs	$30,000,000	$24,500,000	$24,500,000
Less: other site development costs	$9,000,000	$6,000,000	$7,100,000
Net site sales	$21,000,000	$24,600,000	$28,500,000
Daily fee asset value/membership sales[†]	–	$6,700,000	$11,400,000
Total cash flow	$21,000,000	$31,300,000	$39,900,000
Net present value[‡] (1991 dollars)			
Net site sales	$13,600,000	$17,800,000	$20,800,000
Net daily fee asset value/net membership sales	–	$5,800,000	$9,100,000
Total net present value	$13,600,000	$23,600,000	$29,900,000
Less: golf development costs	–	$6,000,000	$10,500,000
Residual land value	$13,600,000	$17,600,000	$19,400,000
Per acre	$27,200	$35,200	$38,800
Per unit	$11,300	$20,100	$22,200

* These values represent operating losses, or required developer subsidies, during the membership sales period.

† Represents stable year net income of $700,000 capitalized at 10.4%. Represents gross membership sales (golf and social) less an allowance for marketing, general, and administrative expenses.

‡ Net present value calculated by discounting projected constant dollar annual cash flow stream at a 14% discount rate.

Source: The authors adapted this residual land value calculation for alternative development programs from data presented in an article prepared by J. Richard McElyea, Austin G. Anderson, and Gene P. Kreporian, "Golf's Real Estate Value" *Urban Land* (February 1991).

CHAPTER TWELVE

CONCLUSIONS AND TRENDS

The need for substantially more golf courses in the next decade is unclear. The supply of new golf courses is outpacing the development of new golfers and increases in participation. Meanwhile, development continues.

About 600 new courses are currently under construction and another 900 or so are in the planning stage. These figures include the expansion of existing facilities. The problem of overdevelopment is not going away. Excess capacity can adversely affect both new and existing projects with an established market through price competition and the dilution of the average number of rounds per facility.

Environmental concerns have had little effect on the development of golf courses throughout the United States. Opposition groups have attempted to rally around issues relating to the alleged ecological damage caused by turf chemicals, drainage, and underwater water levels and quality, but most of these actions have been ineffective. The groups opposed to golf course development have rejected the greenbelt argument and have tended to ignore many of golf's positive contributions to the economy and to the recreational needs of the populace.

To mitigate future water problems, recycling and irrigation with treated waste water will receive greater emphasis. In addition, new design concepts such as "dry lakes" planted with desert flowers or other vegetation will continue to be implemented. Modified or partial link courses have been able to satisfy the concerns of some critics, but opposition to proposed projects based on a variety of real and imagined ecological concerns can be expected to continue.

All of this is not bad news for golf enthusiasts. With more projects available for play and the decline in the hospitality industry, there are more tee times available at lower prices than ever before. Golf management companies are using online reservations and other marketing techniques recently developed by hotels and resorts to fill tee times that would otherwise be lost. Because there is a finite number of golf participants, some facilities will probably gain while others will lose players.

Prices for golf courses have declined in the last three years. Almost one-half of the transactions identified in Table 10.1 involved financial problems, an auction sale, bankruptcy, foreclosure, or other nonperformance issues due to the sluggish economy and the after-effects of September 11, 2001.

One aspect of golf that gets little publicity is its positive impact on local and regional economies. Direct spending by golfers for equipment and playing fees totaled approximately $23 billion in 2001. Indirect spending for golf-related travel and lodging contributed another $26 billion to the GNP, or "golf national product." There are many other categories of spending and investment by golfers and non-golfers such as second homes at golf-related projects and spending on advertising, promotions, tournaments, and other media services. Considering these factors and the business generated by course operations and construction, golf is the most important participant and nonparticipant sport in the country.

Valuation problems will become more complicated for golf course appraisers and analysts and feasibility studies will include consideration of an increasing number of complex variables. Forecasting rounds and greens fees will be more uncertain and projections will need to extend beyond a few years. Increasing expenses and lower rates of revenue growth may mean stable or declining future cash flow. On the positive side, the decline in inflation and low interest rates could balance some of these negative factors.

All of these future industry developments will increase the importance of market feasibility analysis. Future projects cannot be expected to succeed based on past standards of project acceptance, rates of growth, and inflationary expectations. Precise revenue estimates on a department-by-department basis must be prepared and supported by in-depth market research and direct contact with market participants, the managers of competitive facilities, and recognized experts. Attracting capital for financing is becoming increasingly difficult, except for well-established projects; lenders are going to be cautious.

Golf will generate a lot of excitement in the coming decade and there will be abundant opportunities for professional managers. New equipment and products will be introduced and television will continue to exert its inevitable influence on golfers and non-golfers, for better or worse. Well-planned and well-supported projects in niche markets will be successful, while marginal projects will struggle and probably not survive. Tight financial controls will become more and more necessary. New players will be attracted to the game by innovative teaching programs and specialized marketing promotions, and the seniors market will continue to grow in importance as demographic changes increase the number of older players.

There is a growing demand for trained, knowledgeable appraisers and feasibility specialists in the golf course industry; however, the past decade has seen a large increase in this pool of specialists. Appraisal and trade organizations need to continue to promote educational programs and fund additional research to provide more accurate statistics on financial performance, golf facility sales, rates of participation, and terms of rental agreements. We hope that this text has succeeded in providing more information and generating more interest in this important real estate specialty.

APPENDIX

NATIONAL GOLF FOUNDATION PUBLICATIONS

- *Successful Management Practices*
- *An Environmental Approach to Golf Course Development*
- *Golf and the Environment*
- *Improving Golf Car Operations*
- *Golf Business Almanac*
- *Golf Consumer Spending in the U.S.*
- *Golf Participation in the U.S.*
- *Golfer Segmentation and Marketing Implications*
- *Spending Report*
- *U.S. Golf Travel Market*
- *Golf Course Development in Residential Communities*
- *Buying or Leasing a Golf Course*
- *Clubhouse Design & Renovation*
- *Developing Golf Courses on Landfills, Strip-Mines and Other Unusual Locations*
- *Economic Impact and Benefits of Golf Course Development*
- *Golf Course Architecture*
- *Golf Course Design*
- *Golf Course Design and Construction*
- *Golf Course Financing/Refinancing*
- *Guide to Estimating Golf Course Construction*

- *Guidelines for Financing a Golf Course*
- *Guidelines for Planning and Developing a Public Golf Course*
- *Renovating Your Golf Course*
- *Accommodating Disabled Golfers*
- *Accounting Considerations for Public, Resort and Other Daily Fee Golf Courses*
- *Advertising and Promoting Your Golf Facility*
- *Computerizing Your Golf Facility*
- *Conducting Market Research*
- *Golf Course Management and Operations Contracts*
- *Golf Course Operations Policy Manual*
- *Golf Manager's Handbook*
- *Operating and Financial Performance Profiles of Golf Facilities in the U.S.*
- *Risk Management for Golf*
- *2002 Directory of Golf*
- *The Club Tax Book*
- *Contemporary Club Management*
- *Executive and Par-3 Golf Courses*
- *Golf Facility Employee Compensation Study*
- *Golf Practice Facilities in the U.S.*
- *Golf Ranges*
- *Hot Spots For Golf Course Construction Activity in the U.S.A.*
- *Improving Golf Car Fleet Operations*
- *Increasing Your Pro Shop's Bottom Line*
- *Junior Golf*
- *Miniature and Putting Courses NGF's Executive & Par-3 Directory*
- *The Power of the Junior Golf Market*
- *Private Clubs*
- *The Professional Golf Shop*
- *A Strategic Perspective on the Future of Golf*
- *Trends in the Golf Industry*
- *U.S. Golf Travel Market*
- *Pitch and Putt Courses*
- *U.S. 18-Hole Golf Facility Compensation Study*

STATE/REGIONAL MUNICIPAL COURSE AND HOLE SUPPLY—2000

State and Region	Regulation Courses	Regulation Holes	Executive Courses	Executive Holes	Par-3 Courses	Par-3 Holes	Total Courses	Total Holes
Connecticut	30	495	4	45	3	27	37	567
Maine	7	90	1	9	1	9	9	108
Massachusetts	50	738	1	9	1	9	52	756
New Hampshire	3	54	0	0	0	0	3	54
Rhode Island	5	63	0	0	0	0	5	63
Vermont	2	36	0	0	0	0	2	36
New England	**97**	**1,476**	**6**	**63**	**5**	**45**	**108**	**1,584**
New Jersey	44	756	6	99	5	45	55	900
New York	112	1,782	12	135	10	126	134	2,043
Pennsylvania	40	648	4	54	2	18	46	720
Middle Atlantic	**196**	**3,186**	**22**	**288**	**17**	**189**	**235**	**3,663**
Illinois	164	2,601	13	144	14	135	191	2,880
Indiana	59	936	7	81	7	90	73	1,107
Michigan	87	1,296	5	63	4	54	96	1,413
Ohio	92	1,521	9	99	7	81	108	1,701,
Wisconsin	58	900	5	45	10	117	73	1,062
East North Central	**460**	**7,254**	**39**	**432**	**42**	**477**	**541**	**8,163**
Iowa	53	774	2	27	4	36	59	837
Kansas	57	765	2	18	2	18	61	801
Minnesota	82	1,206	14	135	8	81	104	1,422
Missouri	53	792	1	9	2	18	56	819
Nebraska	44	567	2	18	3	27	49	612
North Dakota	43	477	3	27	1	9	47	513
South Dakota	29	360	4	36	1	9	34	405
West North Central	**361**	**4,941**	**28**	**270**	**21**	**198**	**410**	**5,409**
Delaware	2	36	0	0	0	0	2	36
District of Columbia	2	36	1	9	1	9	4	54
Florida	89	1,503	13	171	10	126	112	1,800
Georgia	51	792	2	27	0	0	53	819
Maryland	35	576	5	45	0	0	40	621
North Carolina	33	531	2	27	3	36	38	594
South Carolina	10	162	0	0	1	9	11	171
Virginia	34	585	4	36	3	36	41	657
West Virginia	13	189	0	0	6	90	19	279
South Atlantic	**269**	**4,410**	**27**	**315**	**24**	**306**	**320**	**5,031**
Alabama	34	531	1	18	1	9	36	558
Kentucky	42	639	3	36	7	72	52	747
Mississippi	17	261	0	0	1	9	18	270
Tennessee	55	891	1	9	0	0	56	900
East South Central	**148**	**2,322**	**5**	**63**	**9**	**90**	**162**	**2,475**
Arkansas	16	216	0	0	0	0	16	216
Louisiana	28	414	0	0	0	0	28	414
Oklahoma	66	1,008	2	18	2	27	70	1,053
Texas	184	2,763	2	18	5	54	191	2,835
West South Central	**294**	**4,401**	**4**	**36**	**7**	**81**	**305**	**4,518**
Arizona	36	594	4	54	3	45	43	693
Colorado	80	1,233	4	45	9	81	93	1,359
Idaho	30	432	1	9	0	0	31	441
Montana	21	252	0	0	2	27	23	279
Nevada	20	324	1	18	2	18	23	360
New Mexico	24	342	2	18	4	36	30	396
Utah	53	837	1	9	3	27	57	873
Wyoming	20	279	1	9	0	0	21	288
Mountain	**284**	**4,293**	**14**	**162**	**23**	**234**	**321**	**4,689**
Alaska	2	36	1	9	0	0	3	45
California	155	2,574	26	288	26	279	207	3,141
Hawaii	8	135	0	0	0	0	8	135
Oregon	17	234	1	18	1	18	19	270
Washington	47	756	6	72	6	54	59	882
Pacific	**229**	**3,735**	**34**	**387**	**33**	**351**	**296**	**4,473**
U. S. Totals	**2,338**	**36,018**	**179**	**2,016**	**181**	**1,971**	**2,698**	**40,005**

Source: *Golf Facilities in the U.S.*, 2001 edition

171

APPENDIX

STATE/REGIONAL DAILY FEE COURSE AND HOLE SUPPLY—2000

State and Region	Regulation Courses	Regulation Holes	Executive Courses	Executive Holes	Par-3 Courses	Par-3 Holes	Total Courses	Total Holes
Connecticut	55	810	5	63	7	90	67	963
Maine	103	1,332	3	36	4	36	110	1,404
Massachusetts	163	2,322	8	108	25	351	196	2,781
New Hampshire	77	1,107	5	54	10	90	92	1,251
Rhode Island	24	333	1	9	2	27	27	369
Vermont	50	765	3	27	3	36	56	828
New England	**472**	**6,669**	**25**	**297**	**51**	**630**	**548**	**7,596**
New Jersey	96	1,557	5	63	7	81	108	1,701
New York	422	6,165	48	585	34	342	504	7,092
Pennsylvania	410	6,390	30	342	31	351	471	7,083
Middle Atlantic	**928**	**14,112**	**83**	**990**	**72**	**774**	**1,083**	**15,876**
Illinois	293	4,383	29	315	19	198	341	4,896
Indiana	271	4,257	21	243	21	270	313	4,770
Michigan	651	10,296	33	387	37	387	721	11,070
Ohio	452	7,083	29	378	33	351	514	7,812
Wisconsin	342	4,968	25	279	23	207	390	5,454
East North Central	**2,009**	**30,987**	**137**	**1,602**	**133**	**1,413**	**2,279**	**34,002**
Iowa	247	2,610	10	99	9	81	266	2,790
Kansas	93	1,062	6	72	4	36	103	1,170
Minnesota	280	3,915	44	486	19	189	343	4,590
Missouri	172	2,448	10	108	12	135	194	2,691
Nebraska	109	1,269	8	81	6	54	123	1,404
North Dakota	45	459	5	45	0	0	50	504
South Dakota	56	576	3	36	1	9	60	621
West North Central	**1,002**	**12,339**	**86**	**927**	**51**	**504**	**1,139**	**13,770**
Delaware	11	198	6	72	2	36	19	306
District of Columbia	2	27	1	9	0	0	3	36
Florida	510	8,712	105	1,593	39	423	654	10,728
Georgia	235	3,807	8	99	17	180	260	4,086
Maryland	65	1,125	7	99	7	72	79	1,296
North Carolina	361	6,102	9	108	19	234	389	6,444
South Carolina	269	4,482	6	63	20	252	295	4,797
Virginia	163	2,574	4	45	7	63	174	2,682
West Virginia	72	1,026	2	18	3	27	77	1,071
South Atlantic	**1,688**	**28,053**	**148**	**2,106**	**114**	**1,287**	**1,950**	**31,446**
Alabama	132	2,088	2	27	12	144	146	2,259
Kentucky	131	1,953	4	45	8	81	143	2,079
Mississippi	79	1,233	0	0	3	36	82	1,269
Tennessee	129	1,962	6	72	7	72	142	2,106
East South Central	**471**	**7,236**	**12**	**144**	**30**	**333**	**513**	**7,713**
Arkansas	83	1,107	5	45	7	72	95	1,224
Louisiana	60	882	3	36	4	36	67	954
Oklahoma	88	1,224	6	63	3	36	97	1,323
Texas	360	5,328	14	144	37	360	411	5,832
West South Central	**591**	**8,541**	**28**	**288**	**51**	**504**	**670**	**9,333**
Arizona	154	2,583	38	522	10	108	202	3,213
Colorado	79	1,197	10	126	6	54	95	1,377
Idaho	48	657	4	54	5	45	57	756
Montana	52	639	4	45	6	63	62	747
Nevada	55	927	2	36	3	27	60	990
New Mexico	36	540	1	9	1	9	38	558
Utah	29	423	7	72	2	18	38	513
Wyoming	25	297	2	27	0	0	27	324
Mountain	**478**	**7,263**	**68**	**891**	**33**	**324**	**579**	**8,478**
Alaska	12	162	0	0	4	36	16	198
California	357	5,670	80	1,008	40	450	477	7,128
Hawaii	60	1,008	2	27	2	27	64	1,062
Oregon	113	1,674	23	243	9	108	145	2,025
Washington	141	2,043	20	225	13	126	174	2,394
Pacific	**683**	**10,557**	**125**	**1,503**	**68**	**747**	**876**	**12,807**
U.S. Totals	**8,322**	**125,757**	**712**	**8,748**	**603**	**6,516**	**9,637**	**141,021**

Golf Facilities in the U.S., 2001 edition

ANALYSIS AND VALUATION OF GOLF COURSES AND COUNTRY CLUBS

STATE/REGIONAL PRIVATE COURSE AND HOLE SUPPLY—2000

State and Region	Regulation Only	Regulation All	Executive Only	Executive All	Par-3 Only	Par-3 All	Holes 9	Holes 18	Holes 27	Holes 36	Holes 45+	Total Facilities
Connecticut	75	76	0	1	0	0	17	54	5	0	0	76
Maine	14	14	1	1	1	1	6	10	0	0	0	16
Massachusetts	107	108	2	2	1	2	33	74	4	0	0	111
New Hampshire	13	13	1	1	2	2	6	10	0	0	0	16
Rhode Island	20	20	0	0	0	0	3	17	0	0	0	20
Vermont	7	7	0	0	0	0	1	5	0	1	0	7
New England	**236**	**238**	**4**	**5**	**4**	**5**	**66**	**170**	**9**	**1**	**0**	**246**
New Jersey	120	121	4	4	4	5	25	92	6	5	1	129
New York	228	231	4	5	2	4	38	189	7	2	1	237
Pennsylvania	212	213	2	2	3	4	33	170	12	2	1	218
Middle Atlantic	**560**	**565**	**10**	**11**	**9**	**13**	**96**	**451**	**25**	**9**	**3**	**584**
Illinois	178	180	1	3	2	2	50	124	6	2	1	183
Indiana	90	90	1	1	0	0	16	70	4	1	0	91
Michigan	136	138	4	5	0	1	20	110	6	6	0	142
Ohio	176	178	3	5	0	0	24	145	6	6	0	181
Wisconsin	58	58	0	0	0	0	7	50	1	0	0	58
East North Central	**638**	**644**	**9**	**14**	**2**	**3**	**117**	**499**	**23**	**15**	**1**	**655**
Iowa	77	77	3	3	0	0	51	28	0	1	0	80
Kansas	90	90	2	2	1	1	48	43	1	1	0	93
Minnesota	50	51	1	1	1	2	7	45	1	0	0	53
Missouri	97	97	1	1	3	3	37	56	4	4	0	101
Nebraska	43	43	1	1	1	1	17	26	2	0	0	45
North Dakota	8	9	0	0	0	1	5	3	1	0	0	9
South Dakota	21	22	1	1	0	1	14	8	1	0	0	23
West North Central	**386**	**389**	**9**	**9**	**6**	**9**	**179**	**209**	**10**	**6**	**0**	**404**
Delaware	17	18	0	1	0	0	0	15	1	1	1	18
District of Columbia	0	0	0	0	0	0	0	0	0	0	0	0
Florida	315	324	33	40	20	22	33	253	18	53	20	377
Georgia	121	124	1	1	0	3	24	85	9	5	2	125
Maryland	70	70	0	0	1	1	8	53	3	5	2	71
North Carolina	153	155	0	1	2	3	15	124	6	11	1	157
South Carolina	92	95	0	3	0	3	13	65	7	8	2	95
Virginia	125	125	1	1	3	3	31	89	5	4	0	129
West Virginia	28	28	0	0	0	0	11	17	0	0	0	28
South Atlantic	**921**	**939**	**35**	**44**	**26**	**35**	**135**	**701**	**49**	**87**	**28**	**1,000**
Alabama	91	94	1	2	0	2	26	59	6	4	0	95
Kentucky	86	88	0	1	0	1	26	59	2	1	0	88
Mississippi	74	74	2	2	0	0	39	34	1	2	0	76
Tennessee	90	91	0	0	4	5	24	66	1	3	1	95
East South Central	**341**	**347**	**3**	**5**	**4**	**8**	**115**	**218**	**10**	**10**	**1**	**354**
Arkansas	71	74	0	3	1	2	24	46	2	1	2	75
Louisiana	70	70	0	0	0	0	29	39	1	1	0	70
Oklahoma	47	47	0	0	0	0	10	34	1	2	0	47
Texas	243	247	0	0	5	9	63	146	19	18	6	252
West South Central	**431**	**438**	**0**	**3**	**6**	**11**	**126**	**265**	**23**	**22**	**8**	**444**
Arizona	60	64	11	14	1	2	5	58	4	8	1	76
Colorado	42	45	0	0	1	4	1	37	6	1	1	46
Idaho	15	15	0	0	0	0	2	13	0	0	0	15
Montana	15	15	0	0	0	0	3	11	1	0	0	15
Nevada	16	16	1	1	0	0	2	13	1	0	1	17
New Mexico	19	19	0	0	1	1	7	10	2	1	0	20
Utah	13	13	0	0	1	1	2	11	1	0	0	14
Wyoming	7	7	0	0	0	0	3	4	0	0	0	7
Mountain	**187**	**194**	**12**	**15**	**4**	**8**	**25**	**157**	**15**	**10**	**3**	**210**
Alaska	0	0	0	0	0	0	0	0	0	0	0	0
California	238	245	22	24	13	18	35	206	20	16	3	280
Hawaii	15	15	0	0	0	0	3	11	0	0	1	15
Oregon	35	35	2	2	1	1	7	30	1	0	0	38
Washington	56	56	1	1	3	3	14	45	1	0	0	60
Pacific	**344**	**351**	**25**	**27**	**17**	**22**	**59**	**292**	**22**	**16**	**4**	**393**
U.S. Totals	**4,044**	**4,105**	**107**	**133**	**78**	**114**	**918**	**2,962**	**186**	**176**	**48**	**4,290**

Golf Facilities in the U.S., 2001 edition

Golf Facility Inventory List

Computer Infrastructure

- Internet tee time, POS software & training
- General ledger package
- Computers & printers

Golf Shop

- Golf shop fixtures
- Binders (1½ and 3 inch), 3-ring
- Bull horn
- Cabinet storage
- Calculators
- Calendars
- Window cleaning supplies
- Clocks
- Clothing labeling gun
- Clothing steamer
- Copier
- Credit card duplicate slips
- Credit card slide–manual
- Envelopes
- First aid box
- Filing folders
- Envelopes
- Gift bags & certificates
- Golf pencils
- Hangers–wooden
- Hole punch
- Label maker
- Label stickers
- Laminates–12 inch
- Light bulbs
- Mannequins
- Mirrors
- Office furniture

- Paper
- Paper cutter
- Paper towels
- POS tape
- Postage meter
- Printing labels
- Rack cards–facility, rates, card program
- Rain checks
- Receipt pads
- Rolodex
- Rubber bands
- Safe
- Scissors
- Score cards
- Stackable file trays
- Staplers
- String
- Tape–assorted
- Tape dispensers
- Tees
- Ten-key adding machine
- Trash bags
- Trash cans & liners
- UPS account & software
- Vacuum
- Weighing scale

Tournament Supplies/Equipment

- Baskets–miscellaneous
- Golf car signs
- Misc. tourny equip. & supplies

- Push pins
- Raffle ticket rolls
- Tables–various

- PGA scoresheets
- Proximity markers
- Proxy sheets
- Portable PA system

- Starter case
- Rule books
- Steel yardsticks

Golf Car Equipment & Supplies
- Air compressor–portable
- Ball washer
- Blower
- Golf car towels
- Cleaning agents
- Cleaning brushes, buckets
- Golf car jack & tire iron
- Golf car rags
- Supplies–tires, grease gun, batteries, windshields, etc.
- Golf car wheel ramps
- Clipboards
- Clock
- Dry eraser board
- Extension cords
- First aid kit–large
- Air hoses w/nozzles & reels
- Water hoses–contractor grade, 150 PSI
- Ladder

- Ice machine
- Light bulbs
- Power washer
- Radios–multi-channel
- Rental clubs
- Soft spikes
- Spike wrenches
- Storage cabinet
- Vacuum & brooms
- Work bench w/vise

Practice Range
- Bag stands
- Chairs–outdoor
- Clock
- Hoses–contractor grade
- Pointer boards

- Pyramid ball stackers
- Range balls
- Shag bags
- Podium with shelving

Dining Room
- Bar fixtures
- Bar stools
- Chairs
- DSS cable satellite system
- Tables
- Television
- Deck tables
- BBQ set up

- LP patio warmers
- Umbrellas
- Reception area–couch, tables, phones

Kitchen

- Hand sink
- Wait station w/dispenser & storage
- Coffee, tea machines
- Juice, soda machines
- Dishtable
- Tray rack
- Spray faucet
- Dish machine
- Stainless tables
- Three compartment sink
- Faucet
- Walk-in freezer
- Dry storage shelving
- Ice machine
- Prep table
- Water filter
- Shipping/freight equipment
- Unix slicer
- Walk-in cooler
- Dry storage racks
- Ansel fire system
- Class 1 hood w/exhaust, blower, wall lining
- Convection oven
- Grill with oven
- Countertop char broiler
- Fry dump
- Imperial fryers
- Prep table, dual side
- Chefs table, over shelves, heat lamps
- Four tub steam drop in
- Countertop conveyer toaster
- Mobile prep table
- Beer cooler

Bar

- Dry storage
- Froster
- Remote keg cooler
- Bottle cooler
- Hand sink
- Blender stand
- Jockey box
- Three compartment sink
- Modular bar fixture
- Drink glassware

Restaurant/Dining Equipment

- Beverage cart insert
- China
- Corkboard
- Credit card duplicate slips
- Credit card slide–manual
- Dividers
- First aid box–large
- Hand truck
- Chairs–folding banquet
- Hot carts
- Miscellaneous decorations (plants, etc)
- PA system with cordless mike
- Plate caddy
- Kitchen utensils
- Light bulbs–various sizes
- Glassware/wash racks
- Paper towel rags
- POS tape
- Silver
- Carving station
- Chafers
- Podium
- Salad deck
- Scoreboard
- Speakers

Course Accessories

- Ballwasher
- Wastebaskets
- Benches
- Water coolers
- Tee markers
- Tee yardage plates
- Fairway yardage plates
- 150-yard poles
- Sprinkler head markers
- Putting green cups
- Practice green cups
- Practice green flagsticks
- Flagsticks
- Tee hole signs
- Golf car path distance markers
- Sand/seed containers for golf cars
- Hazard stakes
- OB stakes
- Traffic control chains
- Golf car control signage
- Directional signage
- Bunker rakes
- Scoreboard

Tools

- ½-in. drive rachet
- ½-in. impact wrench
- 10-in. industrial grinder
- 115-piece HSS twist drill bit set
- 1-in. drill press
- 24-piece, ¾-in. socket wrench set
- 250-mig welder & cart
- 25-piece file set
- 26-piece punch chisel set
- 29-piece bit set
- 2-jaw transmission bearing puller
- ⅜-in. drive mini-rachet
- 4-ton manual service jack
- 4-piece posi-lock hub puller
- 4-position variable speed saw
- 52-in.-wide, 14-drawer mobile tool set
- 52-in.-wide, 9-drawer set
- 5 HP 80-gal. horizontal air compressor
- 60/20/2 amp battery charger
- 6-piece pickle fork kit
- 7¼-in. circular saw
- 7-in. angle grinder
- 7-piece, ½-in. impact driver set
- 944-piece pro tool set
- 95-piece impact socket set

Master Lease Items

- 22-in. greens mowers
- Groomers for mowers
- Trailers for mowers
- Triplex mowers
- Verticut reels for triplex
- Five-plex fairway units
- Verticut reels for five-plex units
- Light duty trucksters
- 72-in. riding rotary rough mowers
- Backhoe
- Turf tractors
- Box scraper
- Large volume sweep vac
- PTO drive debris blower
- Motorized bunker rakes
- Provonost trailers
- Truck for superintendent
- Fairway topdresser

- Broom attachment for rotaries
- 84-in. triplex trim mowers
- Rotary gang rough mower
- 22-in. rotary mowers with bag
- 18-in. hover mowers
- Backpack blowers
- Power edges
- String trimmers
- Drag mats
- Heavy duty trucksters
- Equipment lift
- Reel grinder
- Greens topdresser
- Fairway aerator
- Large drop spreader
- Fertilizer spreader
- Fairway spiker
- 200-gal. dedicated sprayer
- 800-gal. nurse tank
- Core harvester
- Trash pump
- Radio communication system
- Bedknife grinder
- Lapping machines

Source: Mark Gurnow, Integrity Golf Company

GLOSSARY

Bunker. An area of bare ground, often a depression, which is usually covered with sand.

Capacity. The total volume of play, typically measured in rounds per year, which a course may physically accommodate without regard to other factors such as waiting time and course maintenance. Capacity is constrained only by sunlight hours and weather conditions.

CC&Rs. Covenants, conditions, and restrictions. A promise between two or more parties, incorporated in a trust indenture or other formal instrument, to perform certain acts or to refrain from performing certain acts.

Course rating. The evaluation of the playing difficulty of a course compared with other rated courses. Courses are rated to provide a uniform, sound basis on which to compute handicaps.

Daily fee facility. A golf facility at which one pays a fee for each daily use.

Demand. The desire and ability to purchase or lease goods and services.

Desired rounds. The ideal, maximum number of rounds played per period or year which results in the highest volume of play while achieving other objectives such as desired course maintenance and waiting time. The number of desired rounds is usually established by the facility's management.

Draw. A stroke, usually deliberate, played across the ball from "in to out" causing it to travel at first to the right and then curve back toward the line required; a half-brother to the hook.

Driving range. A limited area of land with a line of bays or stalls from which golfers can practice shots. Golfers rent the balls, but do not have to pick them up.

Executive course. A short version of a regulation course with a par between 58 and 68 strokes.

Fade. The opposite of a draw; a shot moving slightly from left to right toward the target. A fade is usually deliberate and controlled, unlike a slice.

Fairway. The specially prepared and cut part of the course between the tee and the green. The fairway is surrounded by rough, bunkers, and other hazards.

Focals. The "hot spots" on the golf course, including greens, tees, lakes, bunkers, and first-shot landing areas, which have visual characteristics that command higher lot premiums.

Focus group interview. A market research technique involving comprehensive questioning of a small group of potential consumers. The purpose of the study is to test participants' reactions to specific topics. Those interviewed are not made aware of these topics; the questioning begins on a general basis and gradually focuses on the topics. The objective of the focus group interview is to gather information; there are no correct answers.

Forecast. An individual's expectation of future performance, which may be based on projections or other relevant data and judgment as in a market forecast or financial forecast.

Former golfer. A person who has played golf in the last two years, but not in the last year.

Golf accessibility rate. The total population of a defined area expressed as the number of persons for each 18 holes.

Golf capacity utilization. The actual rounds achieved by a course divided by the number of desired rounds. A private course may prefer to express capacity utilization as the number of actual members of the club divided by the maximum number of desired members.

Golf car. A powered vehicle, usually electric, in which one or two golfers may ride and carry their equipment.

Golf cart. An unpowered hand cart for carrying golf equipment.

Golf frequency rate. The average number of rounds played per year for a defined segment of the golfing population.

Golf participation rate. The percentage of the total population in a defined area, age five and older, who have played golf at least once within the survey year.

Golf playability. The relationship between the design features of a particular layout and the talents of the golfers who will play on it.

Golf revenue multiplier (GRM). A unit of comparison used in the sales comparison approach that is equal to the sale price divided by direct golf revenues (i.e., greens fees, car fees, and driving range).

Golf values. Those qualities, sometimes quite subtle, that make a layout or round of golf either a memorable experience or a forgettable one.

Golfer. One who has played golf at least once in the last year.

Greens. The whole course over which the game is played, not just the area commonly called the *green*, which is, strictly speaking, the putting green.

Greens fee multiplier (GFM). A unit of comparison used in the sales comparison approach that is equal to the sale price divided by gross greens fee revenues (i.e., average greens fee times total annual rounds). The factor equals the price paid per dollar of greens fee.

Hazards. Any bunker or water hazard located within the course of play of a hole.

Heroic holes. Holes with a combination of penal and strategic design. Hazards are placed diagonally, and the golfer shoots accordingly. About 30% to 50% of holes are heroic.

Highest and best use. The reasonably probable and legal use of vacant land or an improved property, which is physically possible, appropriately supported, financially feasible, and results in the highest value.

Hook. A golf stroke in which the ball's flight path begins to the right of the direct line to the target and finishes to the left. For a left-hander, this is reversed.

Internal rate of return (IRR). The annualized rate of return on capital that is generated or capable of being generated within an investment or portfolio over the period of ownership; similar to the equity yield rate. The *IRR* is often used to measure profitability. It is the rate of discount that makes the net present value of an investment equal to zero.

Market segmentation. The process of identifying groups of buyers with different purchasing desires or requirements.

Municipal course. A golf course owned by the public, i.e., a city or county.

Net cash flow. The net operating cash flow plus proceeds of the reversion in the last year of a discounted cash flow analysis.

Net operating cash flow. The actual or anticipated net operating income less an allowance or reserve for periodic replacement of short-lived capital items, before deducting mortgage debt service or depreciation, and before reversion value.

Net operating income. The actual or anticipated net income remaining after deducting all expenses from effective gross income, but before deducting mortgage debt service, depreciation, and any allowance or reserve for the replacement of long-lived capital items.

Nongolfer. An individual who has not played golf within the last two years.

Nonproprietary facility. A golf facility that is owned by a party other than its members, who enjoy a right to use it.

Par. The score an expert golfer would be expected to make for a given hole. Par means errorless play without flukes and, under ordinary weather conditions, allows for two strokes on each putting green. Par is based on the yardage recommended by various governing bodies. Par applies to each individual hole and is governed by the length of the hole, not necessarily its difficulty. Difficulty is measured as the standard scratch score in Britain and elsewhere, and the course rating in America. The standard par for an 18-hole course is 72 strokes.

Par-3 course. A course in which each hole has a par-3 rating and is less than 250 yards in length.

Penal holes. Holes in which sand traps guard the greens in bottleneck or island fashion and force the golfer to shoot accurately or play short. Penal design is usually found on one or two short holes on an 18-hole course.

Pitch-and-putt course. A small course with holes usually less than 100 yards in length.

Price per membership (*PPM*). A unit of comparison used in the sales comparison approach equal to the sale price divided by the number of members in the club.

Price per round (*PPR*). A unit of comparison used in the sales comparison approach equal to the sale price divided by the number of annual rounds played.

Primary data. Information that is gathered firsthand by the researcher, usually through interviews or surveys. Primary data are specific to the topic researched, which may be the subject golf course or its immediate market.

Projection. Extrapolating future events from a series of former events, often by regression analysis. A projection such as a market projection or financial projection is based solely on the former events' trend.

Proprietary facility. A golf facility in which the members share in the equity ownership.

Putting green. The specially prepared part of every golf hole where the cup is situated and the putting takes place. Ideally, greens are closely mowed, creating a smooth and fast surface.

Regulation course. A course that meets these minimum standards: length of 3,200 yards for 9 holes and 6,500 yards for 18 holes, and a par of 35 strokes for 9 holes and 72 strokes for 18 holes. Par will range from three to five strokes per hole.

Reversion value. A lump-sum benefit that an investor receives at the termination of an investment.

Roughs. The part of a golf course that is neither tee, green, fairway, nor hazard. Because roughs are unmanicured areas, play from the rough is difficult.

Round. One golfer playing 18 holes or 9 holes on a 9-hole course.

Secondary data. Data that has been gathered by a source other than the researcher such as the U.S. Bureau of the Census or the National Golf Foundation. This data usually relates to macro conditions and is not specific to the subject property.

Semiprivate facility. A golf course that offers a private membership status (either proprietary or nonproprietary) and also allows daily fee use of the course to the public.

Shoulder season. The period of time between the prime season and the off season, usually in the spring and fall.

Signature golf course. A course designed by a well-recognized, acclaimed architect, which is usually distinguished by characteristics specific to that designer.

Slice. A stroke that starts to the left of the direct line to the target and finishes to the right. For a left-hander, this is reversed.

Slope. The measure of the difficulty of obstacles and hazards encountered on a golf course that was developed by the United States Golf Association. It takes into account the placement of hazards and the degree of difficulty of a hole from 150 yards and in from the green. Distance is only part of the formula. The higher the slope rating, the tougher the course for average golfers. Slope rating also makes an average golfer's handicap portable. More strokes are given on courses with a higher slope rating, fewer strokes on those with a lower rating.

Strategic holes. About one-half the holes on a modern golf course are strategic-i.e., they have fewer traps but are well placed. The golfer can hit at full power but must place the shots.

Supply. The various amounts and types of goods or services that are available for sale at different prices.

Target market. The market segment that a particular facility is designed to serve.

Tee. 1. The raised and suitably marked ground from which the player begins each hole. 2. A wooden or plastic peg on which the ball is placed for the initial shot to each hole.

Total revenue multiplier (*TRM*). A unit of comparison used in the sales comparison approach equal to the sale price divided by total facility revenues.

Value in use. The value a specific property has to a specific person or specific firm as opposed to the value to persons or the market in general. Special-purpose properties such as churches, schools, and public buildings, which are seldom bought and sold in the open market, can be valued on the basis of value in use. The value in use to a specific person may include a sentimental value component. The value in use to a specific firm may be the value of the plant as part of an integrated multiplant operation.

Water hazard. Any sea, lake, pond, or other open water course within the area of play.

Windows. Open areas on the perimeter of the golf course that provide direct views of the golf course.